Galaxy of Origami Stars

37 Original Stellar Designs

Second Edition in Full Color

Other books by John Montroll
www.johnmontroll.com

General Origami

DC Super Heroes Origami
Origami Worldwide
Teach Yourself Origami: Second Revised Edition
Christmas Origami
Storytime Origami
Origami Inside-Out: Second Revised Edition

Animal Origami

Dogs in Origami
Perfect Pets Origami
Dragons and Other Fantastic Creatures in Origami
Bugs in Origami
Horses in Origami
Origami Birds
Origami Gone Wild
Dinosaur Origami
Origami Dinosaurs for Beginners
Prehistoric Origami: Dinosaurs and other Creatures: Third Edition
Mythological Creatures and the Chinese Zodiac Origami
Origami Under the Sea
Sea Creatures in Origami
Origami Sea Life: Third Edition
Bringing Origami to Life
Bugs and Birds in Origami
Origami Sculptures: Fourth Edition
African Animals in Origami: Third Edition
North American Animals in Origami: Third Edition

Geometric Origami

Origami Stars
Origami and Math: Simple to Complex
Origami & Geometry
3D Origami Platonic Solids & More
3D Origami Diamonds
3D Origami Antidiamonds
3D Origami Pyramids
Classic Polyhedra Origami
A Constellation of Origami Polyhedra
A Plethora of Polyhedra in Origami: Second Revised Edition
Origami Polyhedra Design

Dollar Bill Origami

Dollar Origami Treasures
Dollar Bill Animals in Origami: Second Revised Edition
Dollar Bill Origami
Easy Dollar Bill Origami

Simple Origami

Fun and Simple Origami: 101 Easy-to-Fold Projects: Second Edition
Super Simple Origami
Easy Dollar Bill Origami
Easy Origami Animals
Origami Twelve Days of Christmas: And Santa, Too!

Galaxy of Origami Stars

37 Original Stellar Designs

Second Edition in Full Color

John Montroll

With Contributions by
Russell Cashdollar

To Heidi and Glenn

Galaxy of Origami Stars
Second Edition in Full Color

Copyright © 2018 by John Montroll. All rights reserved.
No part of this publication may be copied or reproduced by any means without the express written permission of the author.

ISBN-10: 1-877656-06-2
ISBN-13: 978-1-877656-06-4

Introduction

Stars are mysterious objects that have always fascinated humans, giving us reason to advance science and art. Long depicted as twinkling, pointed objects, in the field of origami, stars are represented as geometric shapes with radial symmetry and pointed arms.

Presented here is a collection of original origami star shapes. Each is folded from a single, uncut, square sheet. Several use both sides of the paper, creating impressive color patterns. Not only do they look beautiful, they are enjoyable to fold. Great care was given to each model to keep the design and folding sequence as elegant as possible.

You can fold a collection of star shapes with varying numbers of points and color patterns. The radiant stars have alternating color patterns, meeting at the center and radiating to the outer points. The magic star resembles a modular model composed of eight sheets, with the same pattern on both sides—yet it is easily folded from one square in less than two dozen steps. The twelve-pointed woven star appears impossible to fold from a single square. Along the way are the double five-pointed star, the six-pointed propeller, the two-toned, eight-pointed star, and the omega star.

Most of the stars are two-dimensional; a few are three-dimensional. Most are my designs; several are by Russell Cashdollar, with his name indicated on the pages showing his models. Working on this project we inspired each other to design, improve, and make more discoveries. We developed many more designs, including variations and related sets, but lack of space prevented including them in this collection. So we wrote a sequel, *Origami Stars*, which contains those designs, and many more.

Folding these shapes is different than folding animals—no crimp folds or rabbit ears. Instead, there are geometric methods for folding the square into polygons such as pentagons and hexagons, and several twist-fold maneuvers. The Basic Folds section has detailed explanation of the square twist fold that is used throughout this work. Models range from simple to complex, but not too complex. Difficulty levels are shown in the book's contents.

I hope this work inspires you to create your own stars. The diagrams are drawn in the internationally approved Randlett-Yoshizawa style, which is easy to follow once you learn the basic folds. You can use any kind of square paper for these models, but the best results will be achieved with standard origami paper, which is colored on one side and white on the other (in the diagrams in this book, the shading represents the colored side). Duo origami paper, which has a different color on each side, is ideal for several of these star models and gives impressive results. Large sheets are easier to use than small ones.

Origami supplies are found at arts and crafts stores, or at Origami USA: www.origamiusa.org. Online sites such as OrigamiUSA will help you find local, national, and international groups practicing the art of origami around the world.

I thank Russell Cashdollar for his contributions to this book, which include the radiant star models, and the design of the book cover. Thanks also to Joan Mentzer for editing and proofreading the text, and to Yakntoro Udoumoh for photographing the models for the cover.

John Montroll
www.johnmontroll.com

Contents

Symbols 9
Basic Folds 10

★ Simple
★★ Intermediate
★★★ Complex

Radiant Bipolar Star
★
page 14

Three-Pointed Star
★★
page 15

Radiant Three-Pointed Star
★★
page 17

Pinwheel
★★
page 20

Shiruken
★★
page 22

Patterned Pinwheel
★★
page 23

Patterned Shiruken
★★
page 26

Four-Pointed Star
★★
page 27

Radiant Four-Pointed Star
★★
page 29

Two-Toned Four-Pointed Star
★★
page 30

Double Four-Pointed Star
★★★
page 33

Five-Pointed Asterisk
★★★
page 37

Double Five-Pointed Star
★★★
page 40

6   *Galaxy of Origami Stars*

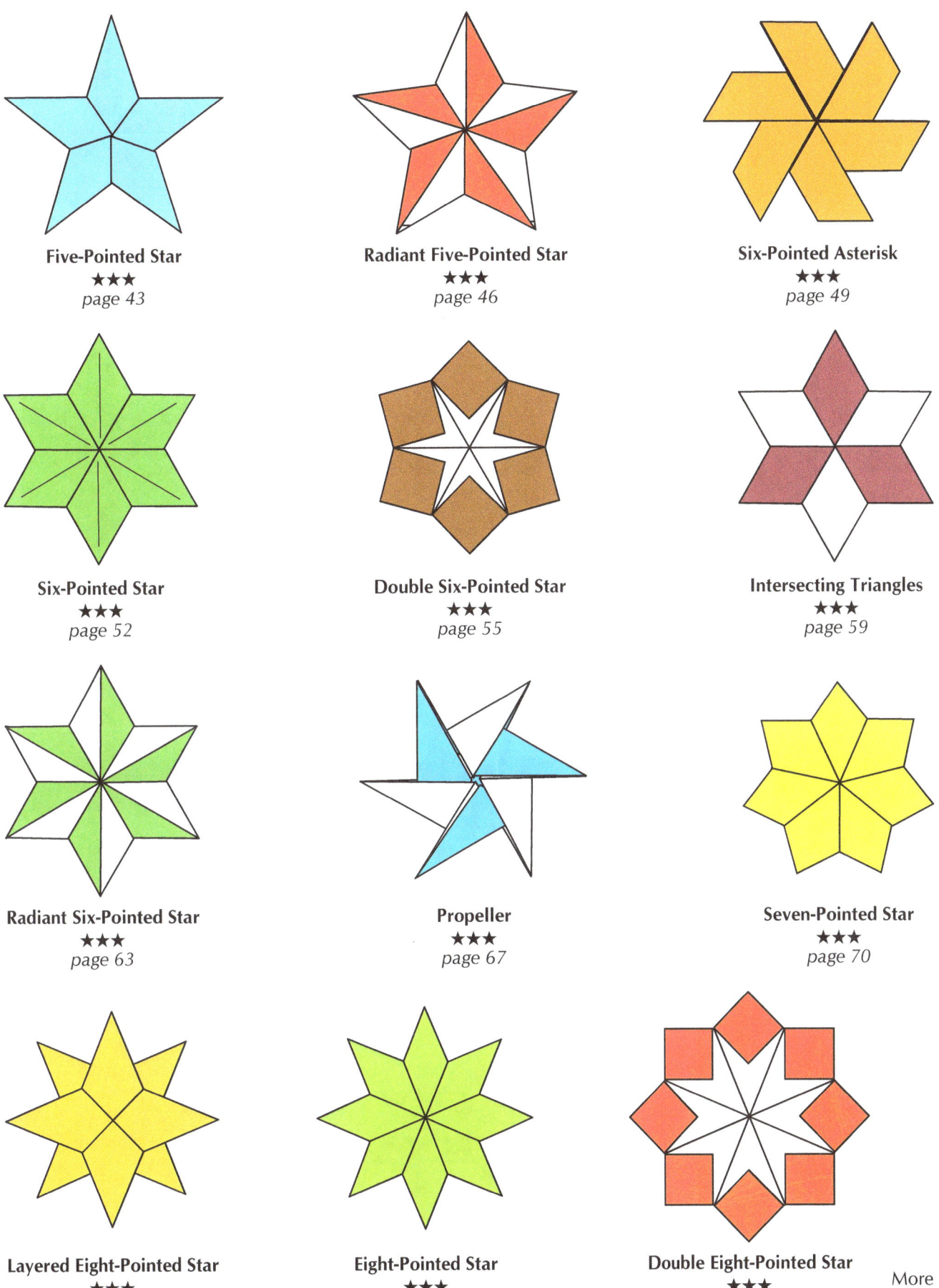

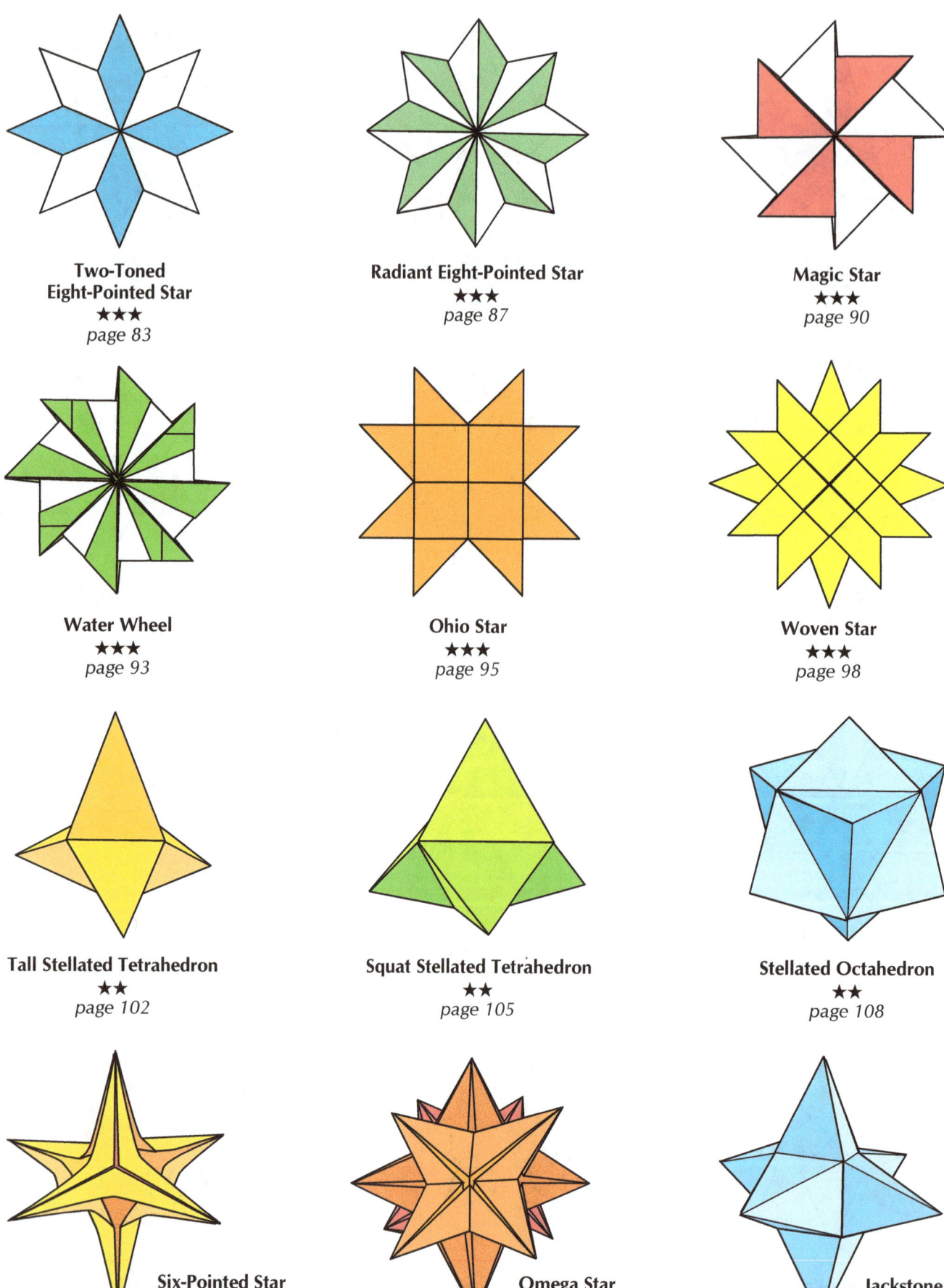

Symbols

Lines

— — — — — — — — —   Valley fold, fold in front.

— ·· — ·· — ·· — ·· —   Mountain fold, fold behind.

_____   Crease line.

················   X-ray or guide line.

Arrows

⌒⟶   Fold in this direction.

⌒⟶   Fold behind.

⌒▷   Unfold.

◁⌒▷   Fold and unfold.

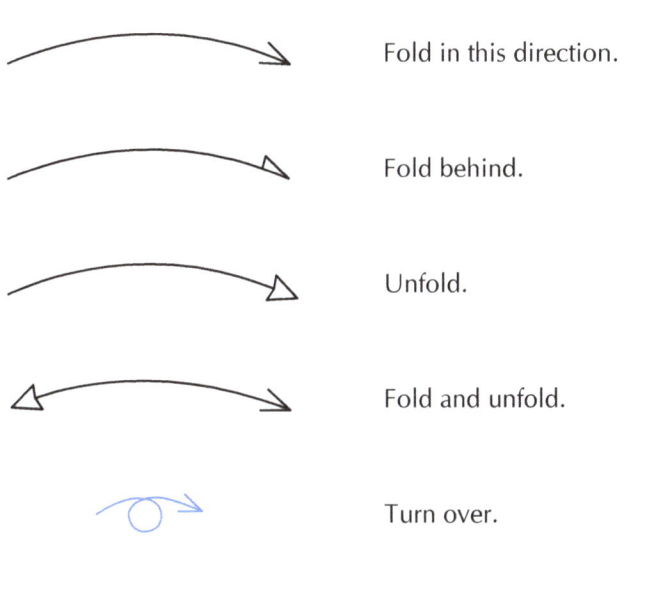   Turn over.

⇨   Sink or three dimensional folding.

⇨   Place your finger between these layers.

Basic Folds

Pleat Fold.

Fold back and forth. Each pleat is composed of one valley and mountain fold. Here are two examples.

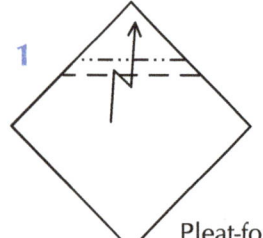
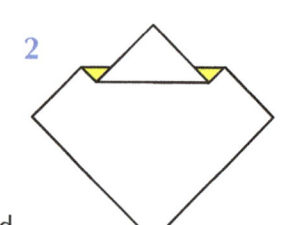
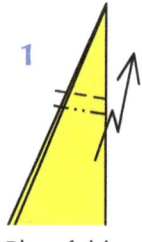

Pleat-fold.   Pleat-fold.

Squash Fold.

In a squash fold, some paper is opened and then made flat. The shaded arrow shows where to place your finger.

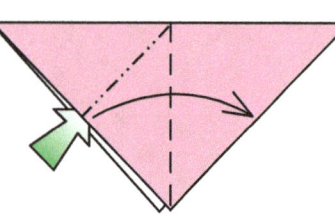
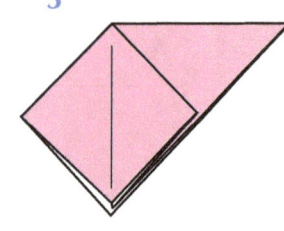

Squash-fold.   A 3D step.

Petal Fold.

In a petal fold, one point is folded up while two opposite sides meet each other.

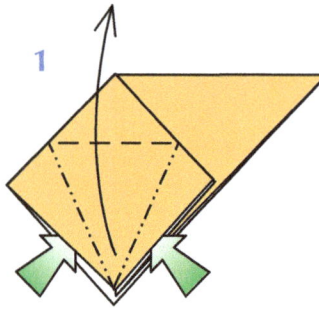
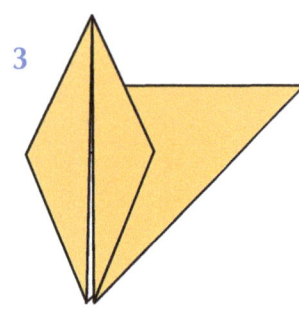

Petal-fold.   A 3D step.

Inside Reverse Fold.

In an inside reverse fold, some paper is folded between layers. Here are two examples.

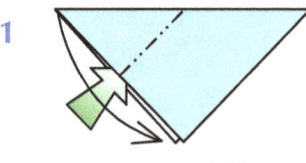
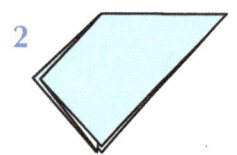
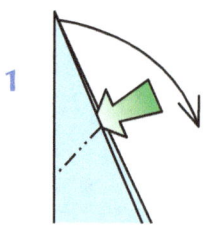
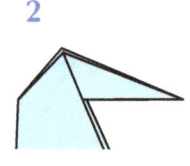

Reverse-fold.   Reverse-fold.

Sink.

For a sink, some of the paper without edges is folded inside. To do this fold, much of the model must be unfolded.

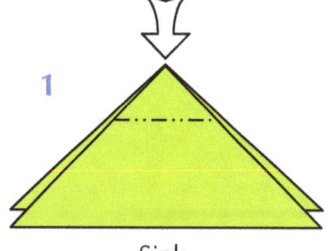
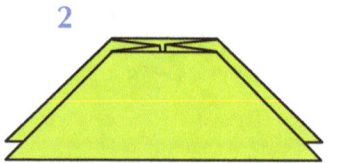

Sink.

10   *Galaxy of Origami Stars*

Square Twist Fold.

Several models use the twist fold. Here is a detailed method for making the square twist fold. This sample model can be used as a base to create many stars, see what you can design from it.

1

Fold and unfold.

2

Fold to the center.

3

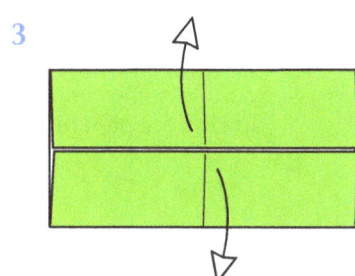
Unfold and rotate 90°.

4

Fold and unfold.

5

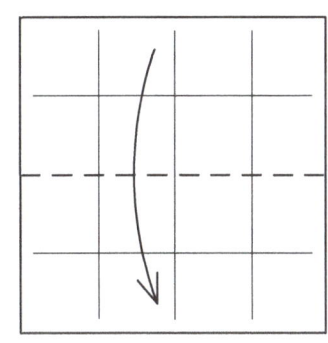
Fold in half.

6

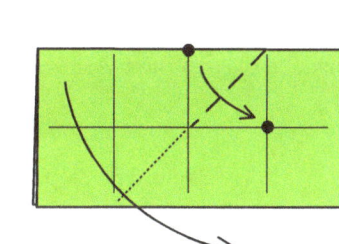
Crease on the upper part.

7

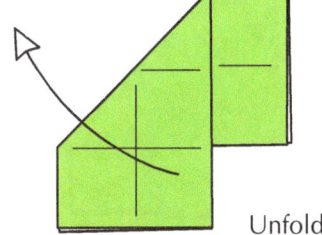
Unfold.

8

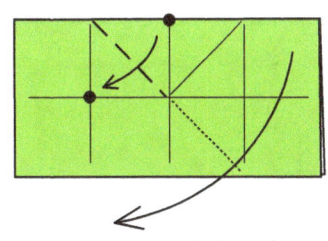
Repeat steps 6–7 in the opposite direction.

9

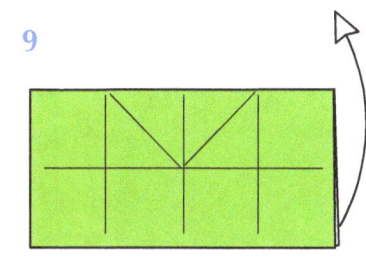
Unfold.

Basic Folds 11

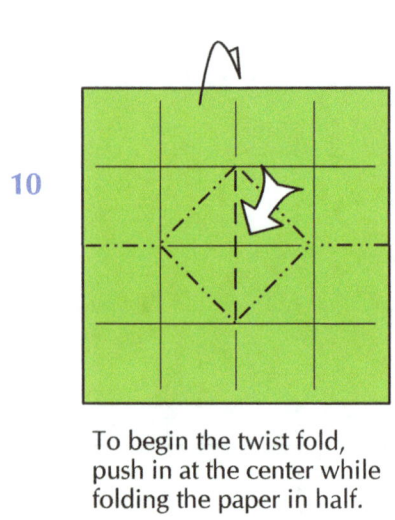

10. To begin the twist fold, push in at the center while folding the paper in half.

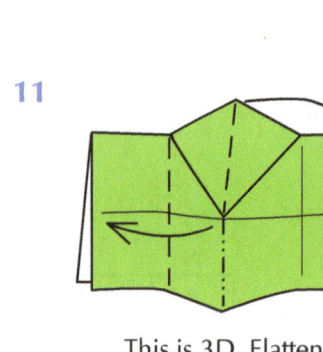

11. This is 3D. Flatten.

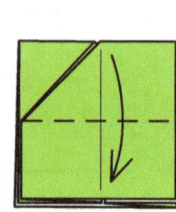

12.

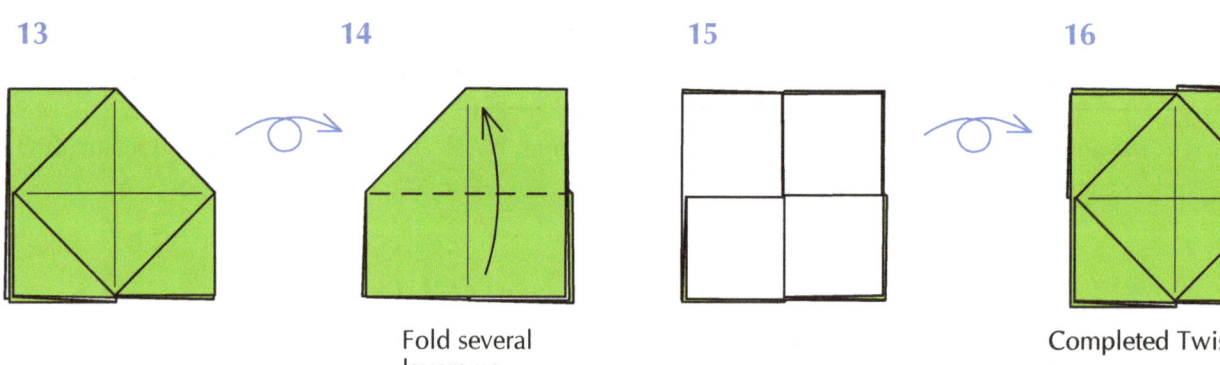

13.

14.

15.

16. Completed Twist Fold.

Fold several layers up.

Throughout this work, steps 6–16 will be diagrammed as shown below.

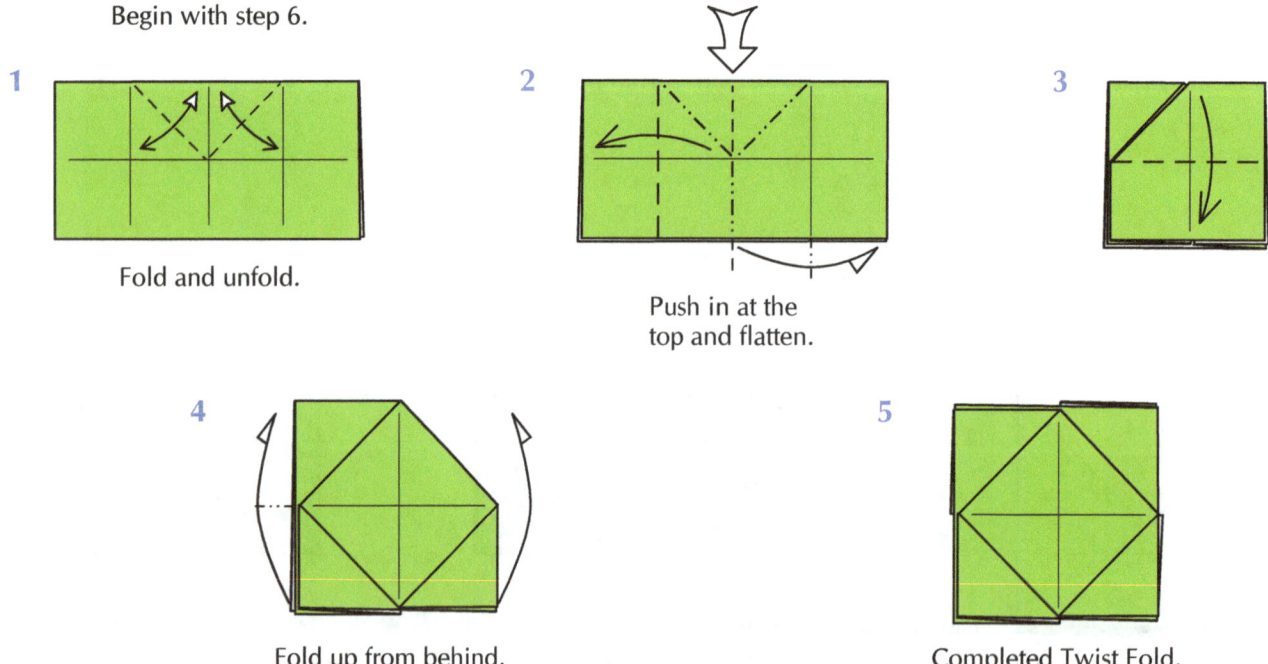

Begin with step 6.

1. Fold and unfold.

2. Push in at the top and flatten.

3.

4. Fold up from behind.

5. Completed Twist Fold.

12 Galaxy of Origami Stars

Groups of Stars

Several stars belong to groups. Here are some of them.

Solid Colored Stars

Two-Toned Stars

Double Stars

Radiant Stars

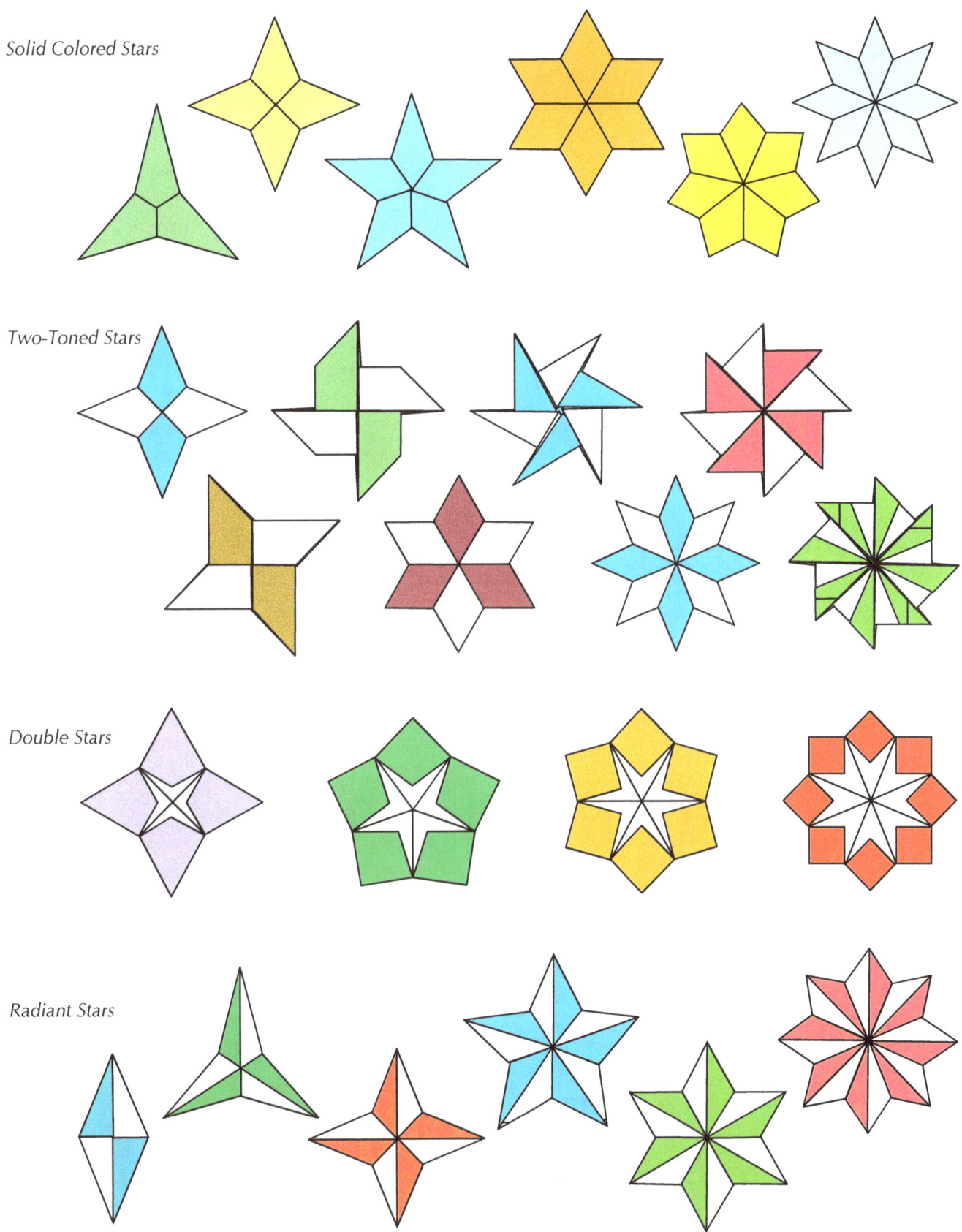

Groups of Stars   13

Radiant Bipolar Star

Designed by Russell Cashdollar

This simple two-pointed star is the first in the series of radiant stars. For the radiant stars, each point shows both white and color from the two sides of the paper. The radiant stars make for a stunning display.

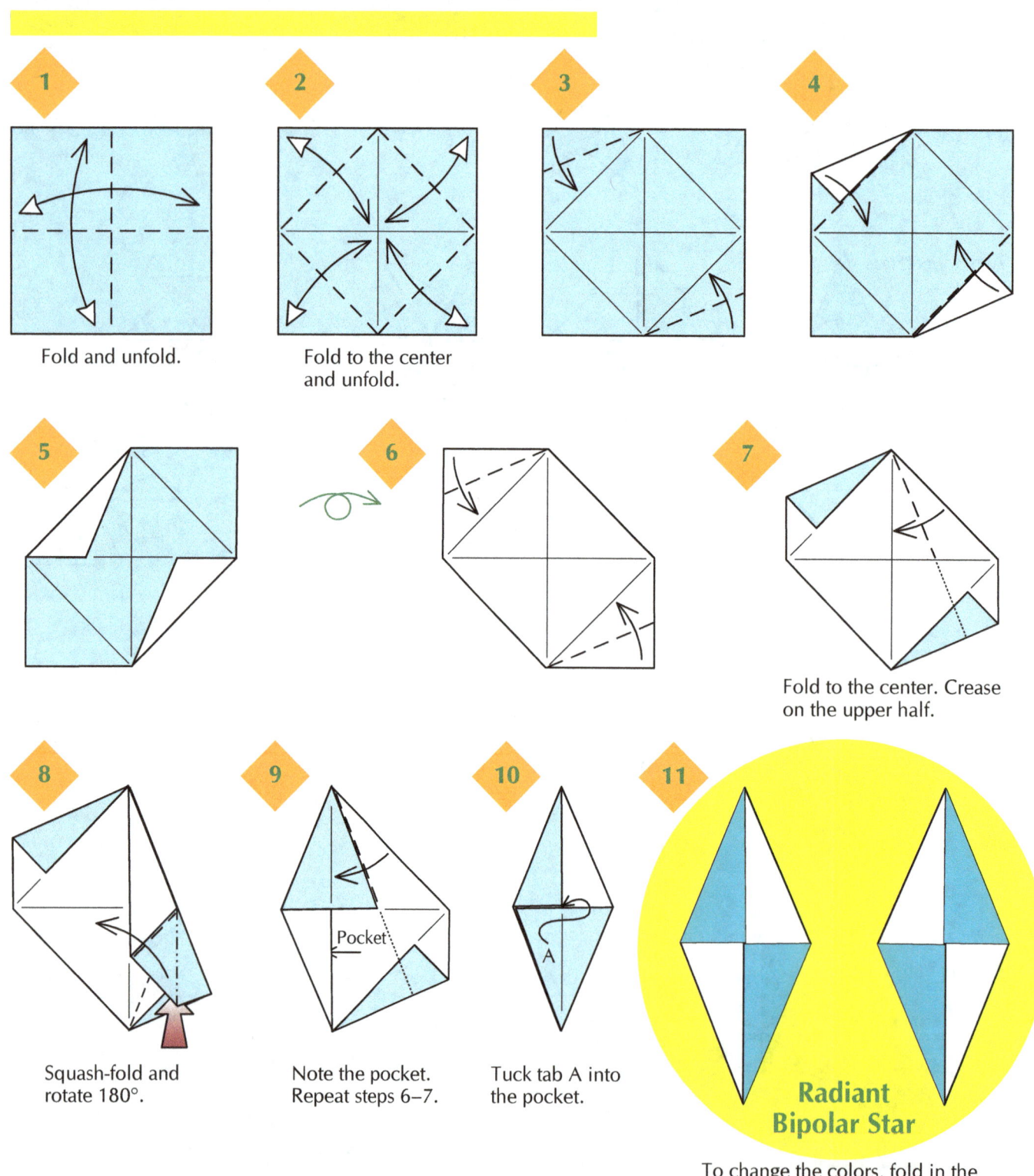

1. Fold and unfold.
2. Fold to the center and unfold.
7. Fold to the center. Crease on the upper half.
8. Squash-fold and rotate 180°.
9. Note the pocket. Repeat steps 6–7.
10. Tuck tab A into the pocket.
11. Radiant Bipolar Star

To change the colors, fold in the mirror image beginning in step 3.

14   *Galaxy of Origami Stars*

Three-Pointed Star

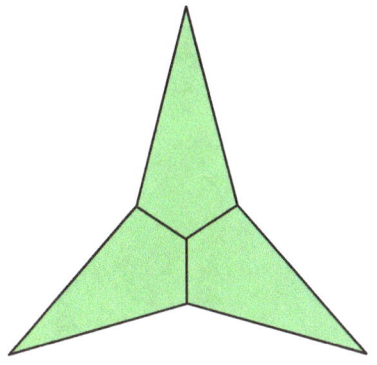

This three-pointed star is the first in a series of solid colored stars. The square is folded into a triangle and a twist fold is used. The basic plan is similar to many stars.

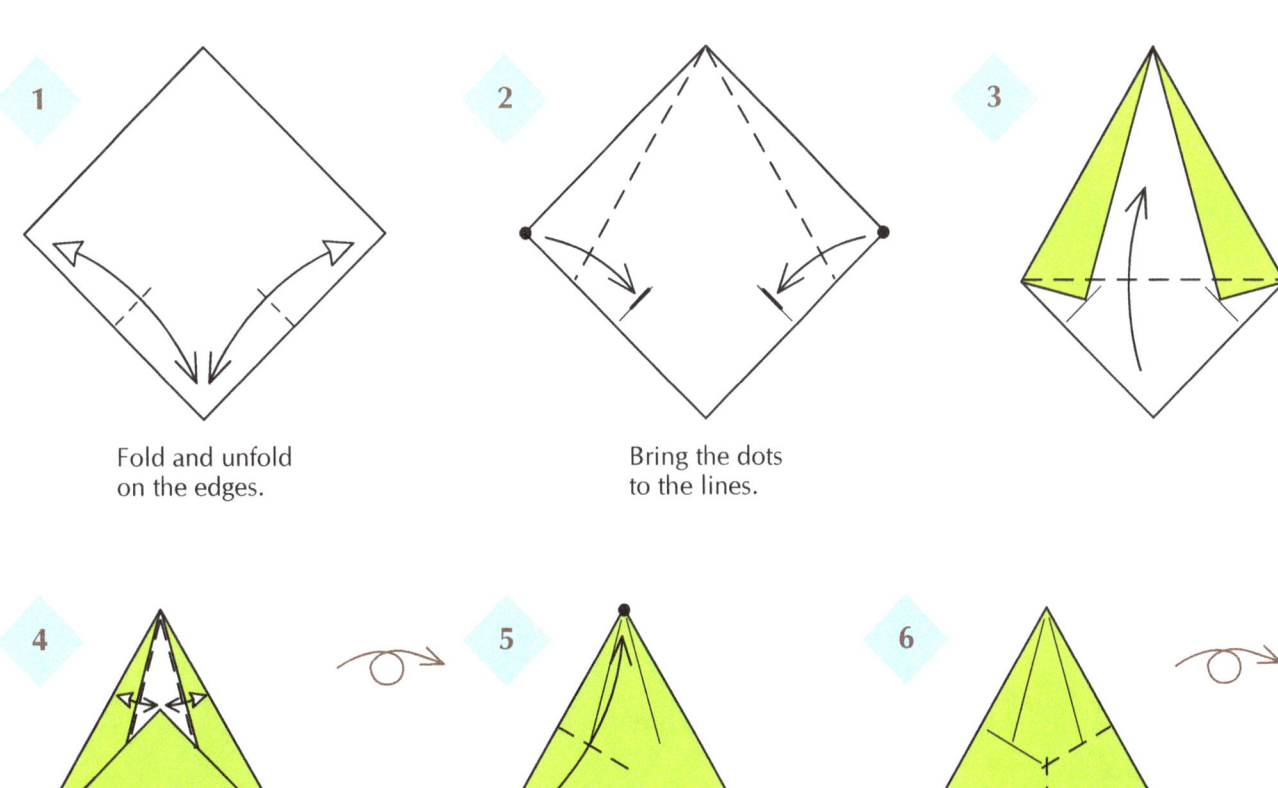

1. Fold and unfold on the edges.
2. Bring the dots to the lines.
3.
4. Fold to the center and unfold. Crease on the upper half.
5. Fold and unfold from the edge to the center.
6. Fold and unfold.

Three-Pointed Star 15

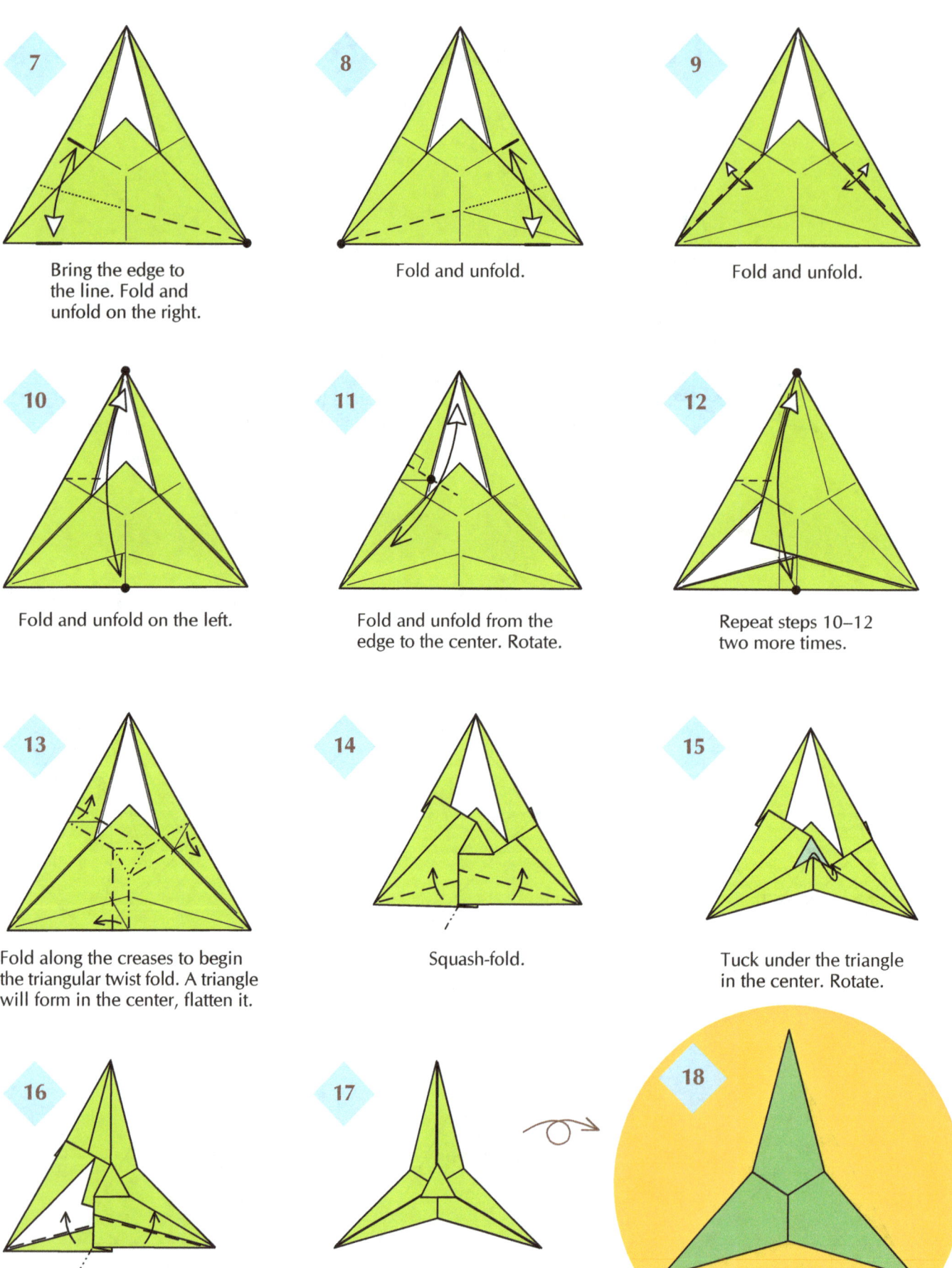

Radiant Three-Pointed Star

Designed by Russell Cashdollar

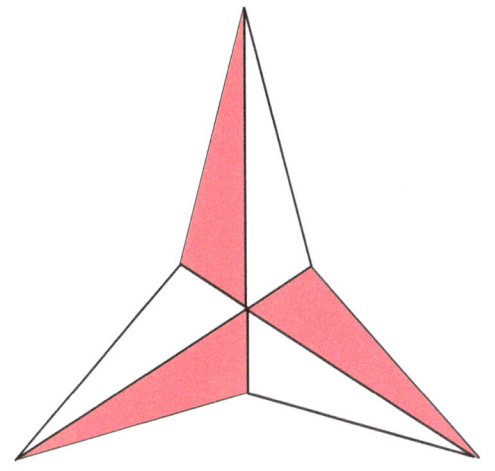

By folding the square into the largest possible triangle, shown in step 7, the two sides of the paper are oriented in an elegant way to create the alternating color pattern for this radiant star. You can experiment by folding in its mirror image to change the pattern, or begin on the opposite side so the back will be white. A triangular twist fold is used in step 17.

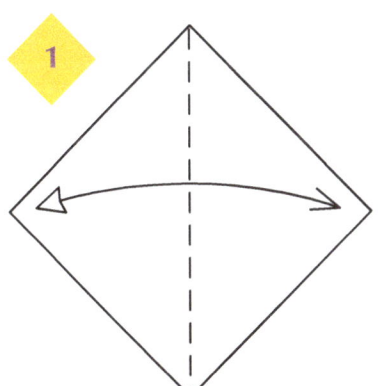

Fold and unfold.

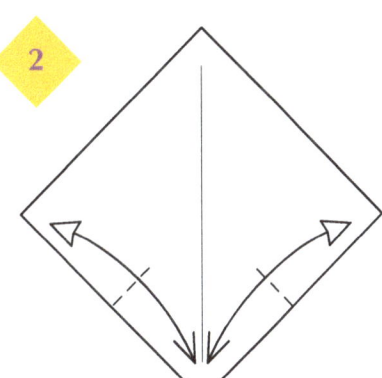

Fold and unfold on the edges.

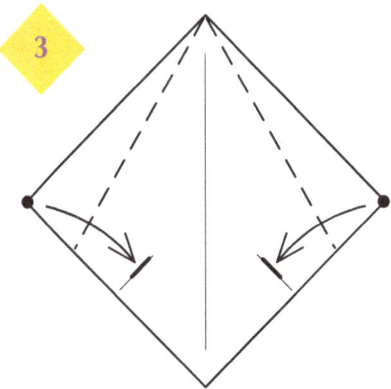

Bring the dots to the lines.

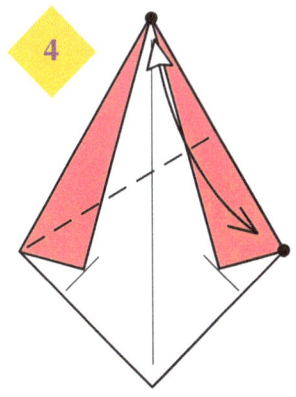

Fold and unfold.

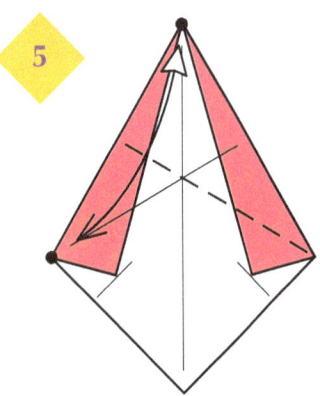

Fold and unfold.

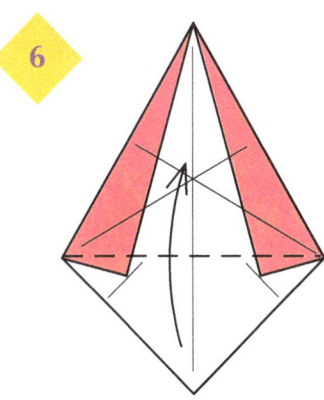

Radiant Three-Pointed Star 17

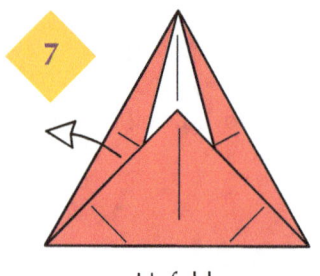

Unfold.

Fold along a hidden crease.

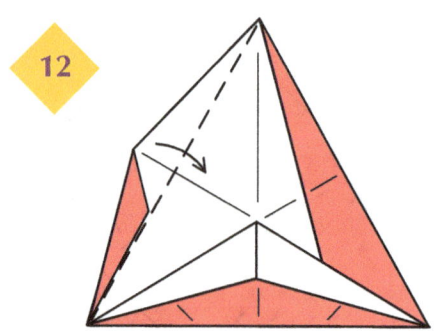

Fold along the creases.

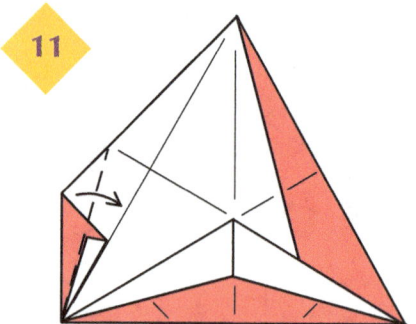

Fold to the crease.

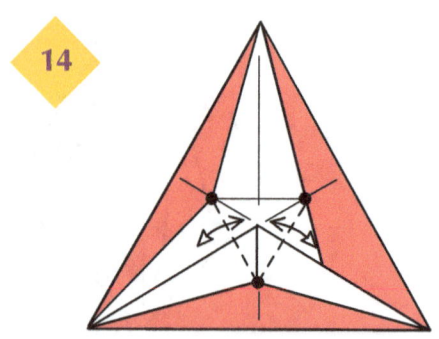

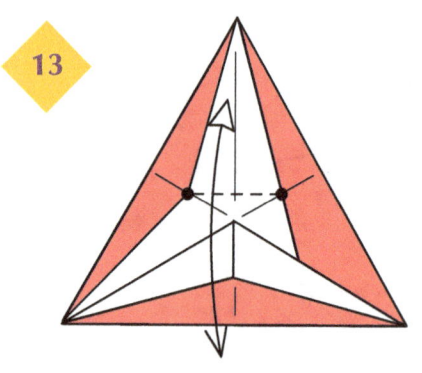

Fold and unfold.

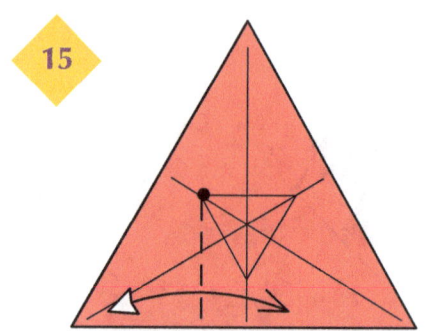

Fold and unfold.

Fold and unfold. Rotate.

18 *Galaxy of Origami Stars*

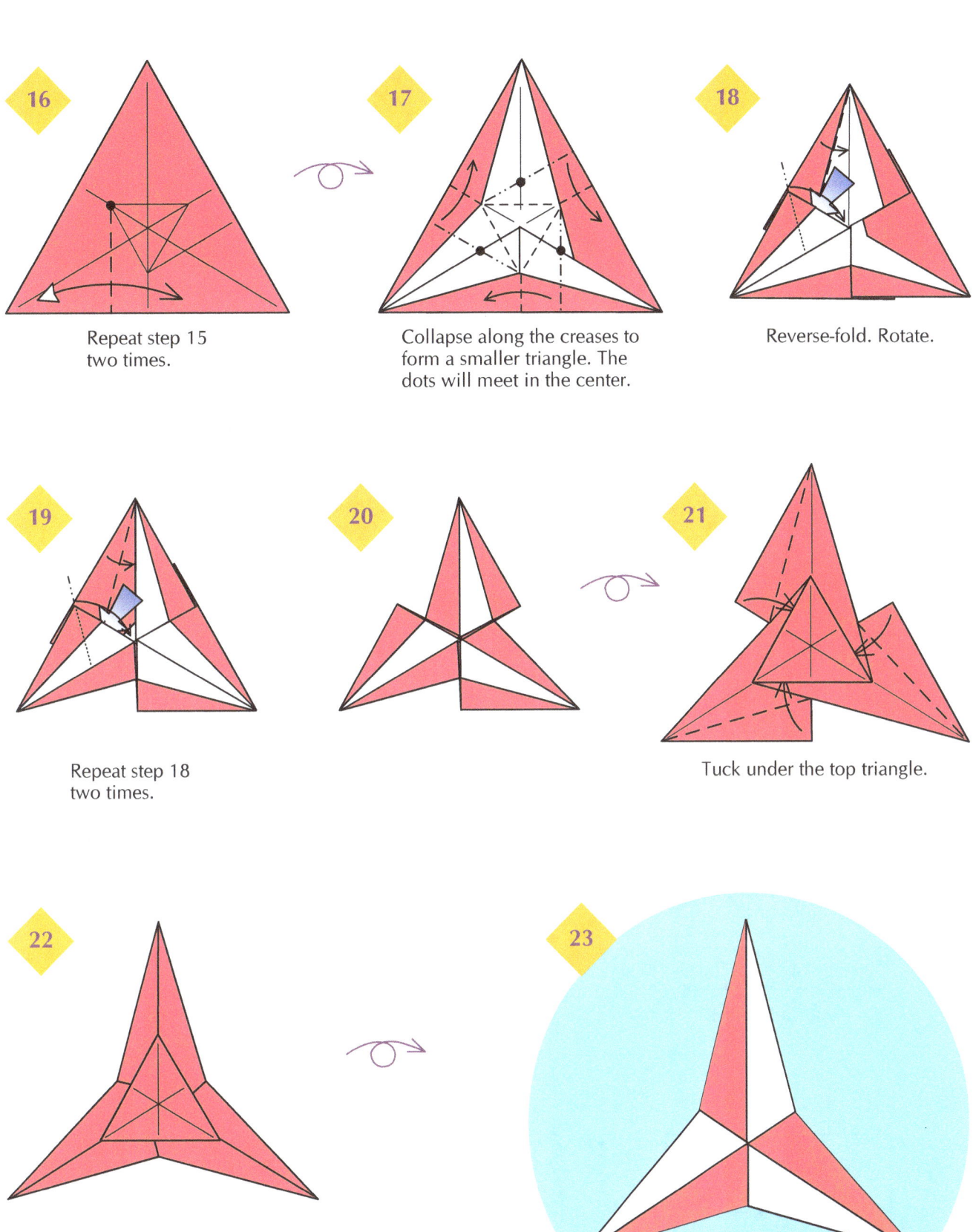

Radiant Three-Pointed Star

Pinwheel & Shiruken

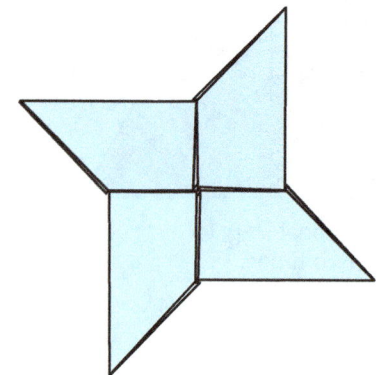

The pinwheel and shiruken start the same way and both require a square twist fold. The paper is divided into sixths horizontally and vertically.

Pinwheel

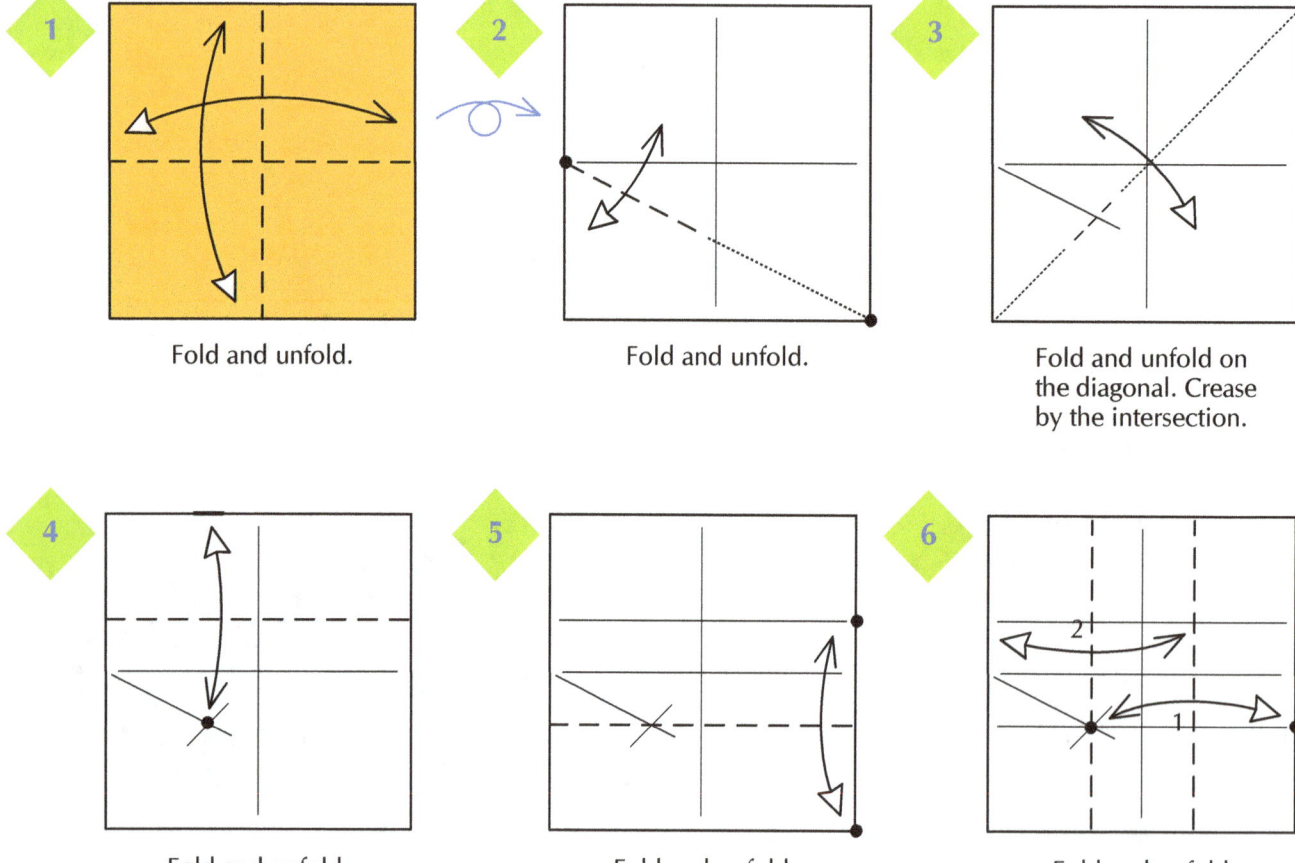

1. Fold and unfold.
2. Fold and unfold.
3. Fold and unfold on the diagonal. Crease by the intersection.
4. Fold and unfold.
5. Fold and unfold.
6. Fold and unfold.

20   *Galaxy of Origami Stars*

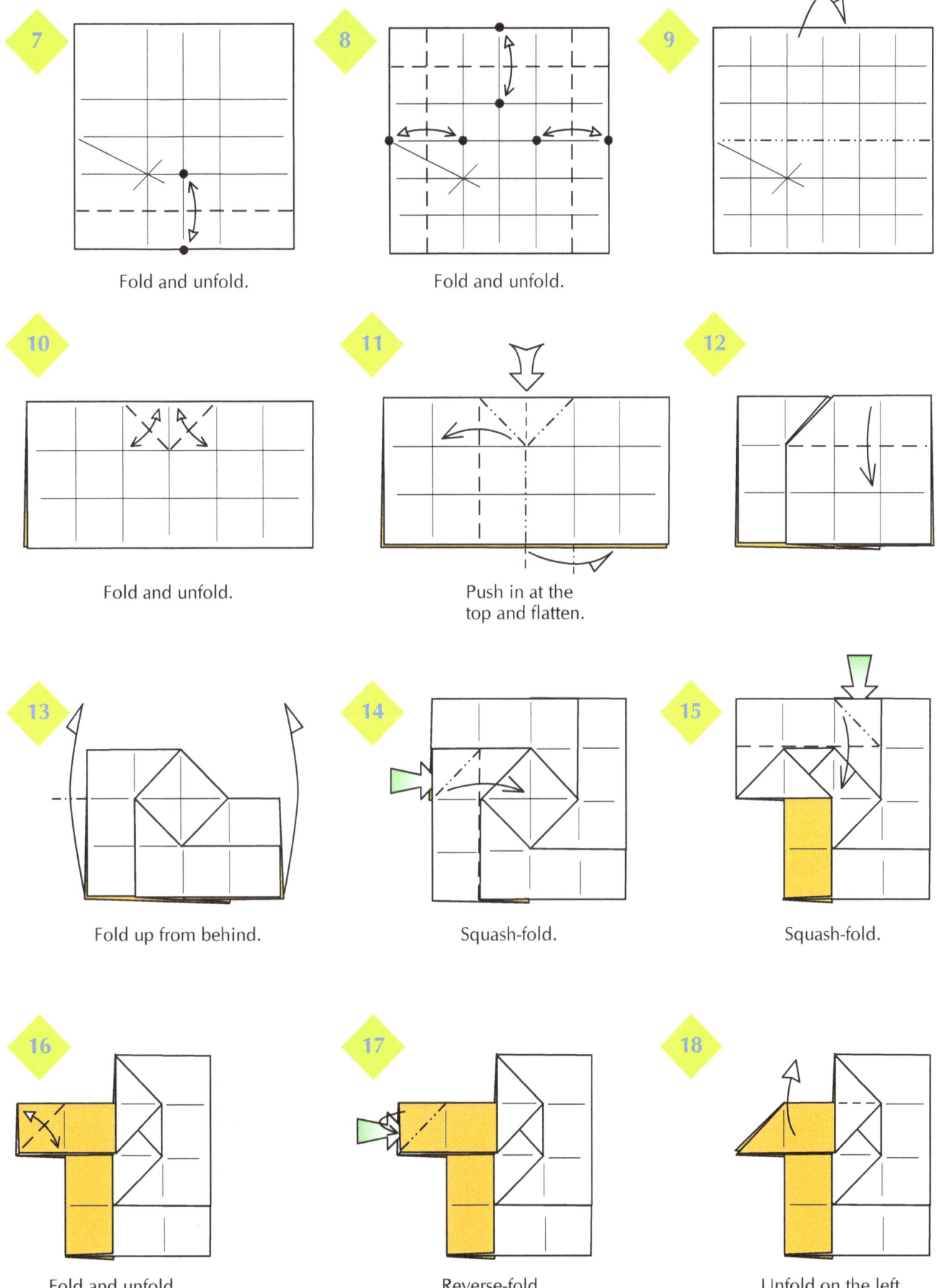

Pinwheel 21

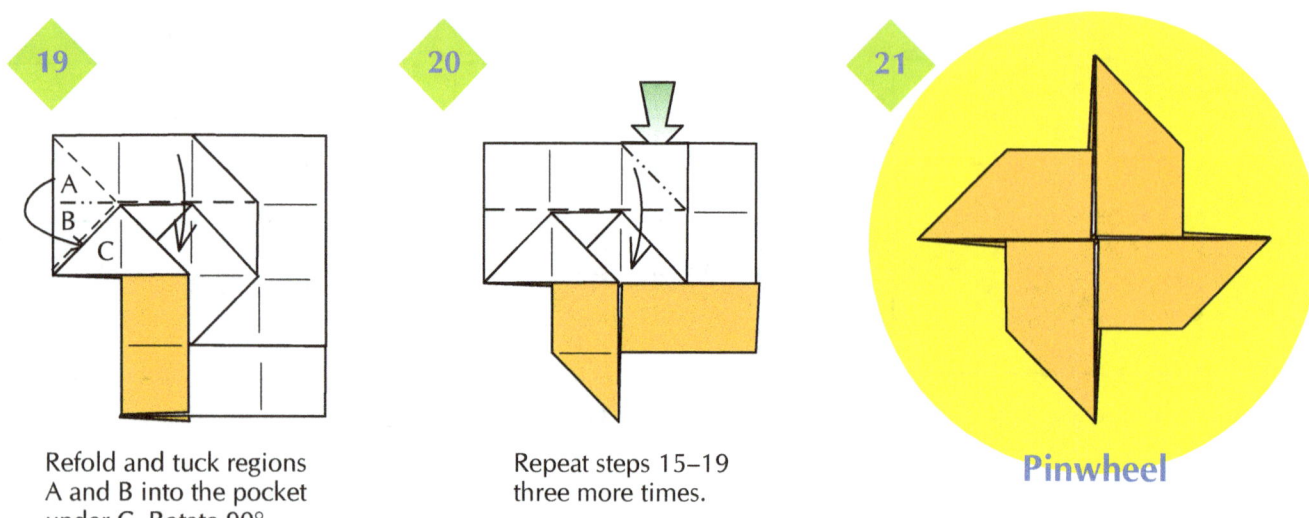

19. Refold and tuck regions A and B into the pocket under C. Rotate 90°.

20. Repeat steps 15–19 three more times.

21. Pinwheel

Shiruken

Begin with step 15 of the Pinwheel.

1. 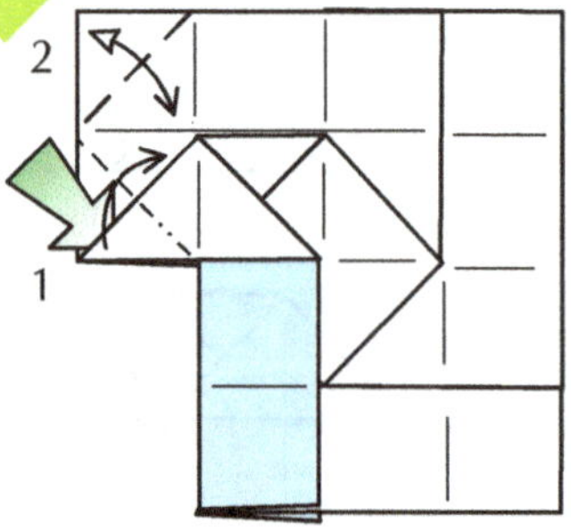
1. Reverse-fold.
2. Fold and unfold.

2. Note the pocket. Squash-fold.

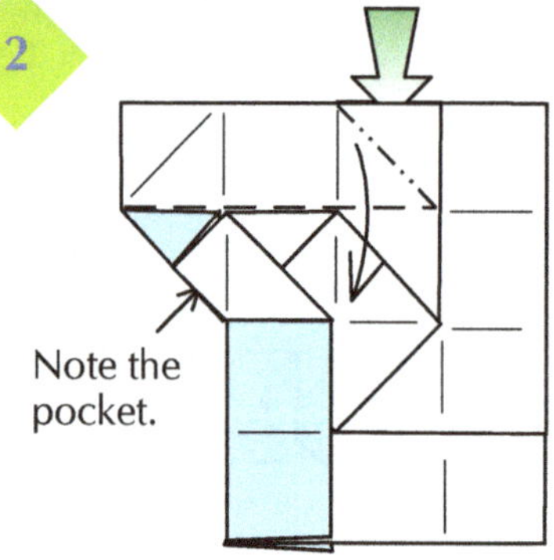

3. Tuck into the pocket. Rotate 90°.

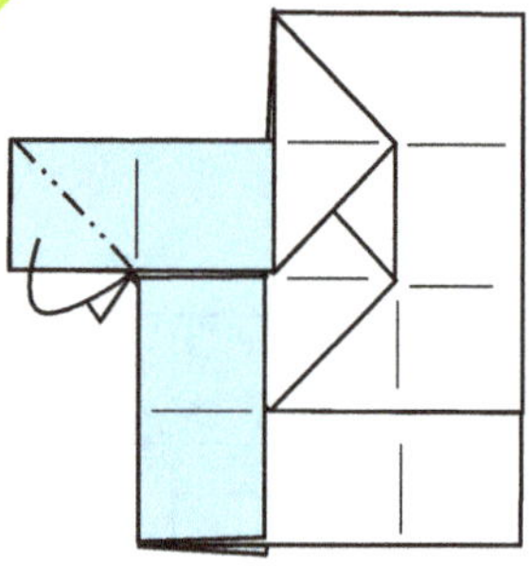

4. Repeat steps 1–3 three more times.

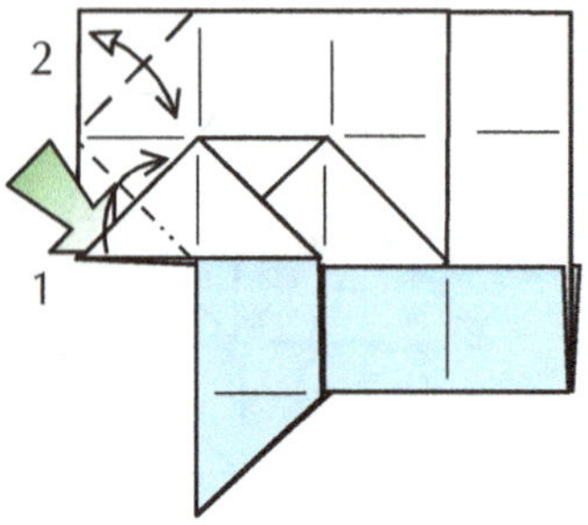

5. Shiruken

22 *Galaxy of Origami Stars*

Patterned Pinwheel

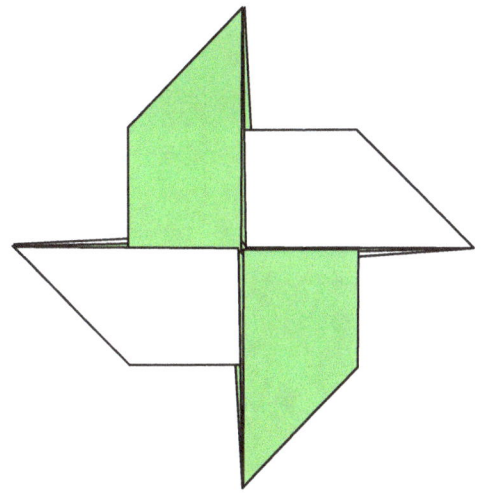

Clever folds are used to create the alternating color pattern, see steps 13–17. The pinwheel has the same pattern on the front and back.

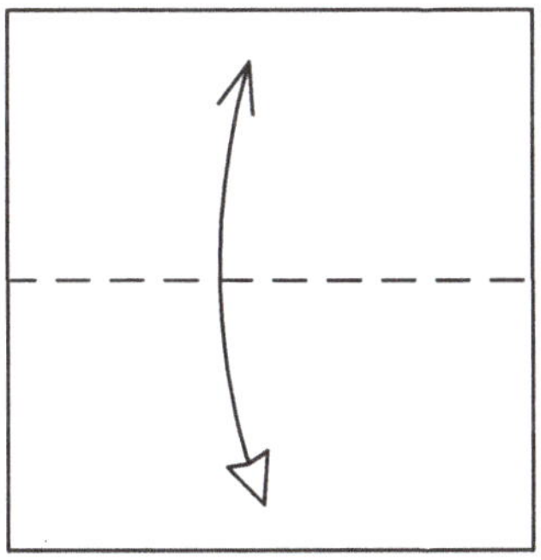

1. Fold and unfold.

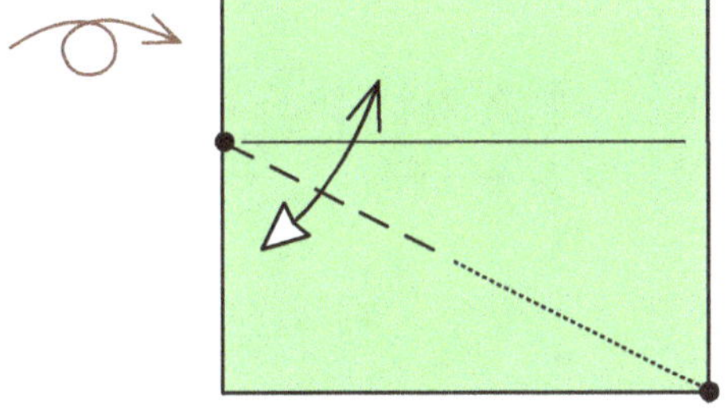

2. Fold and unfold.

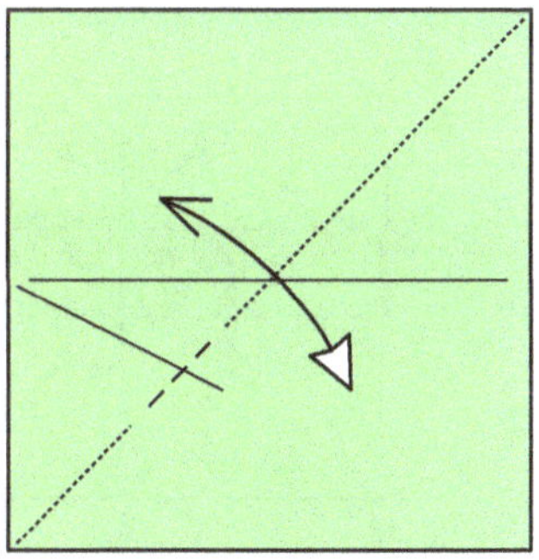

3. Fold and unfold on the diagonal. Crease by the intersection.

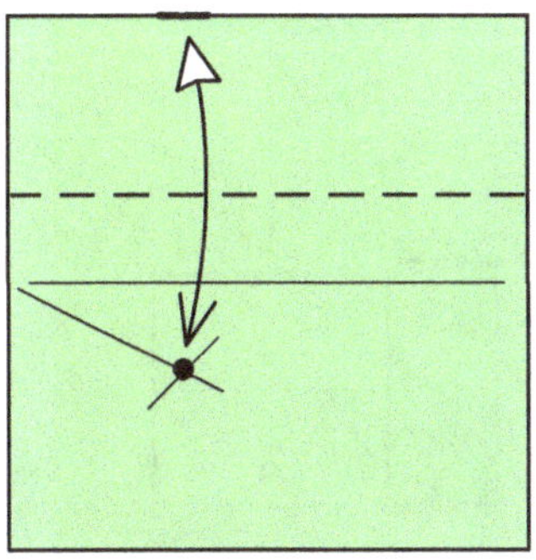

4. Fold and unfold.

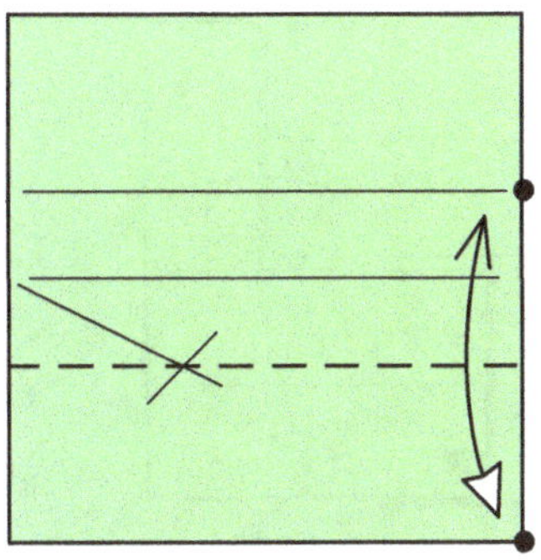

5. Fold and unfold.

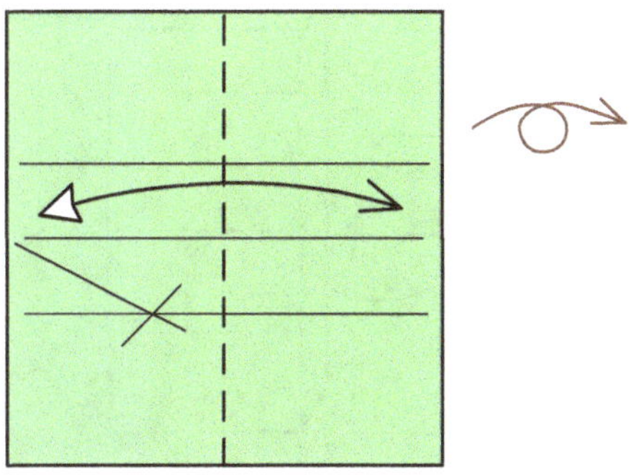

6. Fold and unfold.

Patterned Pinwheel 23

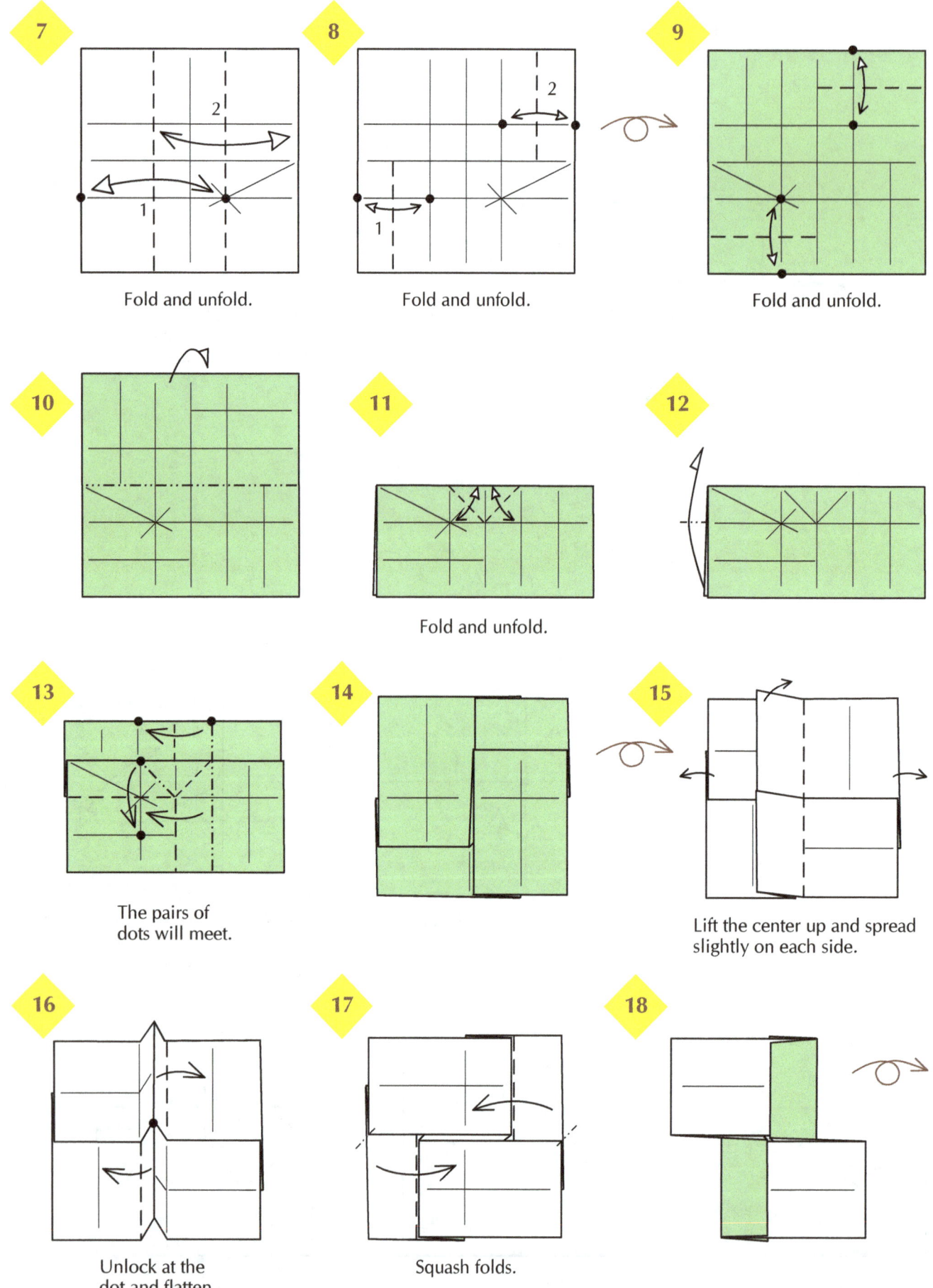

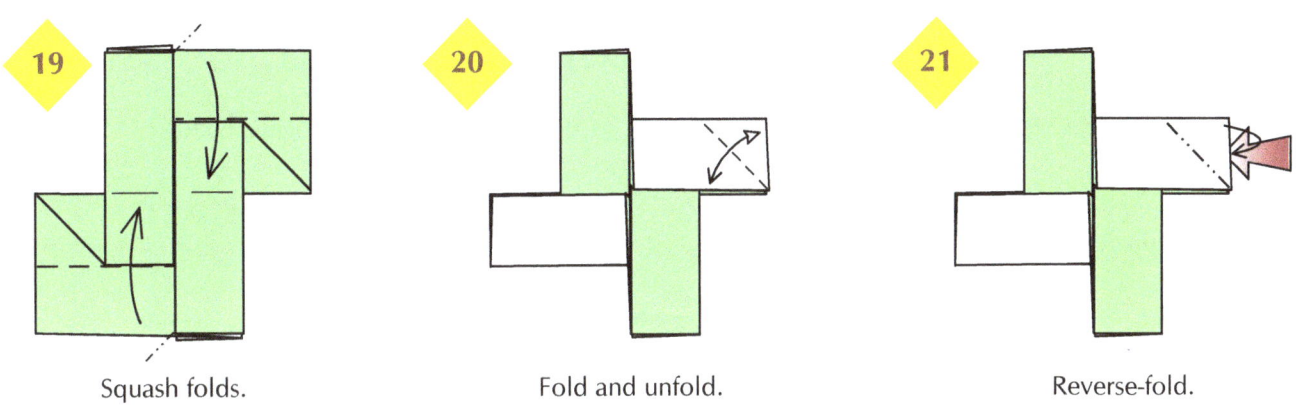

19. Squash folds.

20. Fold and unfold.

21. Reverse-fold.

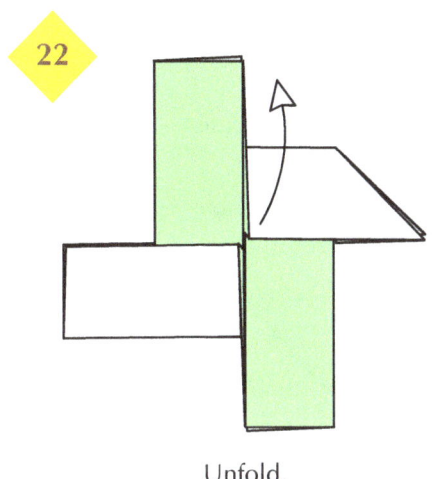

22. Unfold.

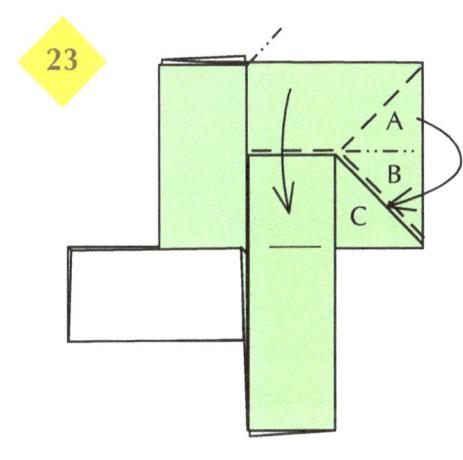
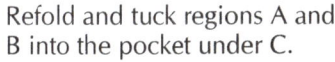

23. Refold and tuck regions A and B into the pocket under C.

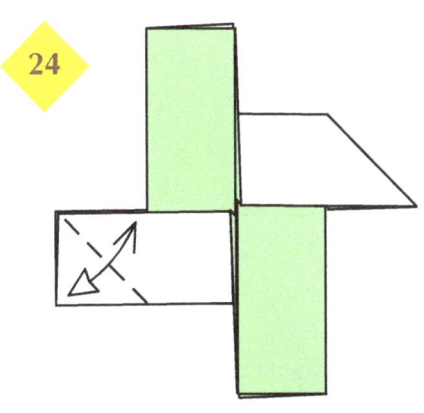

24. Repeat steps 20–23 three more times, on the left and behind.

25. **Patterned Pinwheel**

Patterned Pinwheel 25

Patterned Shiruken

The pattern is the same on the front and back.

Designed by Russell Cashdollar

Begin with step 19 of the Patterned Pinwheel.

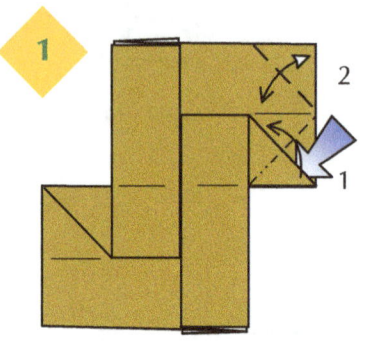

1. Reverse-fold.
2. Fold and unfold.

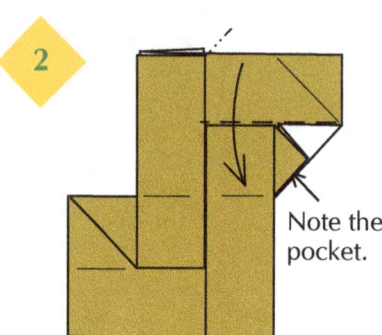

Squash-fold.

Note the pocket.

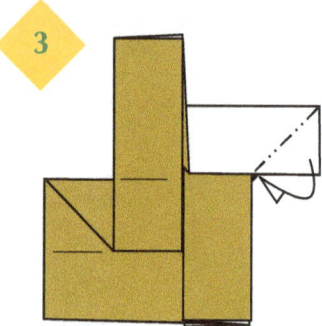

Tuck into the pocket. Rotate 180°.

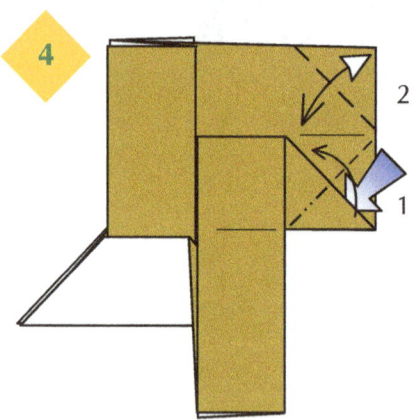

Repeat steps 1–3.

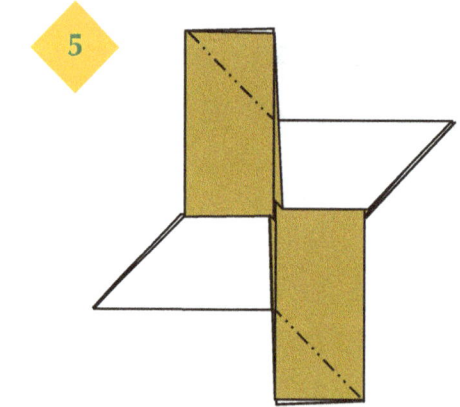

These are similar to the reverse folds in steps 1 and 4.

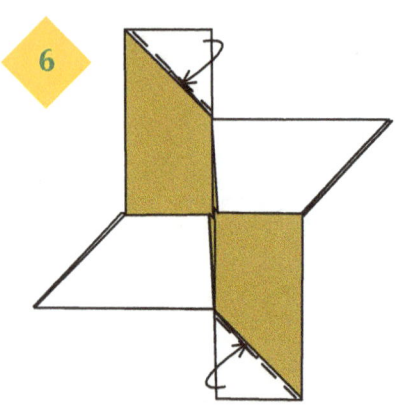

Tuck into the pockets.

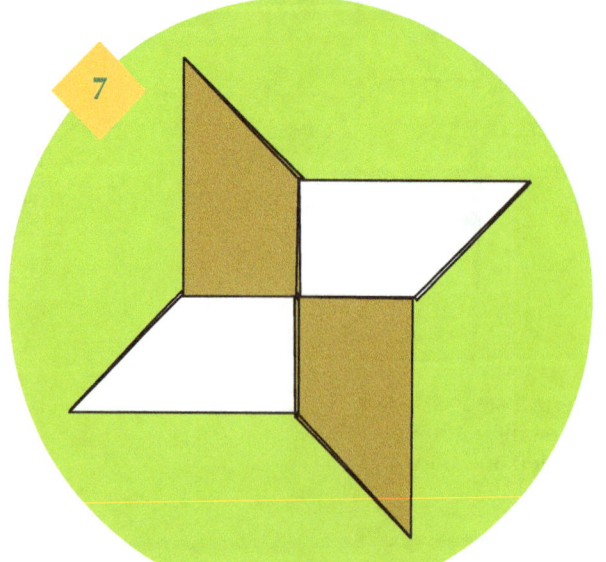

Patterned Shiruken

Four-Pointed Star

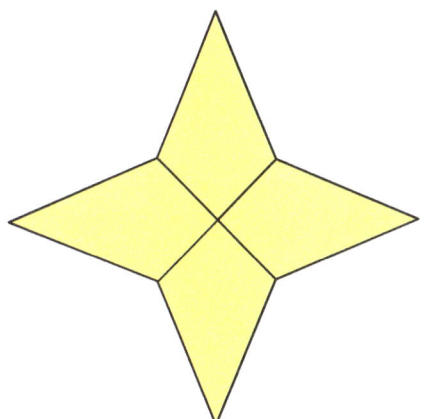

This solid colored star uses a square twist fold.

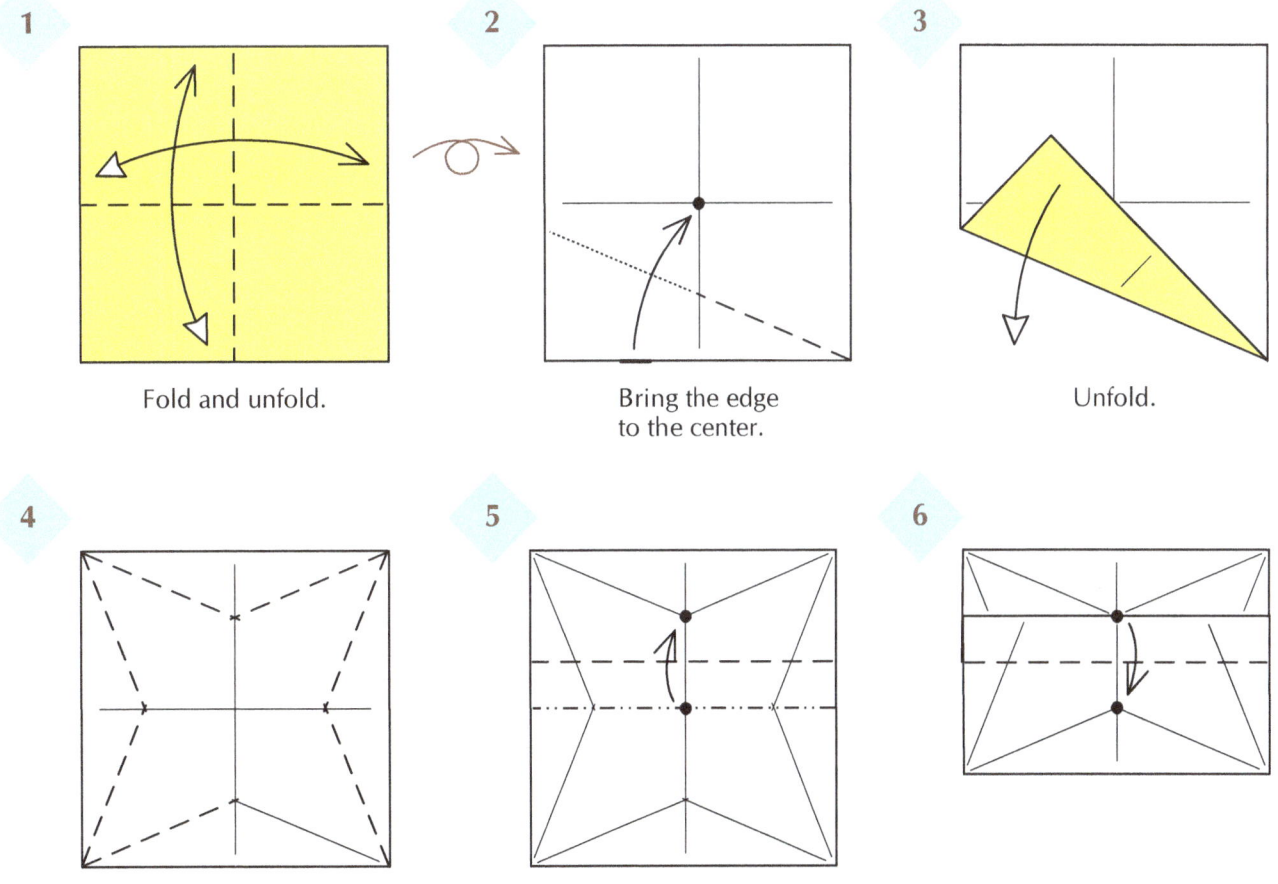

1. Fold and unfold.
2. Bring the edge to the center.
3. Unfold.
4. Repeat steps 2–3 all around.
5. Pleat-fold.

Four-Pointed Star 27

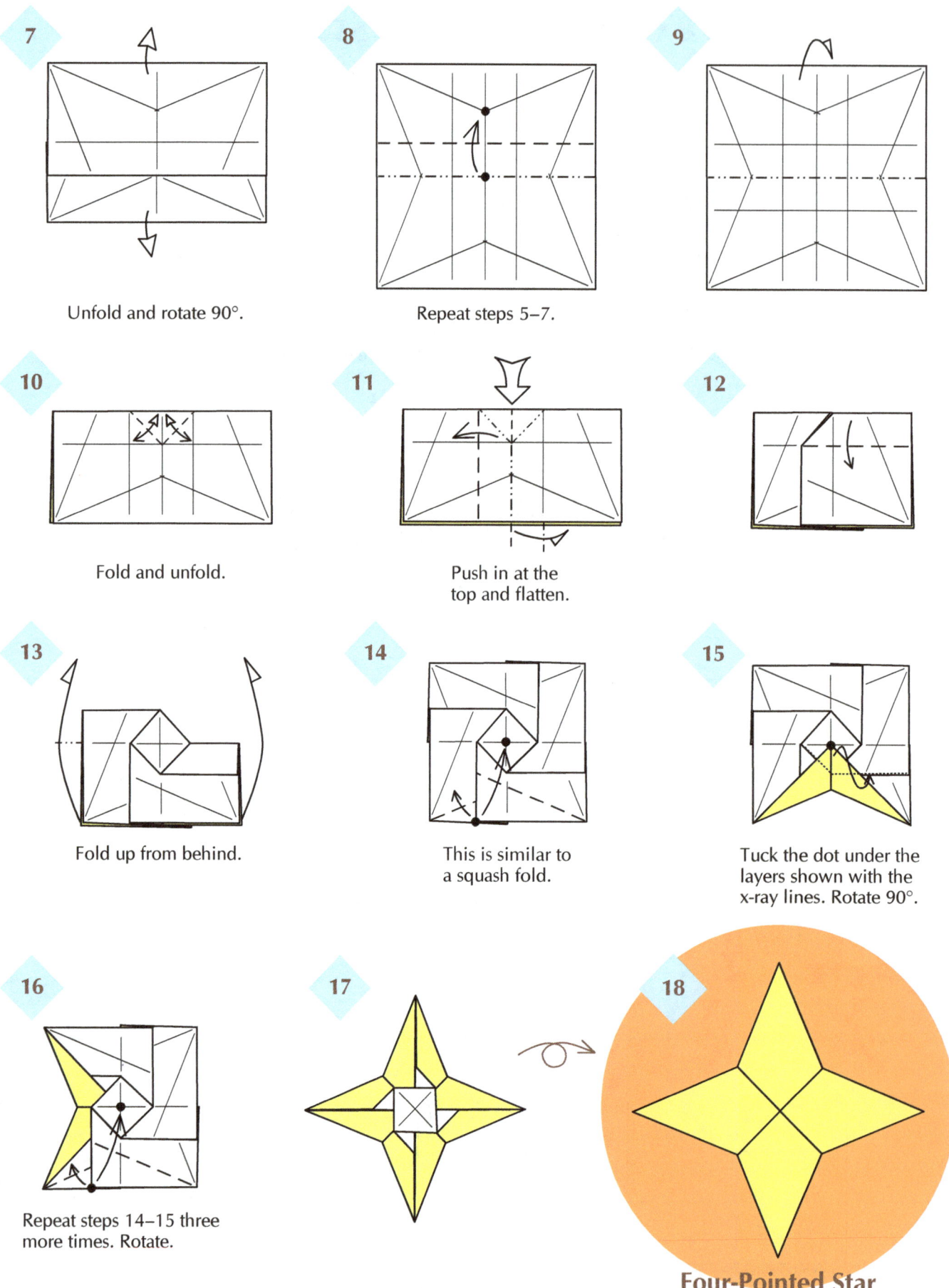

28 *Galaxy of Origami Stars*

Radiant Four-Pointed Star

Designed by Russell Cashdollar

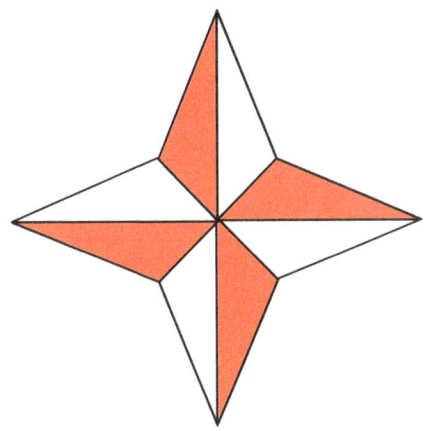

This radiant four-pointed star uses the same starting method as the four-pointed star and is the same size. Clever folds at the end of the folding sequence provides for the alternating colors.

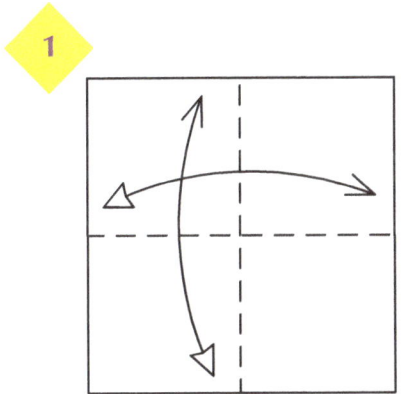

1. Fold and unfold. Continue with steps 2–13 of the Four-Pointed Star (page 27) with colors reversed.

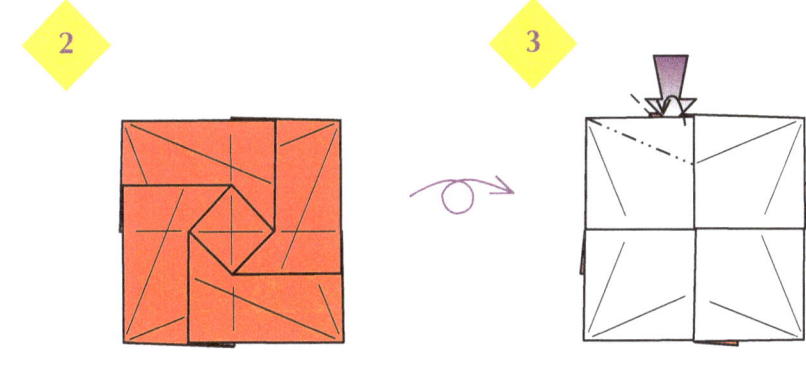

2.

3. Reverse-fold.

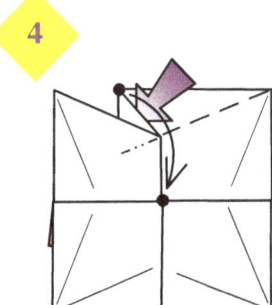

4. Reverse-fold and rotate 90°.

5. Repeat steps 3–4 three more times. Rotate.

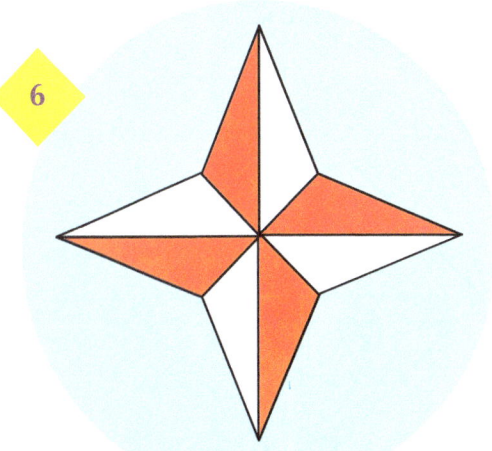

6. **Radiant Four-Pointed Star**

Two-Toned Four-Pointed Star

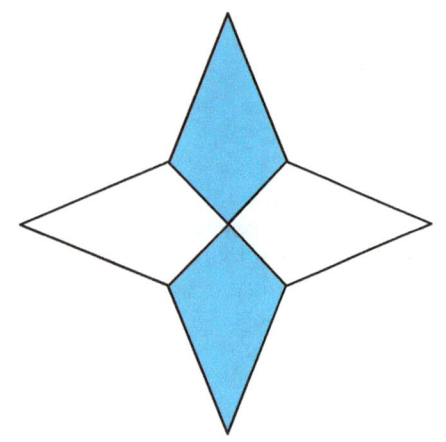

This two-toned star uses a similar folding method as the solid four-pointed star. By creating a smaller square with color patterns (see step 10) the end results in points of alternating colors.

1 Fold and unfold.

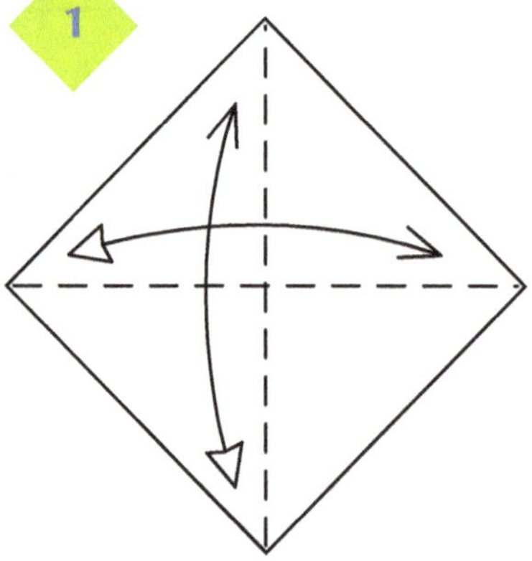

2 Fold and unfold on the edge.

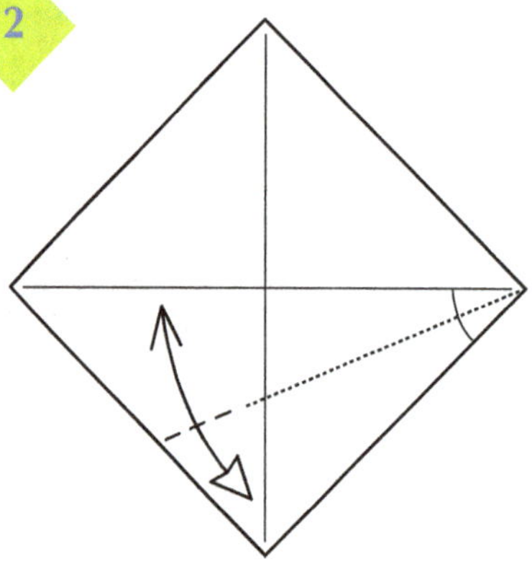

3 Fold and unfold on the edge. Rotate 90°.

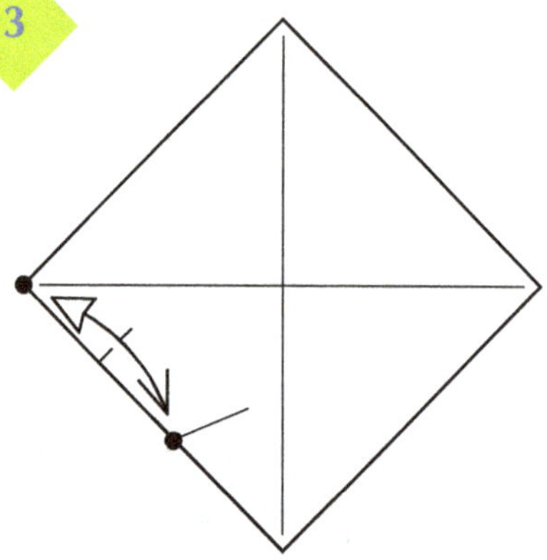

4 Repeat steps 2–3 three times.

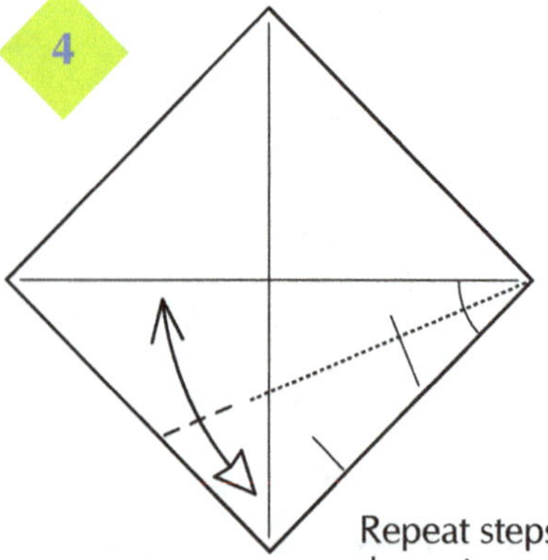

5

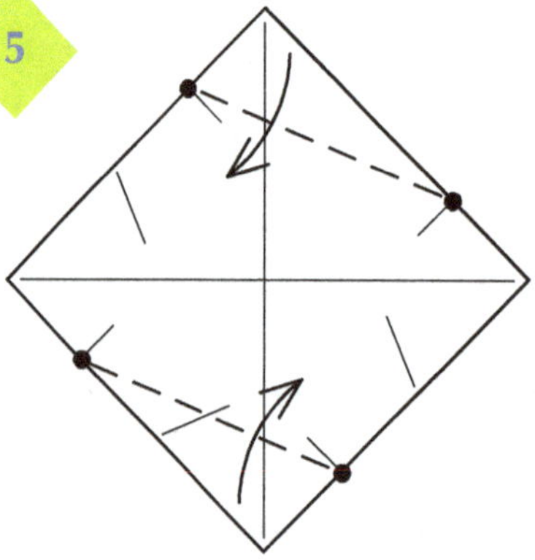

6 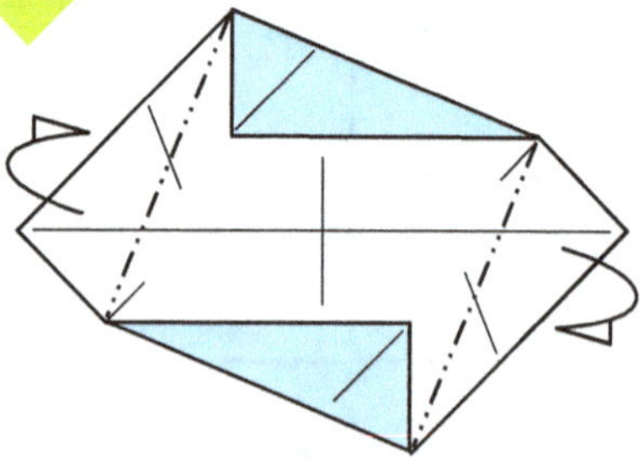 Rotate.

30   *Galaxy of Origami Stars*

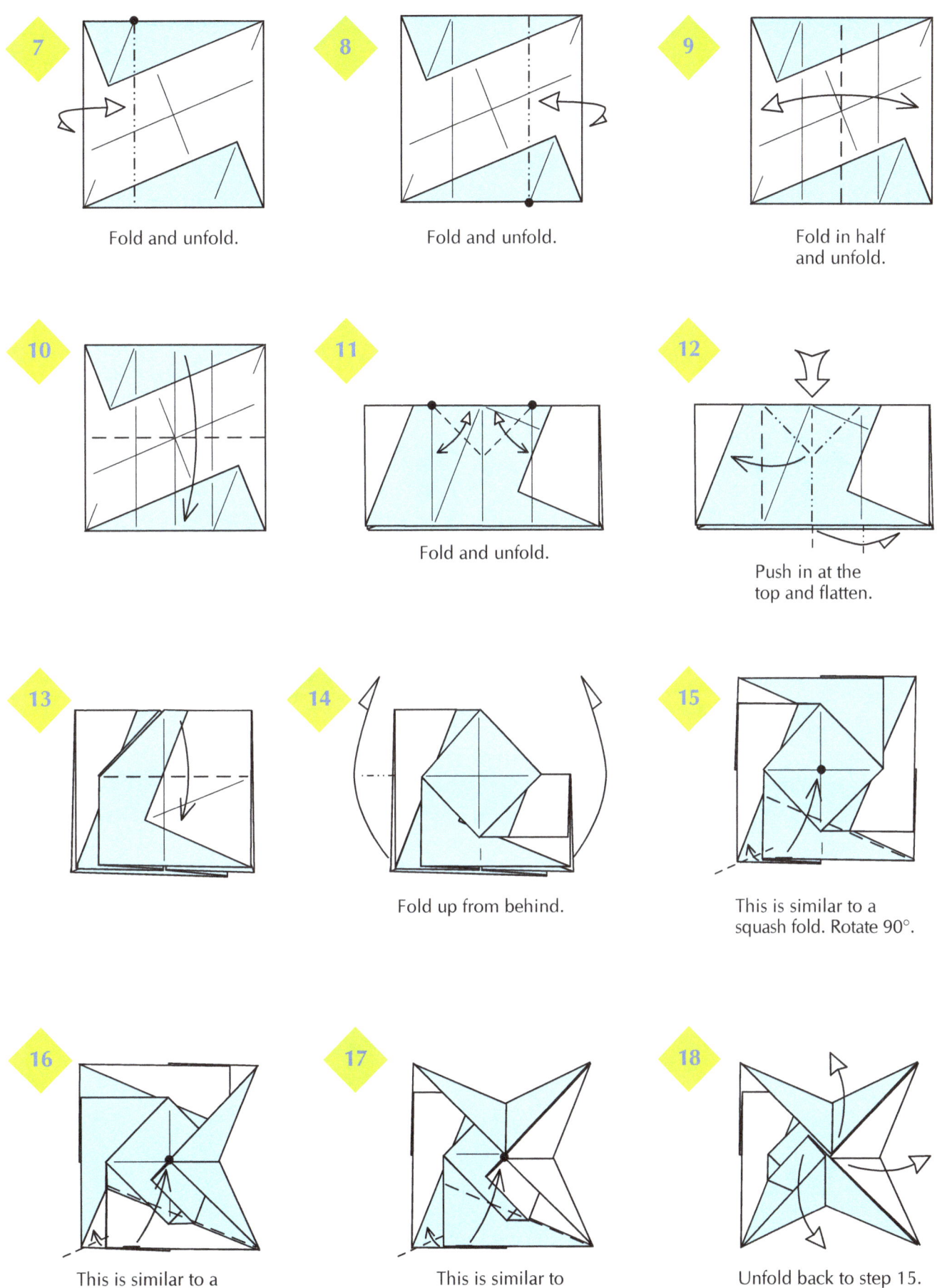

Two-Toned Four-Pointed Star 31

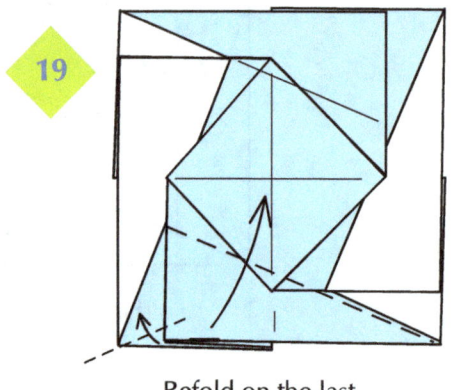

Refold on the last creases. Rotate 90°.

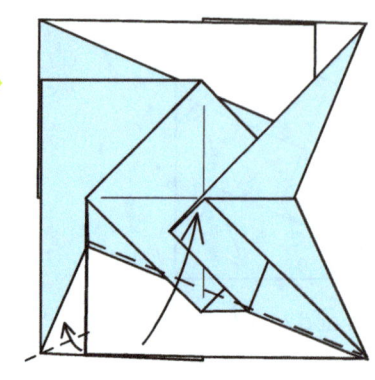

Repeat steps 16–17. Rotate 90°.

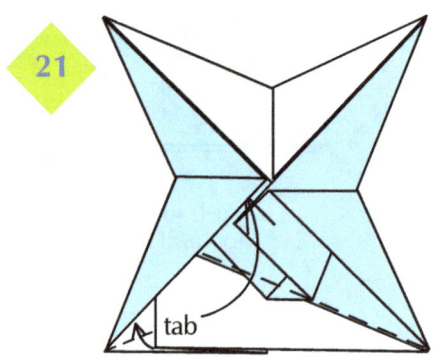

Fold along the creases and tuck the tab inside.

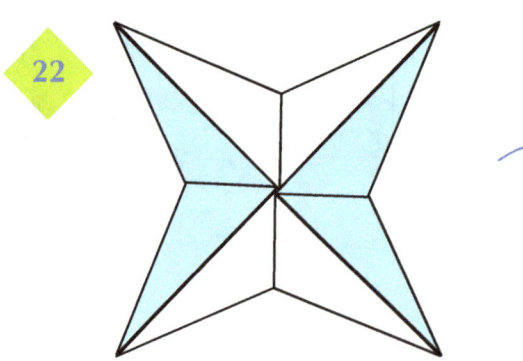

Rotate.

Two-Toned Four-Pointed Star

32 Galaxy of Origami Stars

Double Four-Pointed Star

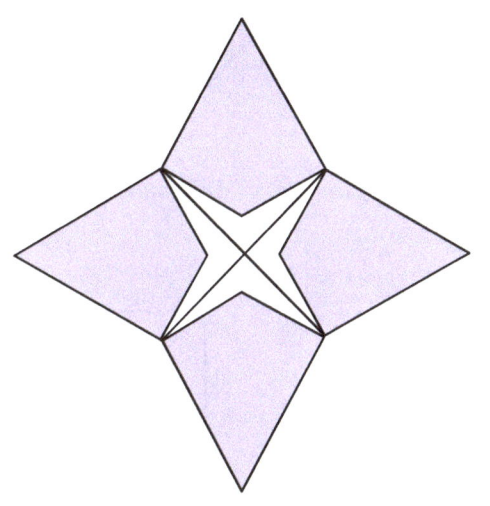

This is the first in a series of double stars, with a white star in the center of a larger, colored star. A small twist fold is used.

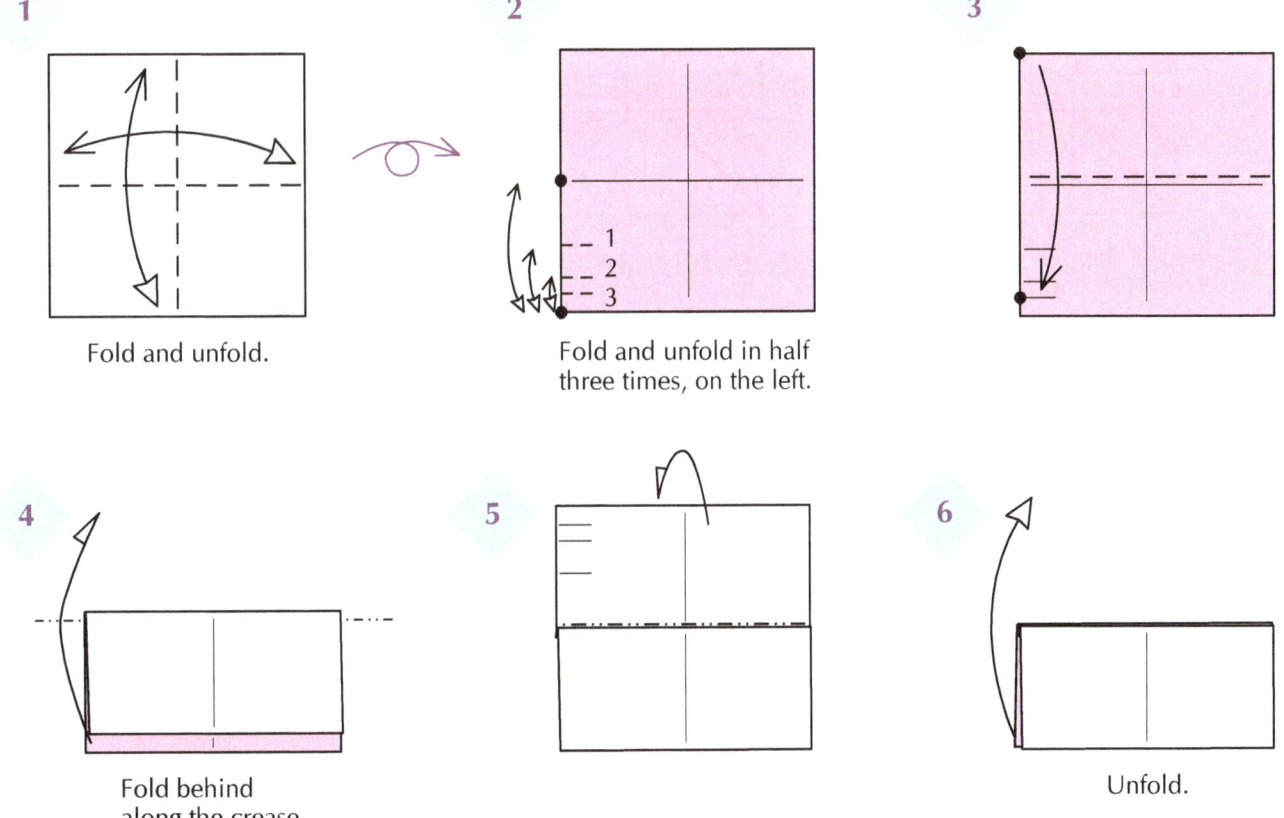

1. Fold and unfold.
2. Fold and unfold in half three times, on the left.
3.
4. Fold behind along the crease.
5.
6. Unfold.

Double Four-Pointed Star 33

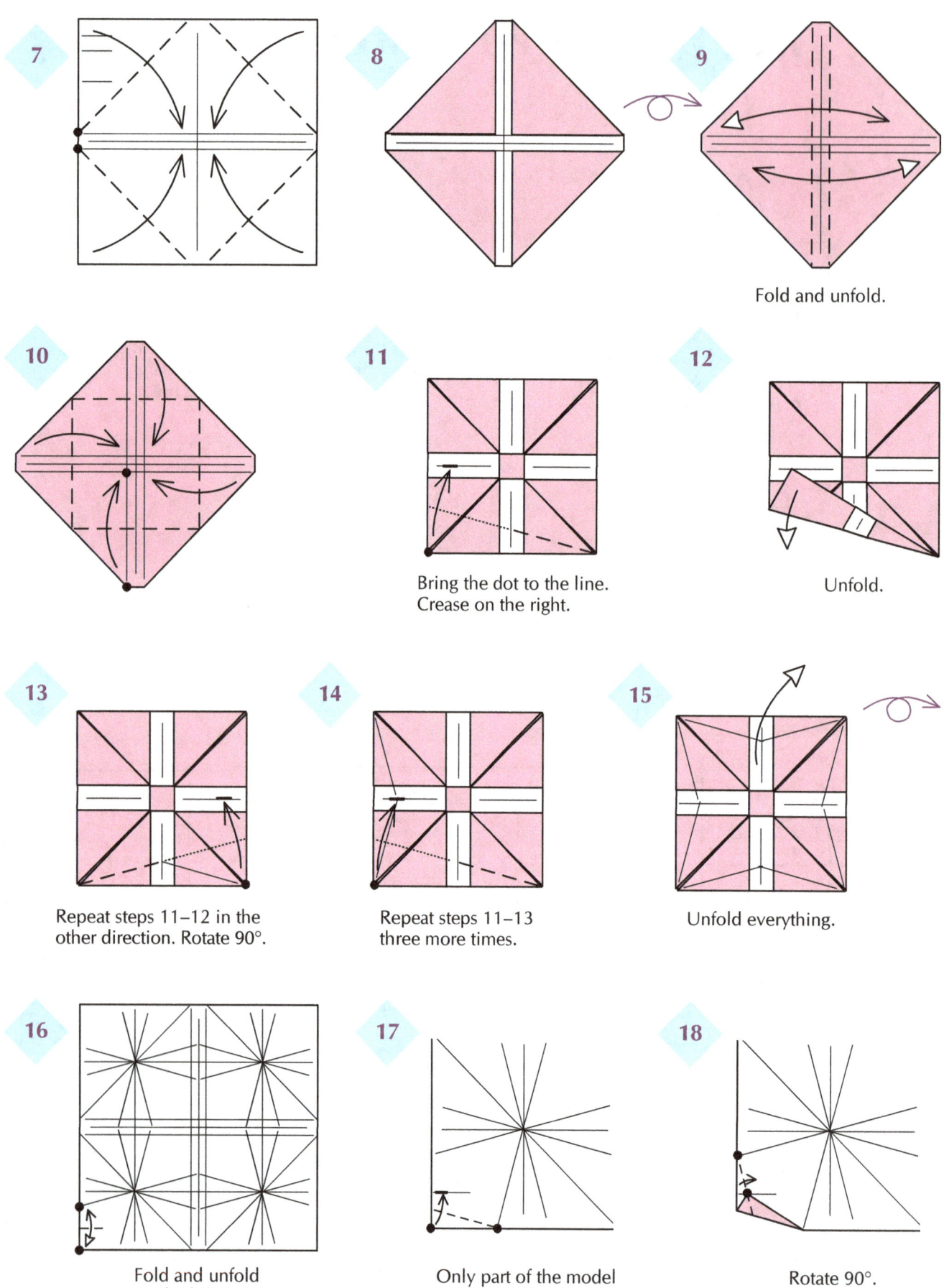

34 Galaxy of Origami Stars

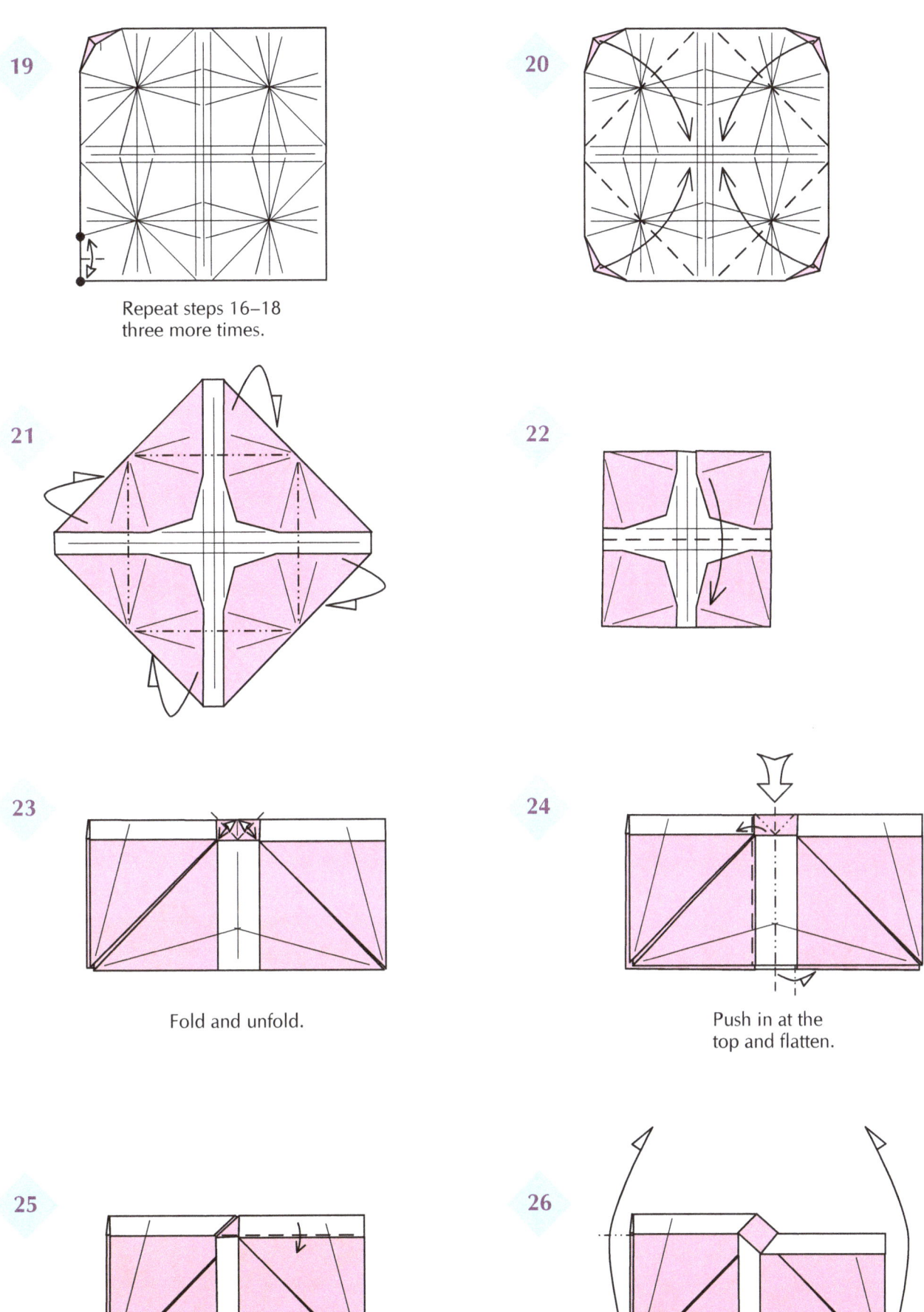

19 Repeat steps 16–18 three more times.

23 Fold and unfold.

24 Push in at the top and flatten.

Double Four-Pointed Star 35

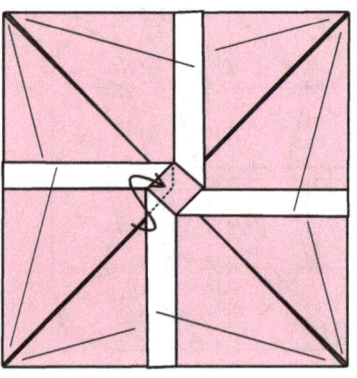

27

Bring the layers to the front.

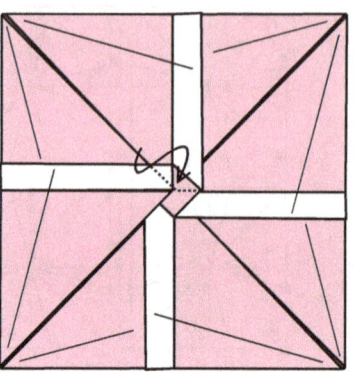

28

Repeat step 27 three more times.

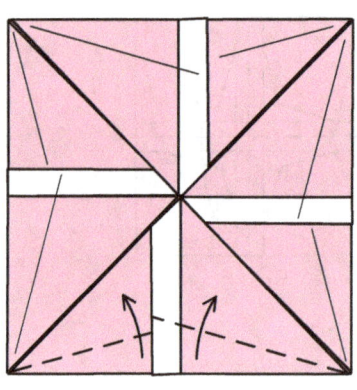

29

Rotate 90°.

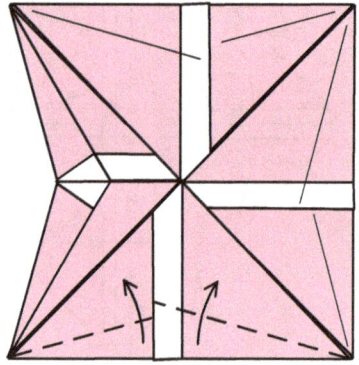

30

Repeat step 29 three more times.

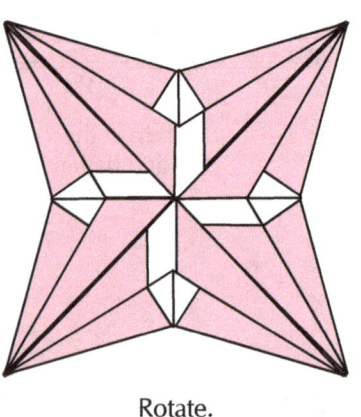

31

Rotate.

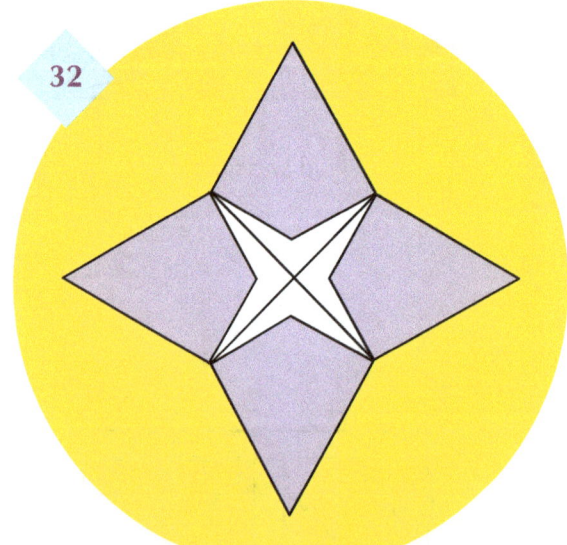

32

Double Four-Pointed Star

36 *Galaxy of Origami Stars*

Five-Pointed Asterisk

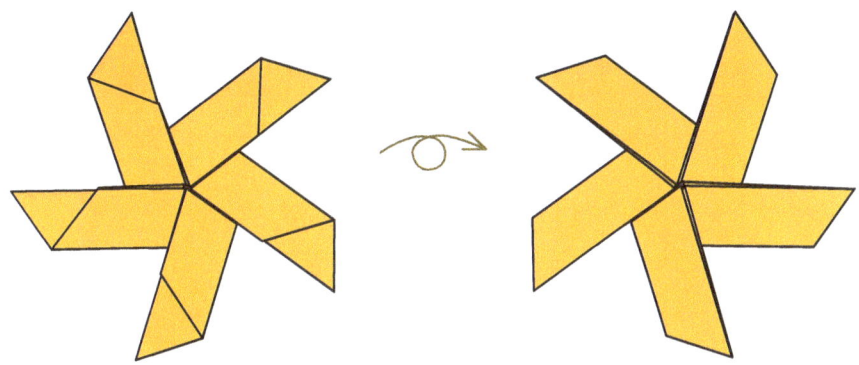

This star begins by folding the square into a pentagon. I have worked out an efficient and exact method for folding a pentagon. A series of squash folds give the model its shape. There is also a six-pointed asterisk in this work.

1. Fold and unfold on the edge.

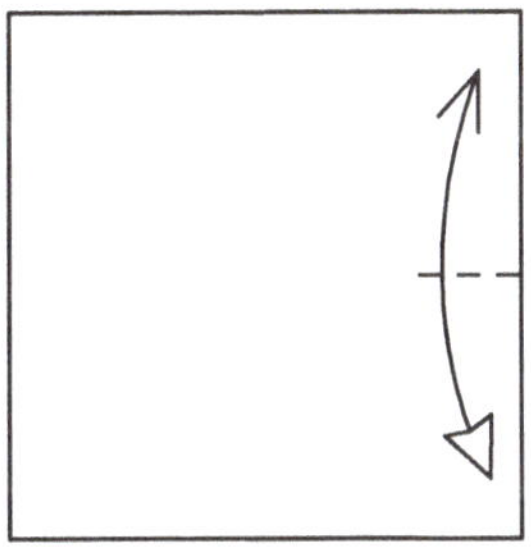

2. Fold and unfold, creasing lightly.

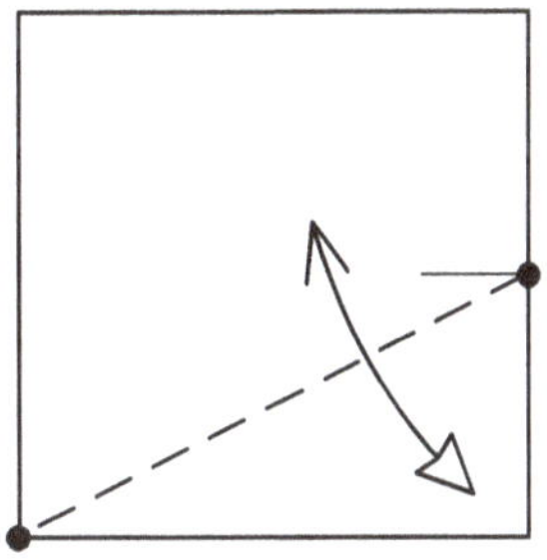

3. Fold and unfold at the bottom to bisect the angle.

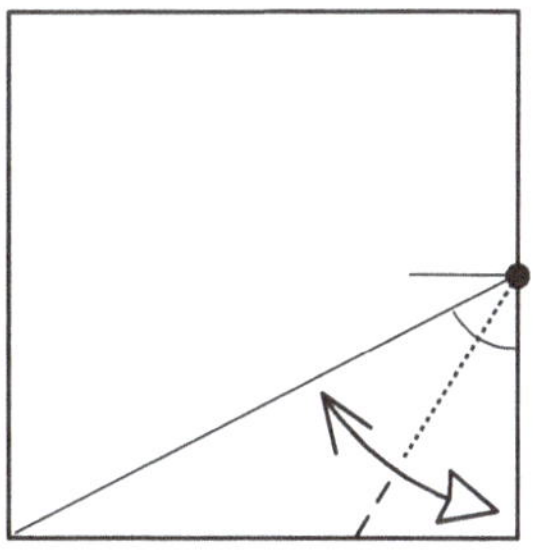

4. Fold and unfold in the center.

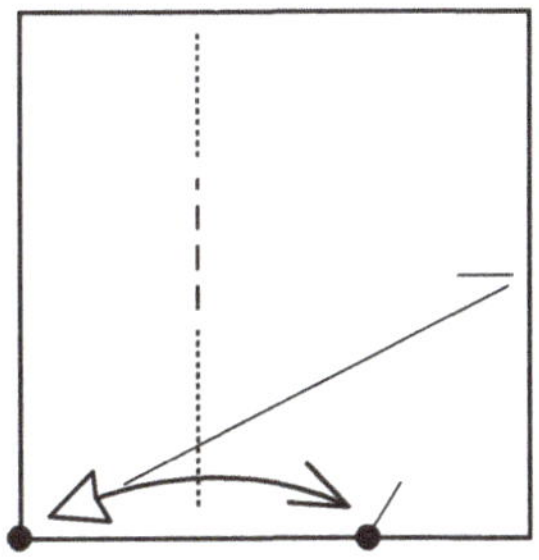

5. Fold in half.

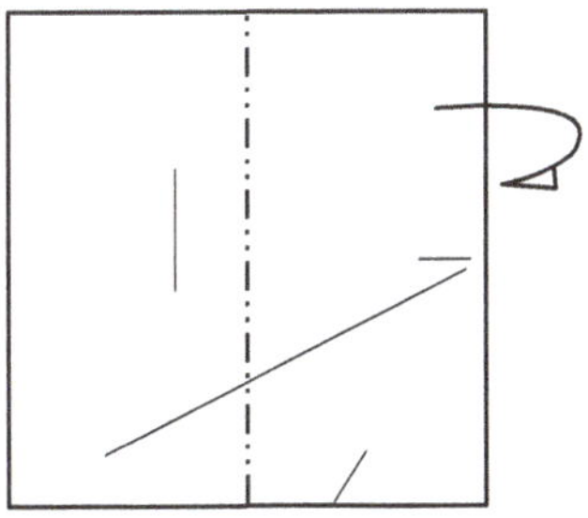

6. Bring the corner to the crease. Repeat behind. The 36° angle is exact.

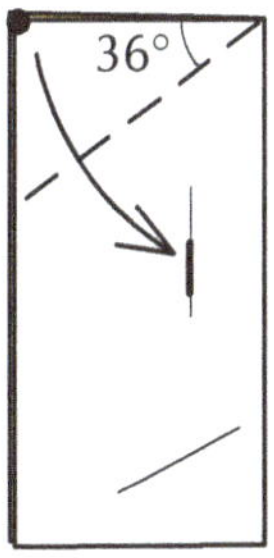

7. Fold and unfold the top layer at the bottom to bisect the angle.

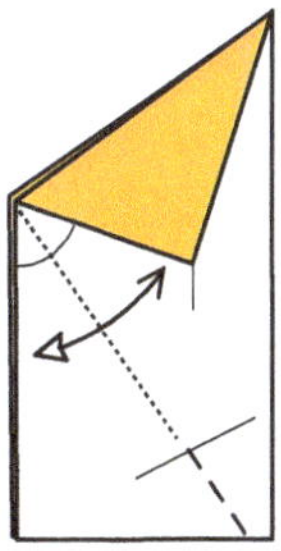

Five-Pointed Asterisk 37

8 Bisect the angle and repeat behind.

9 Unfold.

10 Mountain-fold so the dot meets the edge.

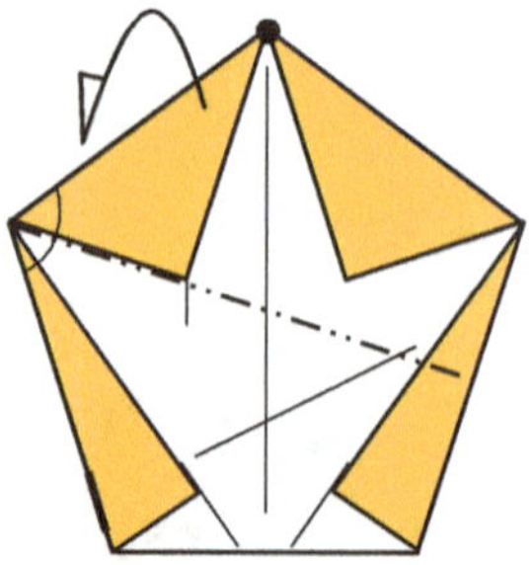

11 Fold along the hidden edge.

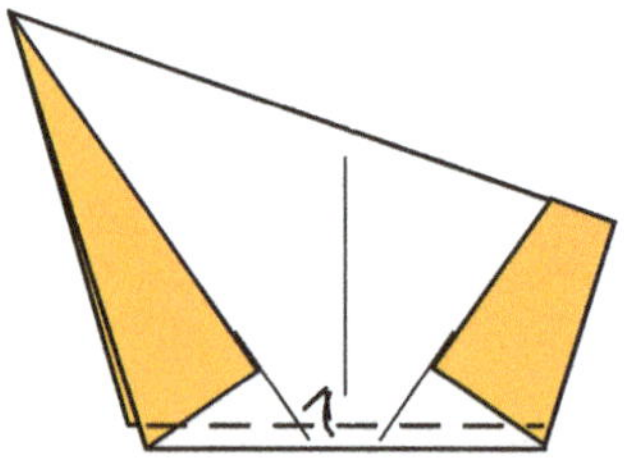

12 Unfold.

13 Fold and unfold along the creases.

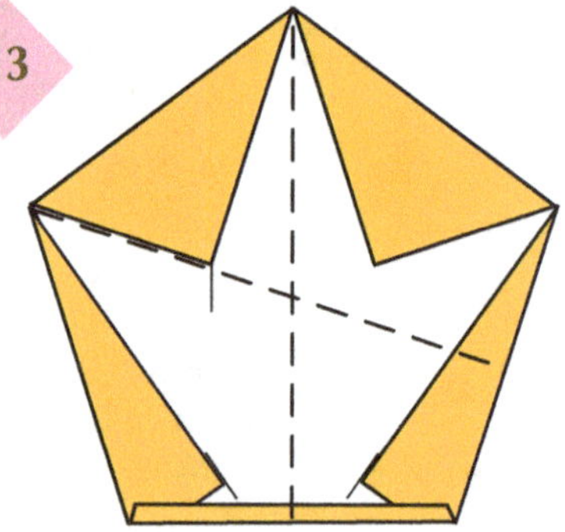

14 Fold and unfold.

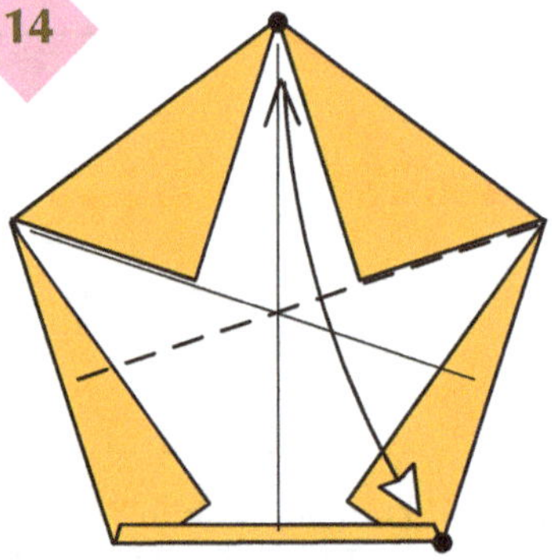

15 Fold and unfold.

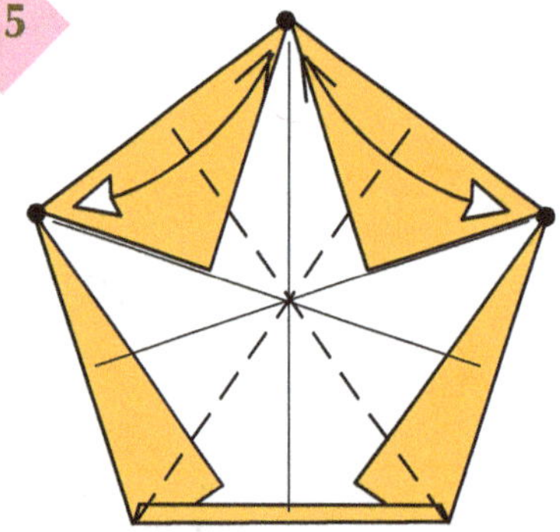

16

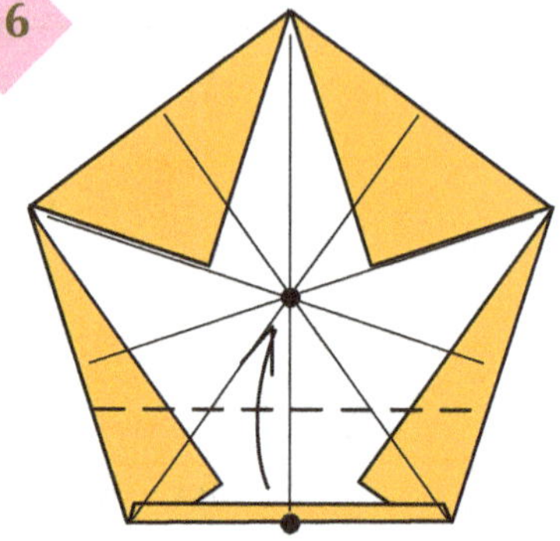

17 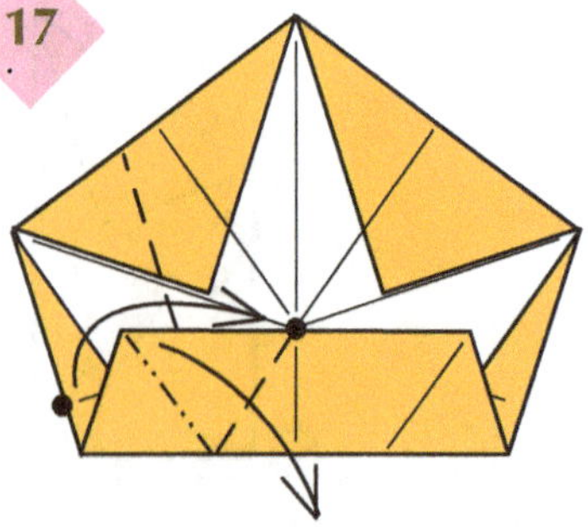 The dots will meet. Squash-fold and rotate.

18 Squash-fold and rotate.

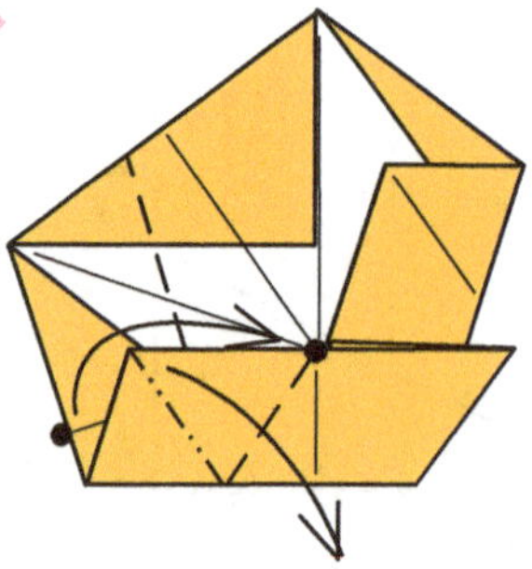

19 Squash-fold and rotate.

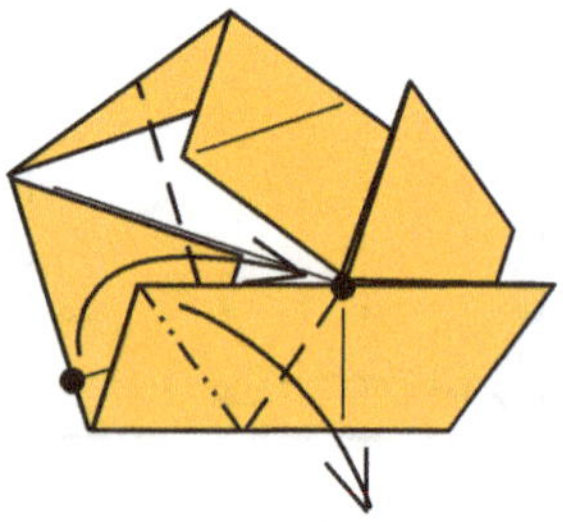

38   *Galaxy of Origami Stars*

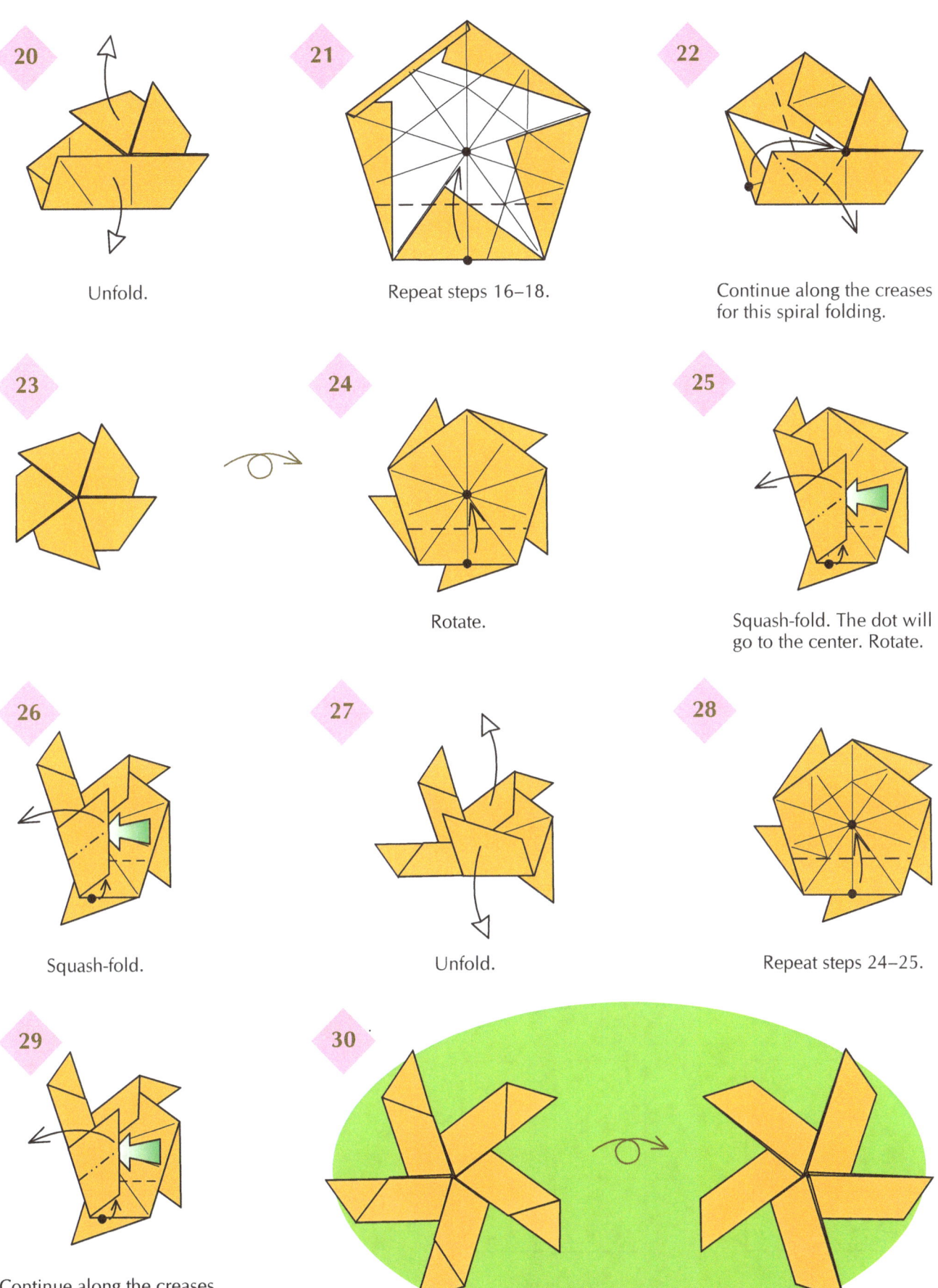

Five-Pointed Asterisk 39

Double Five-Pointed Star

In the series of double stars, this one begins with a pentagon and uses a pentagonal twist fold.

1
Fold and unfold on the edge.

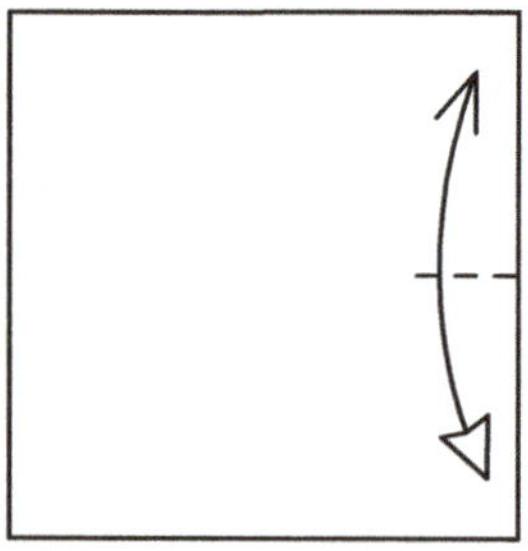

2
Fold and unfold, creasing lightly.

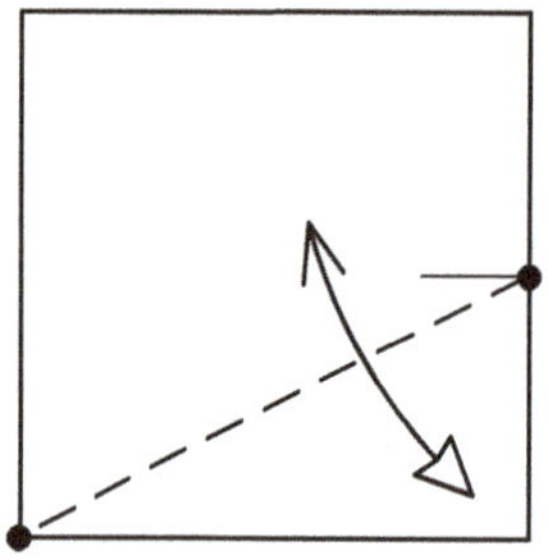

3
Fold and unfold at the bottom to bisect the angle.

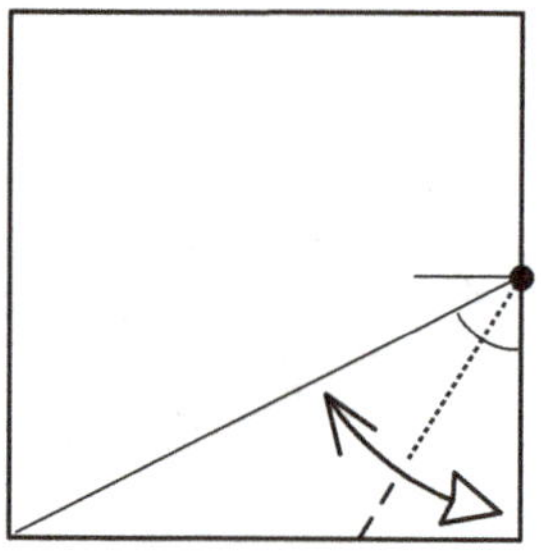

4
Fold and unfold in the center.

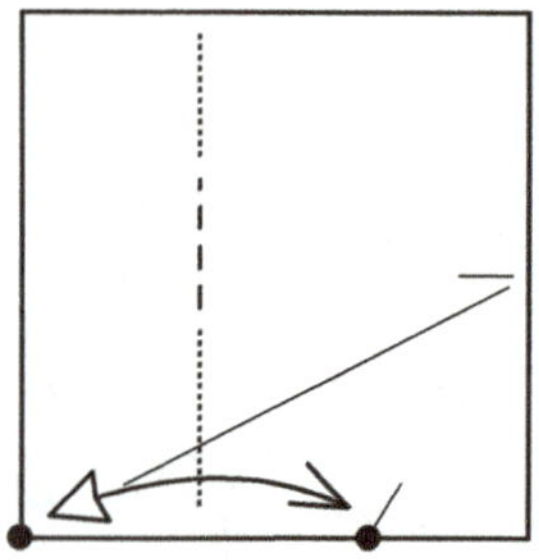

5
Fold in half.

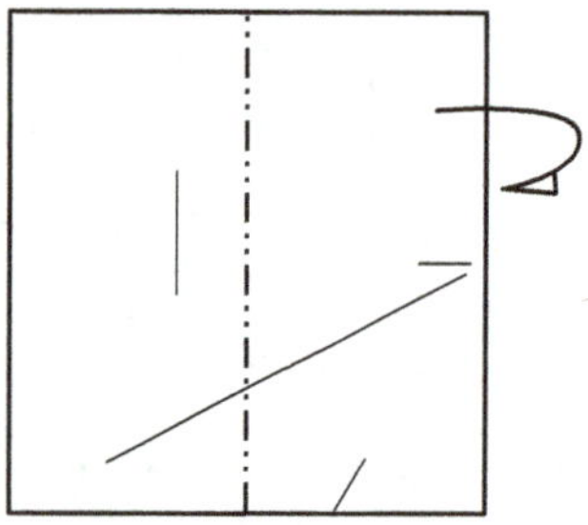

6
Bring the corner to the crease. Repeat behind. The 36° angle is exact.

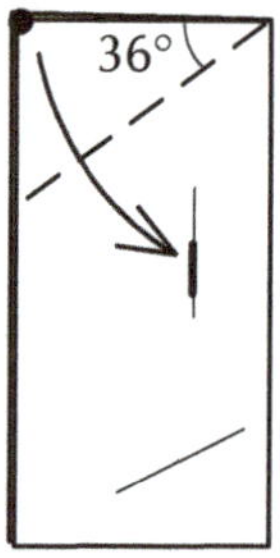

7
Fold and unfold the top layer at the bottom to bisect the angle.

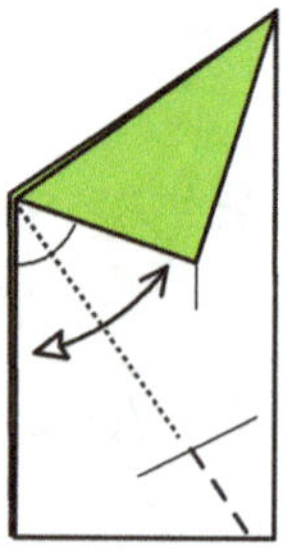

40 *Galaxy of Origami Stars*

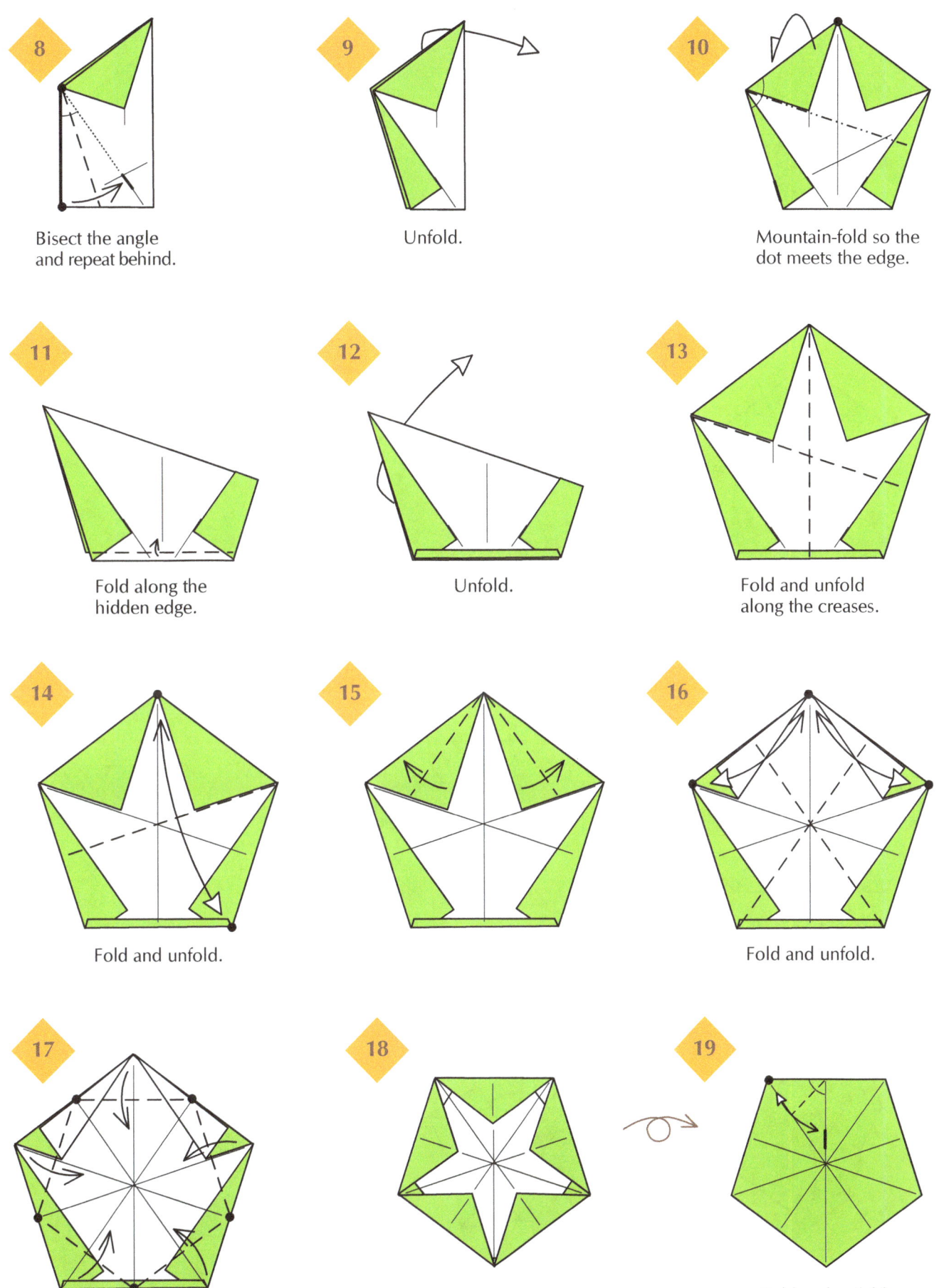

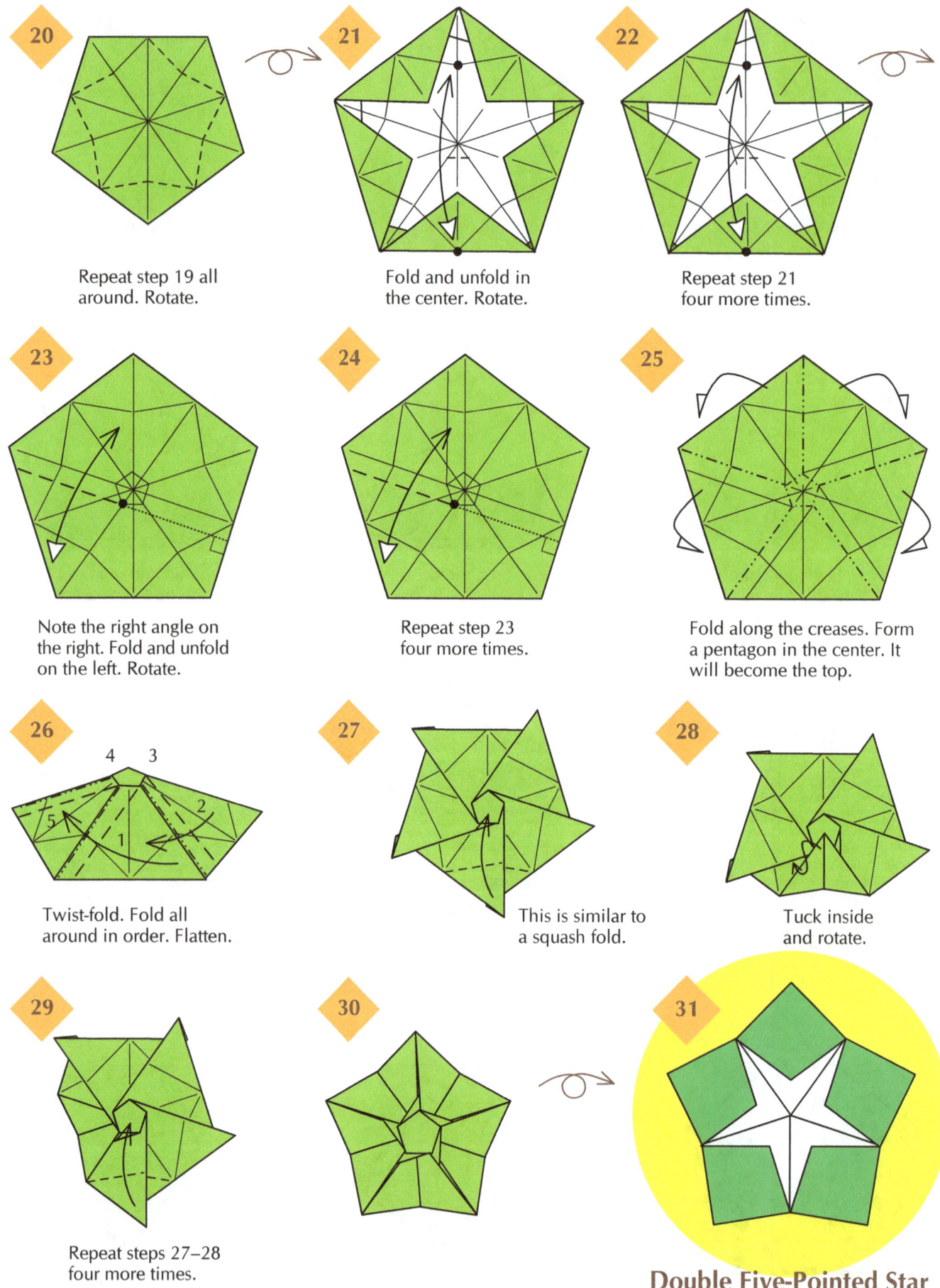

Double Five-Pointed Star

42   Galaxy of Origami Stars

Five-Pointed Star

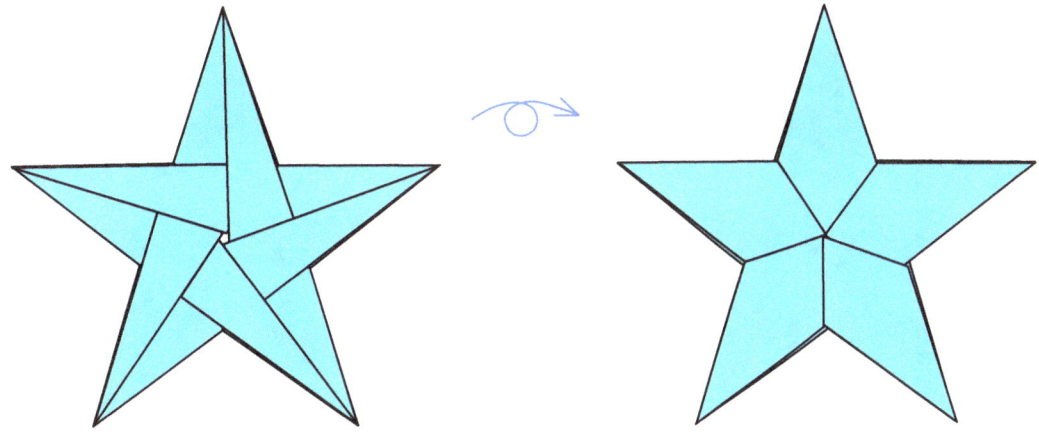

This solid colored star has a woven pattern on one side. Making a pentagon and using a twist fold are part of the folding procedure.

1. Fold and unfold on the edge.

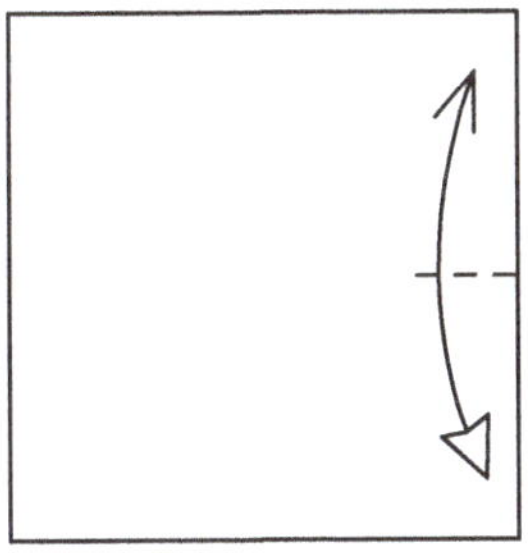

2. Fold and unfold, creasing lightly.

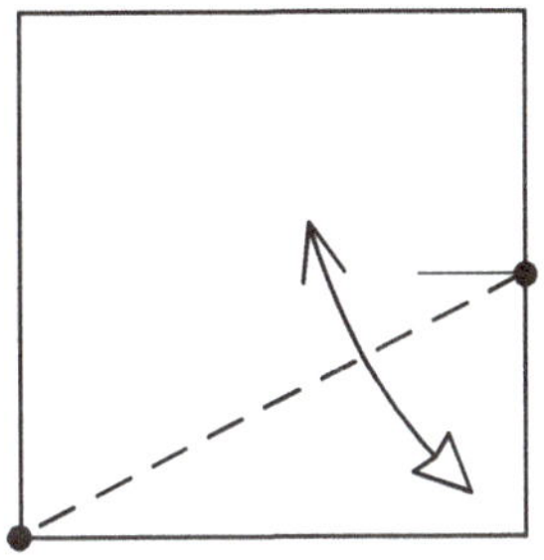

3. Fold and unfold at the bottom to bisect the angle.

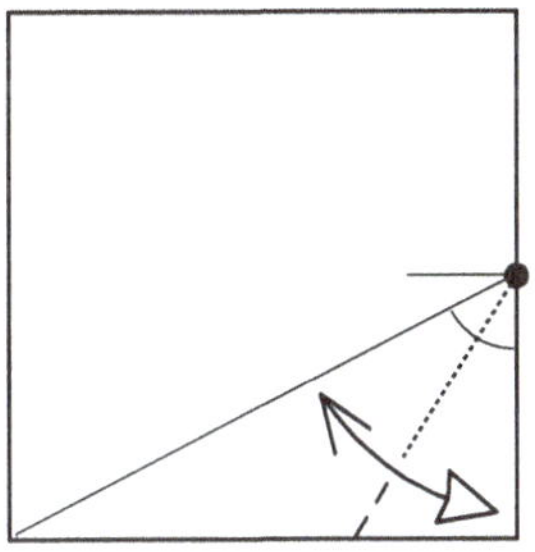

4. Fold and unfold in the center.

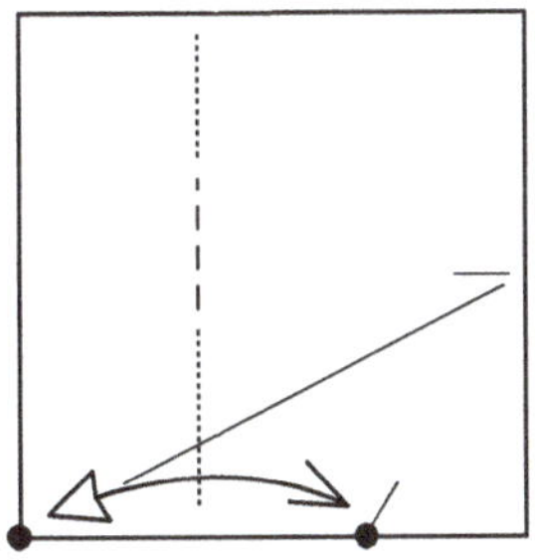

5. Fold in half.

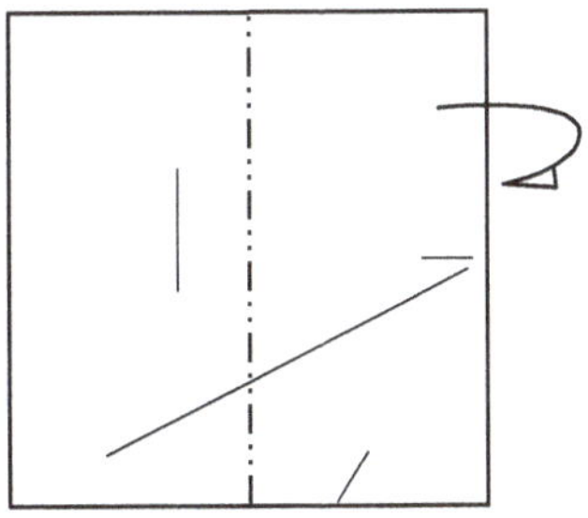

6. Bring the corner to the crease. Repeat behind. The 36° angle is exact.

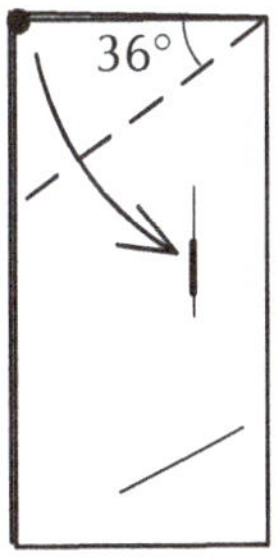

7. Unfold.

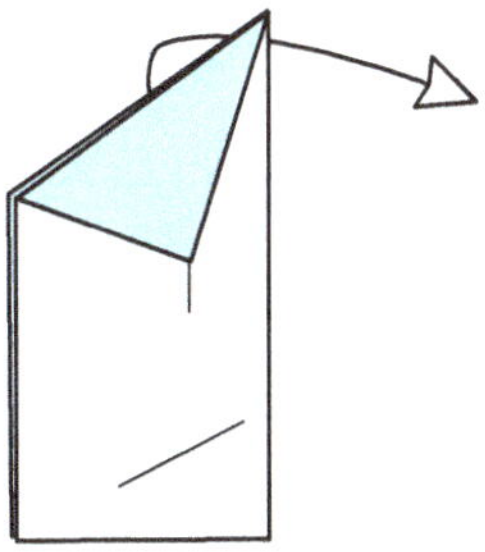

Five-Pointed Star 43

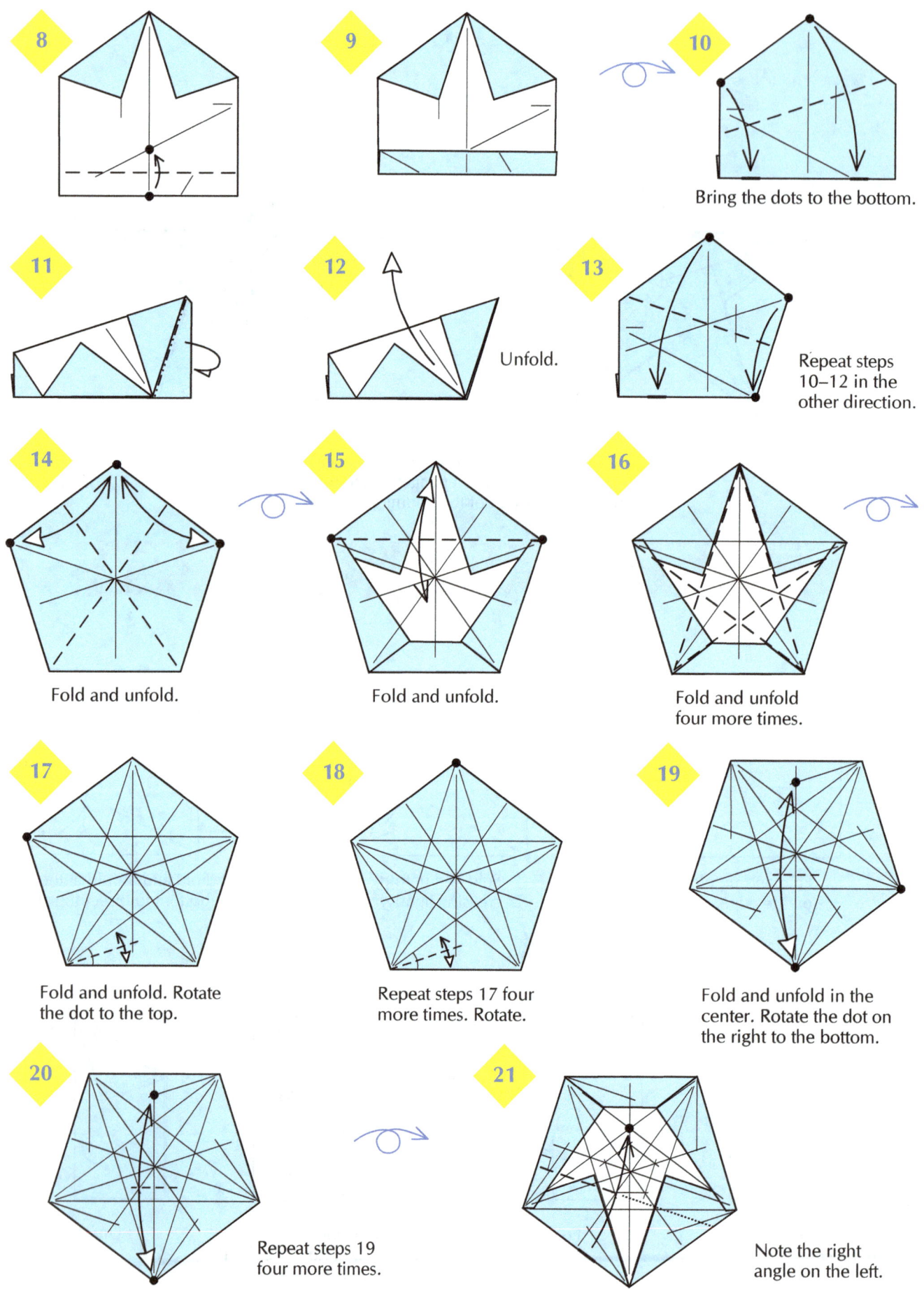

44 Galaxy of Origami Stars

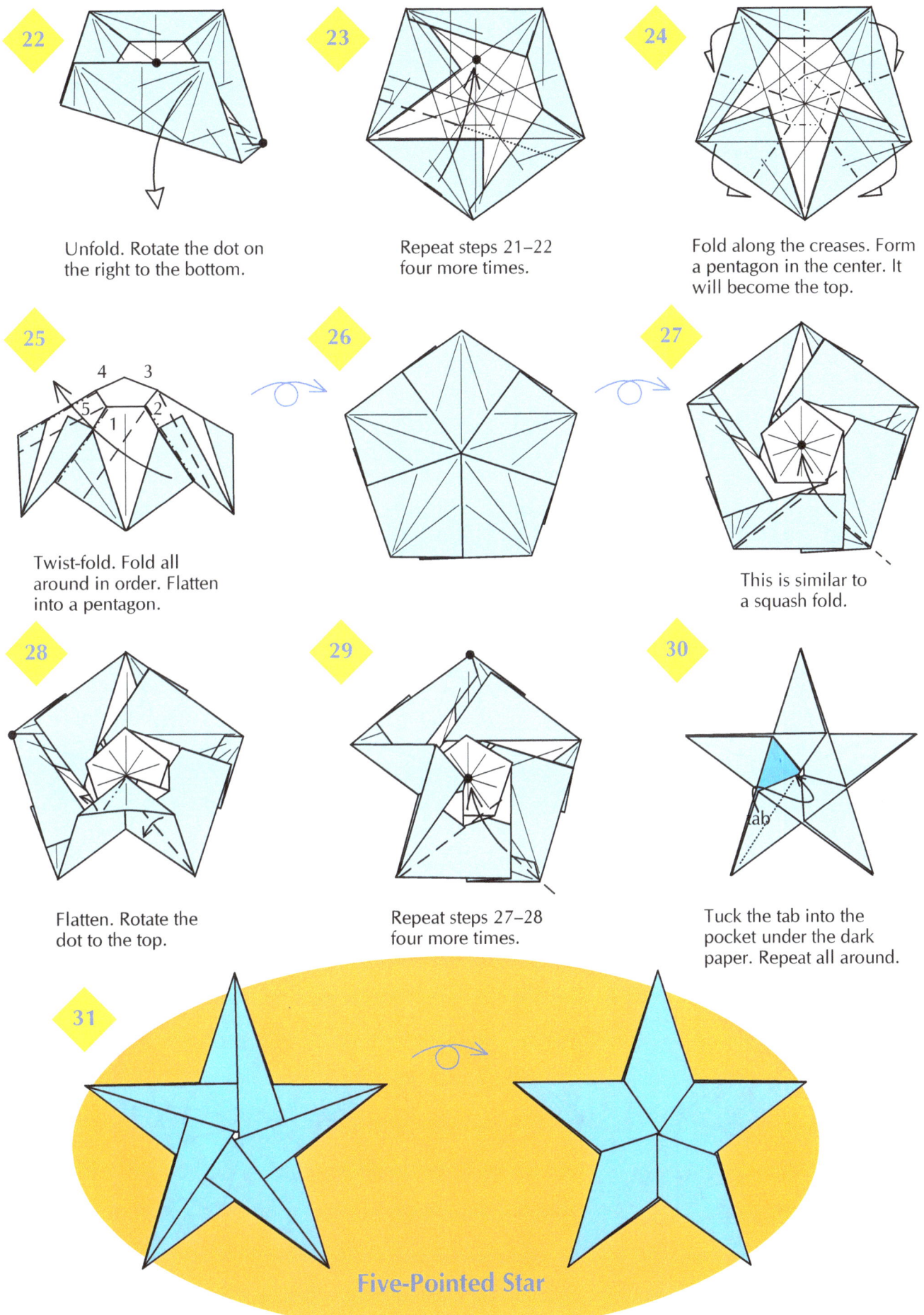

Radiant Five-Pointed Star

Designed by Russell Cashdollar

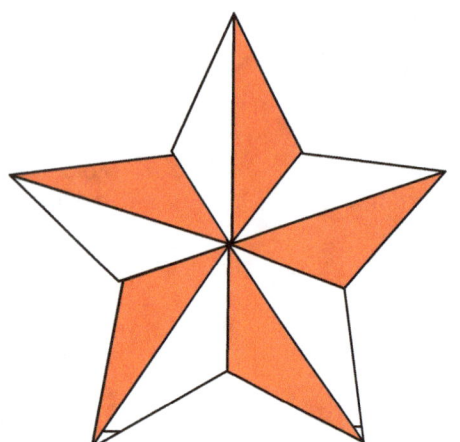

This radiant star begins by folding a pentagon and uses a twist fold. It can also be folded with the colors reversed.

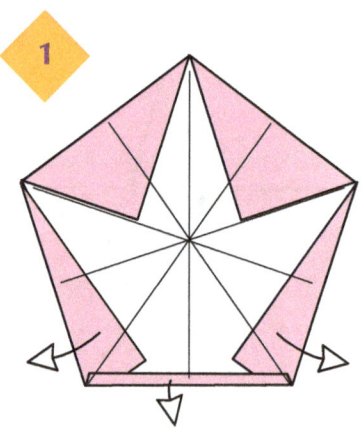

1. Begin with step 16 of the Five-Pointed Asterisk (page 37). Unfold.

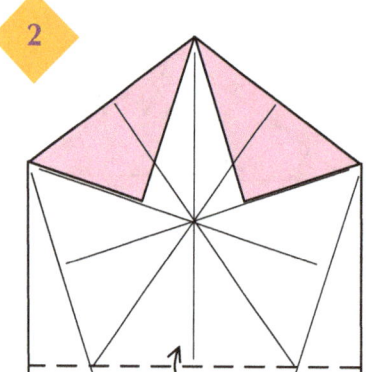

2. Fold along the crease.

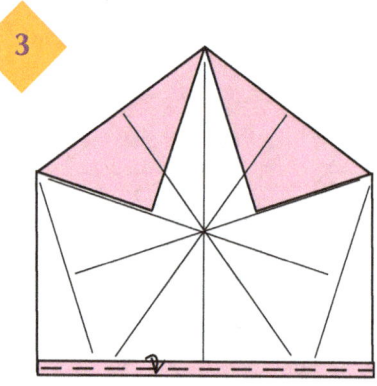

3. Fold the thin strip in half.

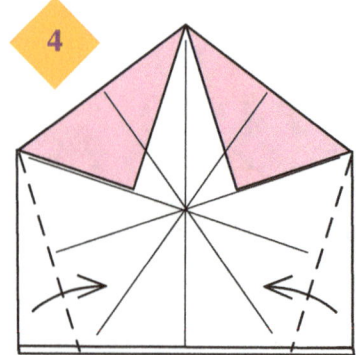

4. Fold along the creases.

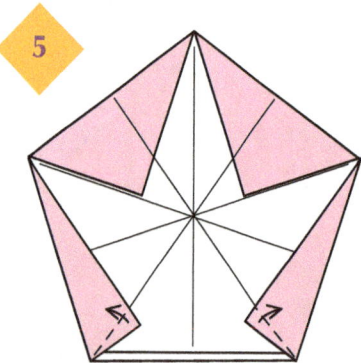

5. Fold along hidden creases.

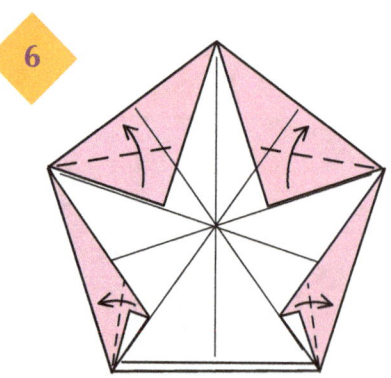

6. Fold to the edges.

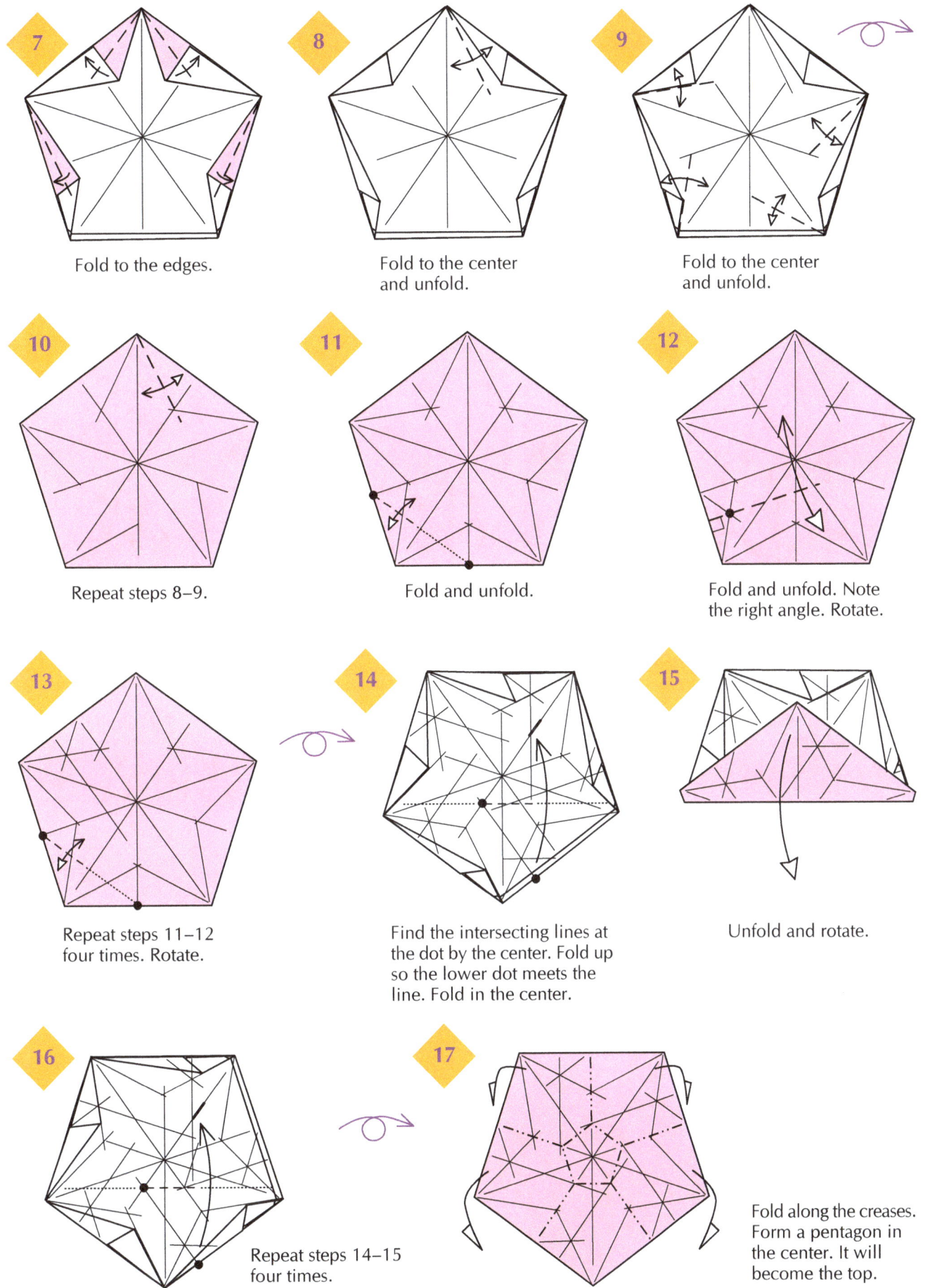

Radiant Five-Pointed Star 47

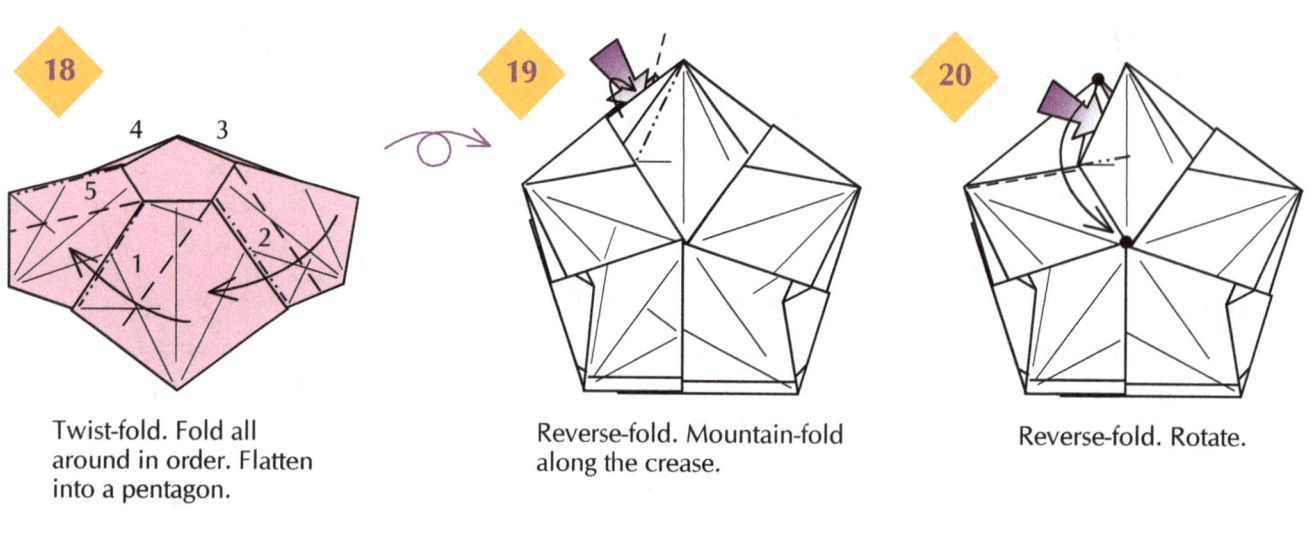

18. Twist-fold. Fold all around in order. Flatten into a pentagon.

19. Reverse-fold. Mountain-fold along the crease.

20. Reverse-fold. Rotate.

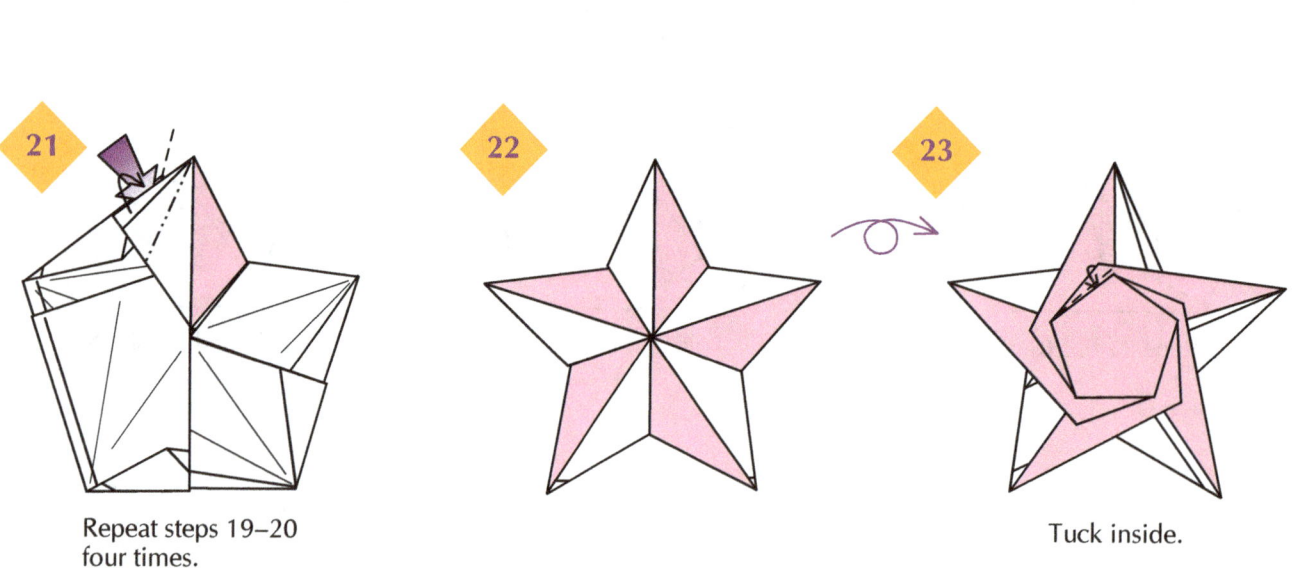

21. Repeat steps 19–20 four times.

23. Tuck inside.

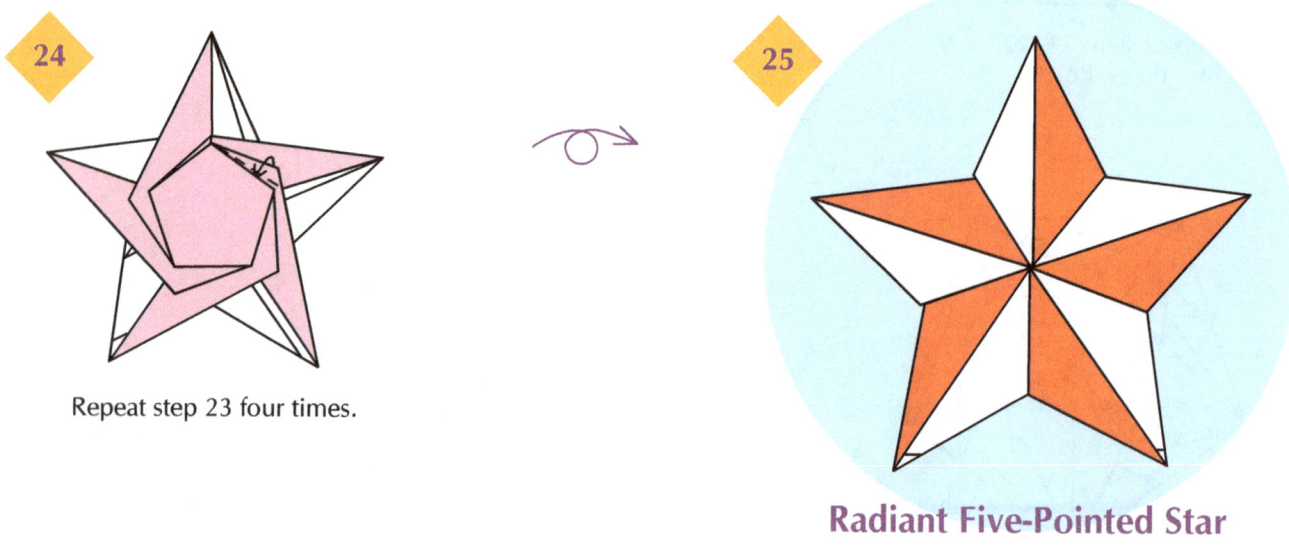

24. Repeat step 23 four times.

Radiant Five-Pointed Star

48   *Galaxy of Origami Stars*

Six-Pointed Asterisk

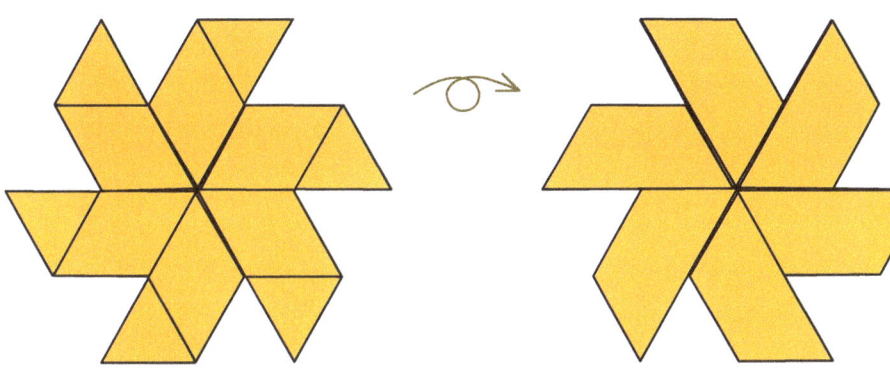

There are six six-pointed stars in this collection. They all begin by folding the square into a hexagon, though the specific hexagons are not all the same. The folding method for this asterisk is similar to the five-pointed asterisk. A variation of this star is the Double-Sided Six-Pointed Star.

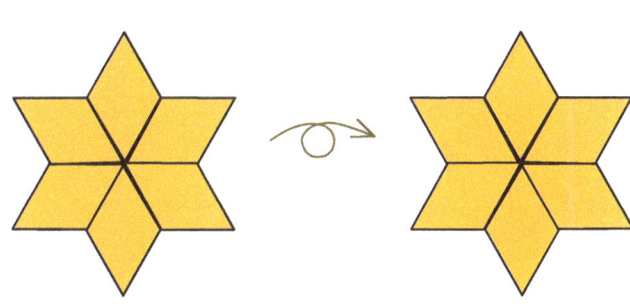

Double-Sided Six-Pointed Star

1.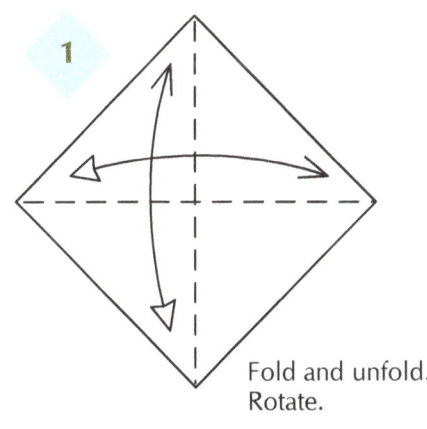
Fold and unfold. Rotate.

2.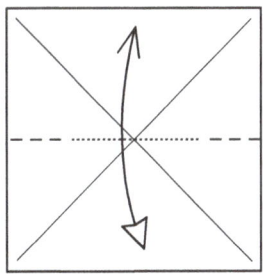
Fold and unfold on the edges.

3.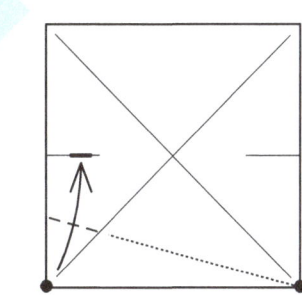
Bring the corner to the crease.

4.
Unfold.

5.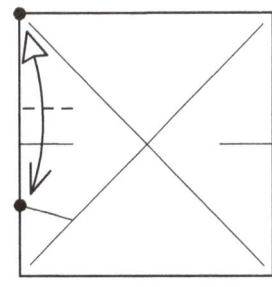
Fold and unfold. Rotate 180°.

6.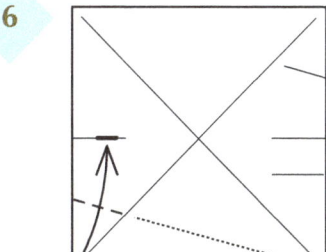
Repeat steps 3–5.

Six-Pointed Asterisk 49

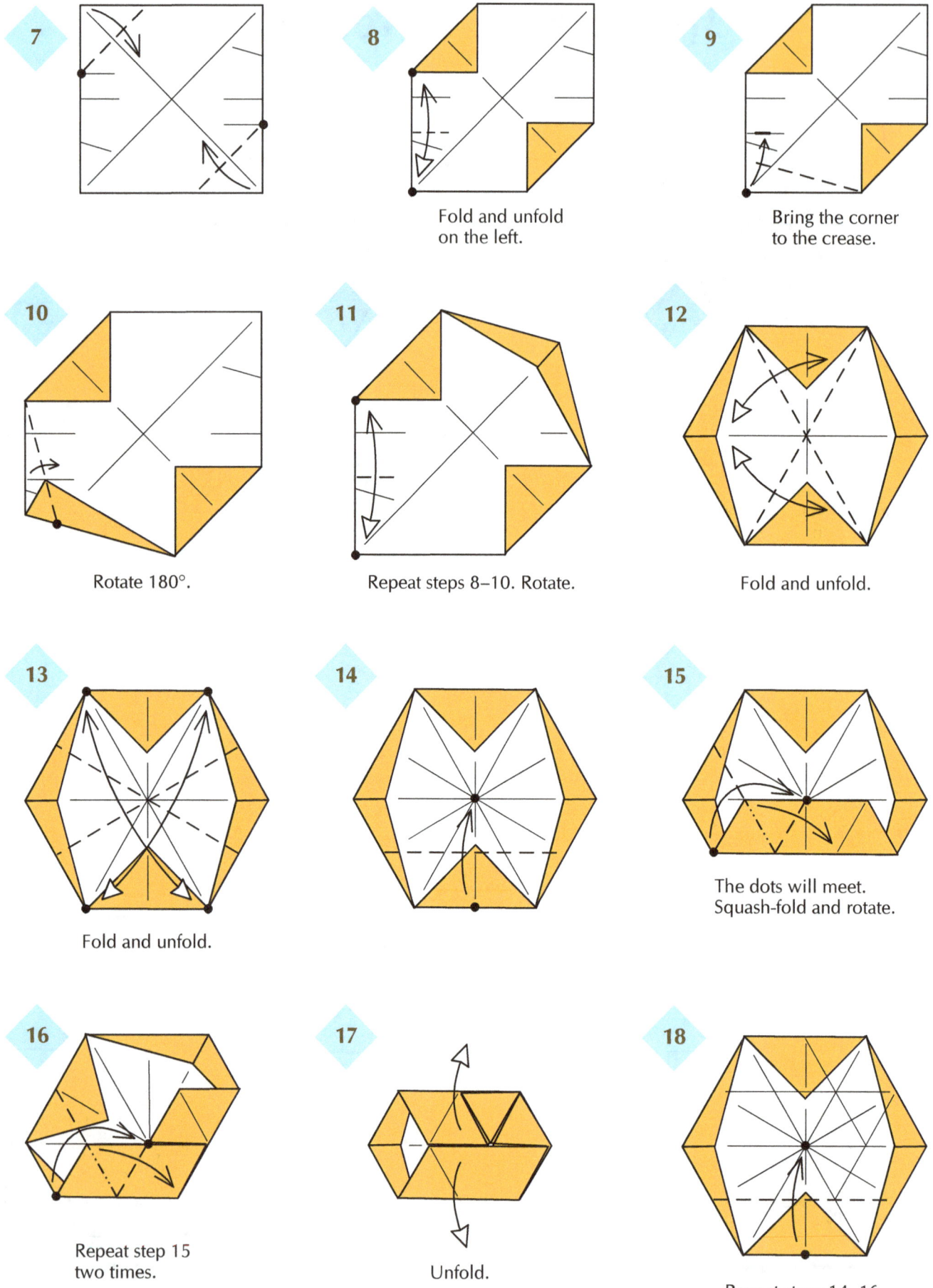

50 *Galaxy of Origami Stars*

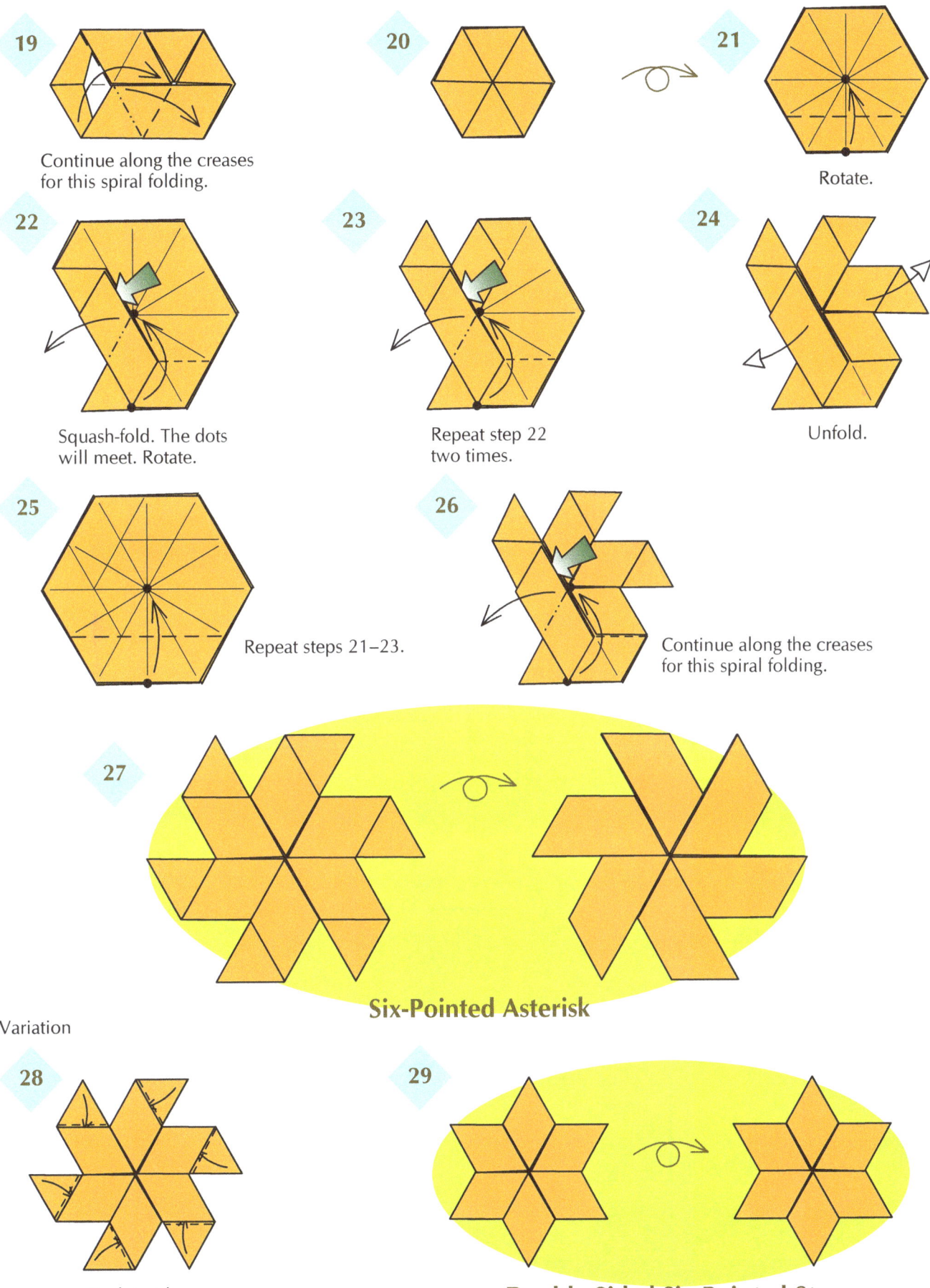

19 Continue along the creases for this spiral folding.

20

21 Rotate.

22 Squash-fold. The dots will meet. Rotate.

23 Repeat step 22 two times.

24 Unfold.

25 Repeat steps 21–23.

26 Continue along the creases for this spiral folding.

27 **Six-Pointed Asterisk**

Variation

28 Tuck inside.

29 **Double-Sided Six-Pointed Star**

Six-Pointed Asterisk 51

Six-Pointed Star

This solid colored star begins by folding the square into a hexagon. Later, a hexagonal twist fold is used.

1 Fold and unfold. Rotate.

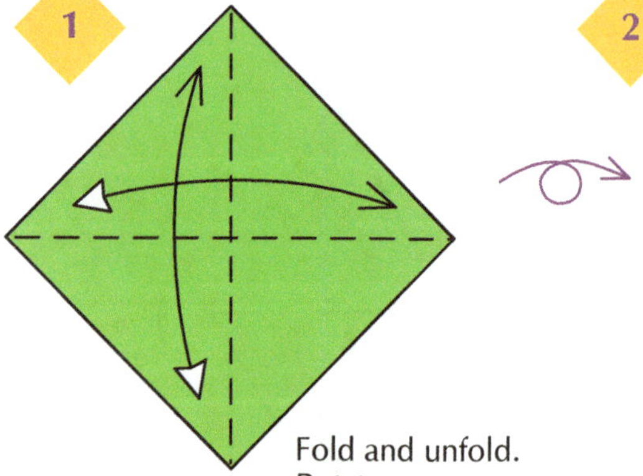

2 Fold and unfold on the edges.

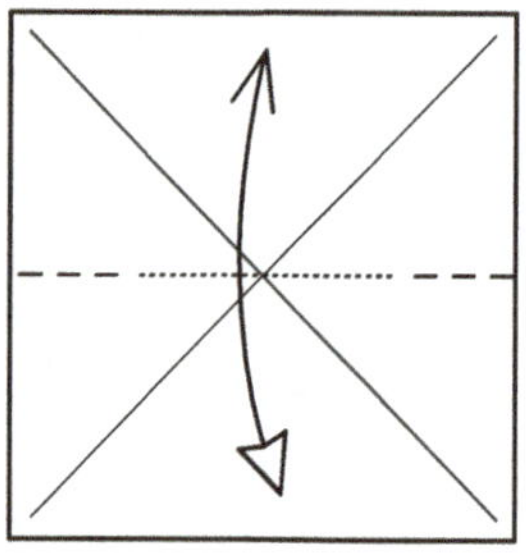

3 Bring the corner to the crease.

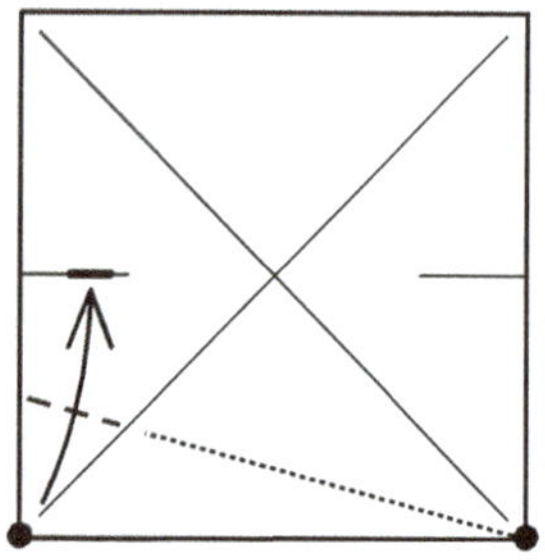

4 Unfold.

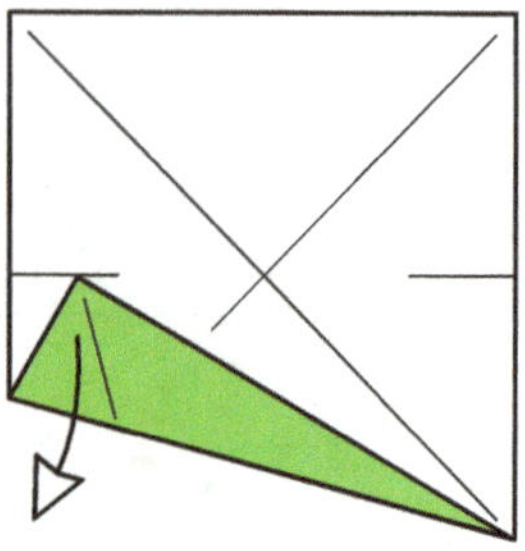

5 Fold and unfold. Rotate 180°.

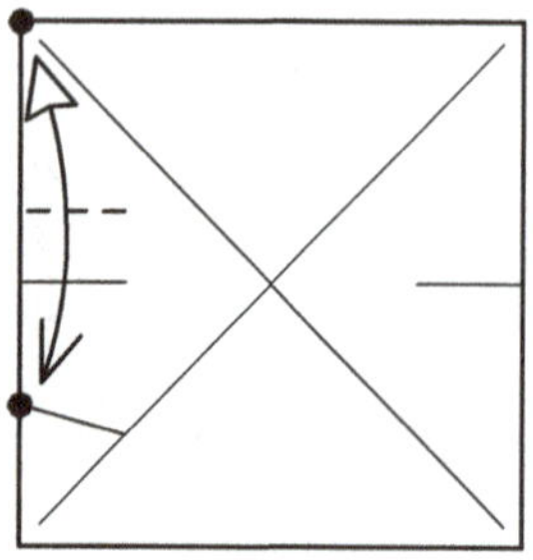

6 Repeat steps 3–5.

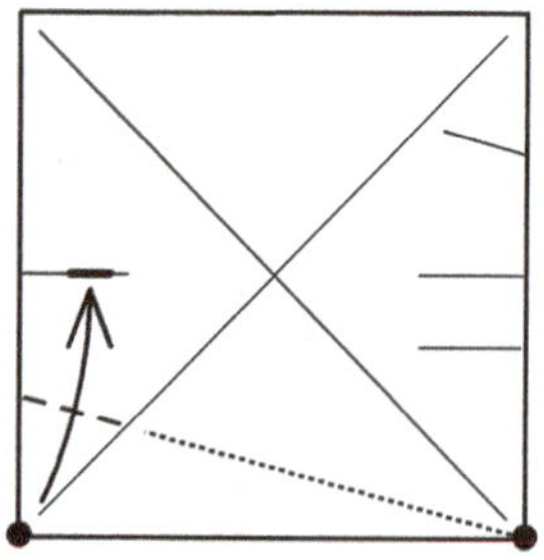

52   *Galaxy of Origami Stars*

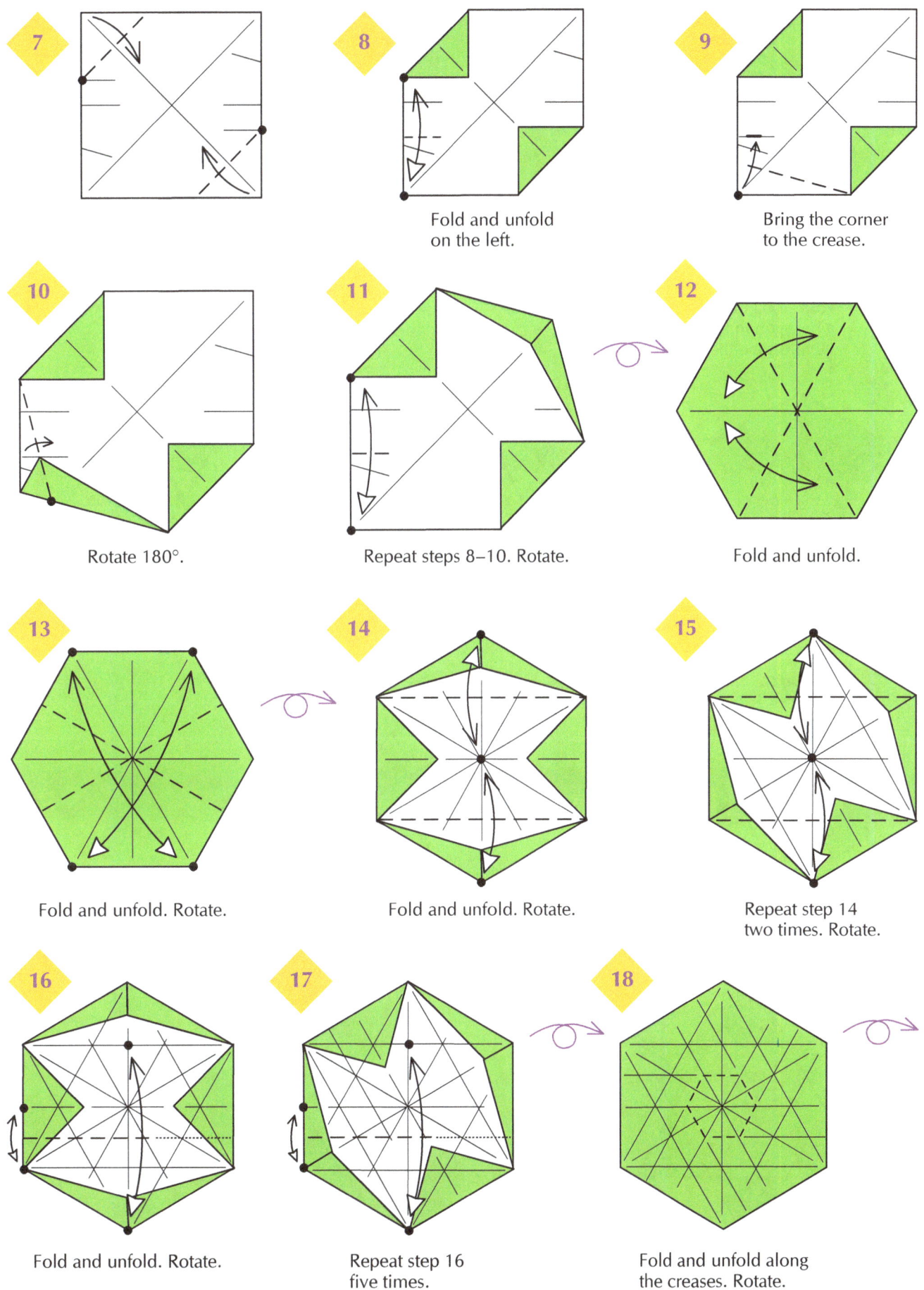

Six-Pointed Star

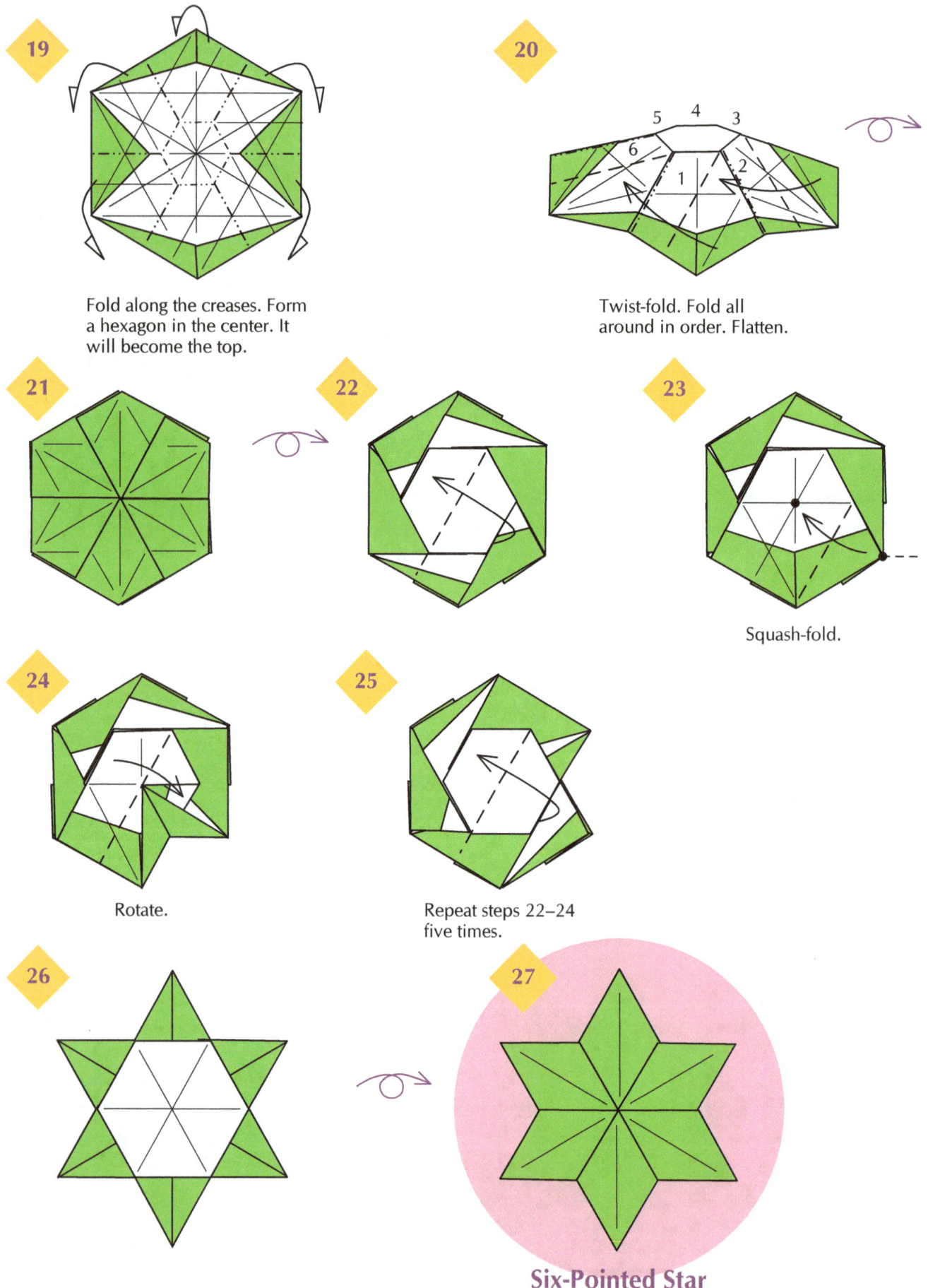

Double Six-Pointed Star

This double star begins by folding a hexagon and uses a hexagonal twist fold.

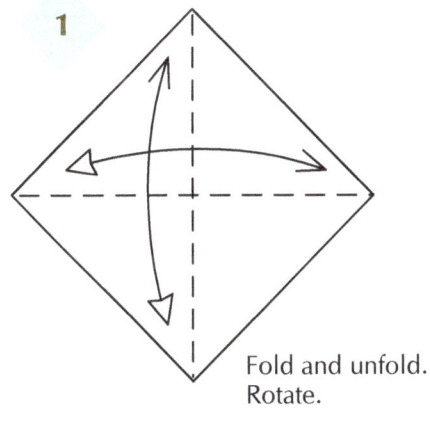

Fold and unfold. Rotate.

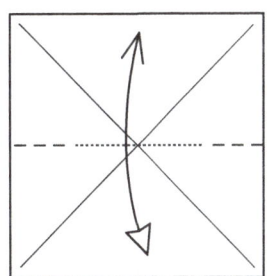

Fold and unfold on the edges.

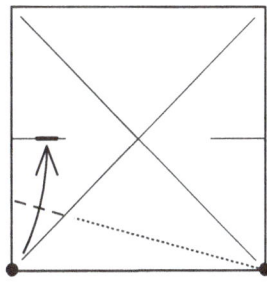

Bring the corner to the crease.

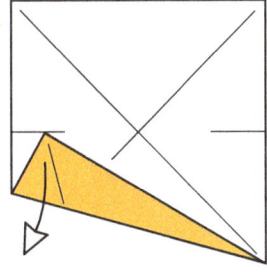

Unfold.

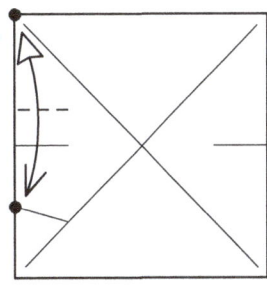

Fold and unfold. Rotate 180°.

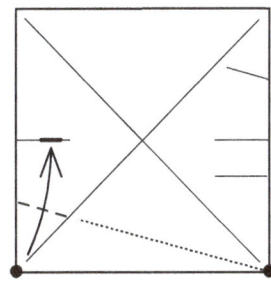

Repeat steps 3–5.

Double Six-Pointed Star 55

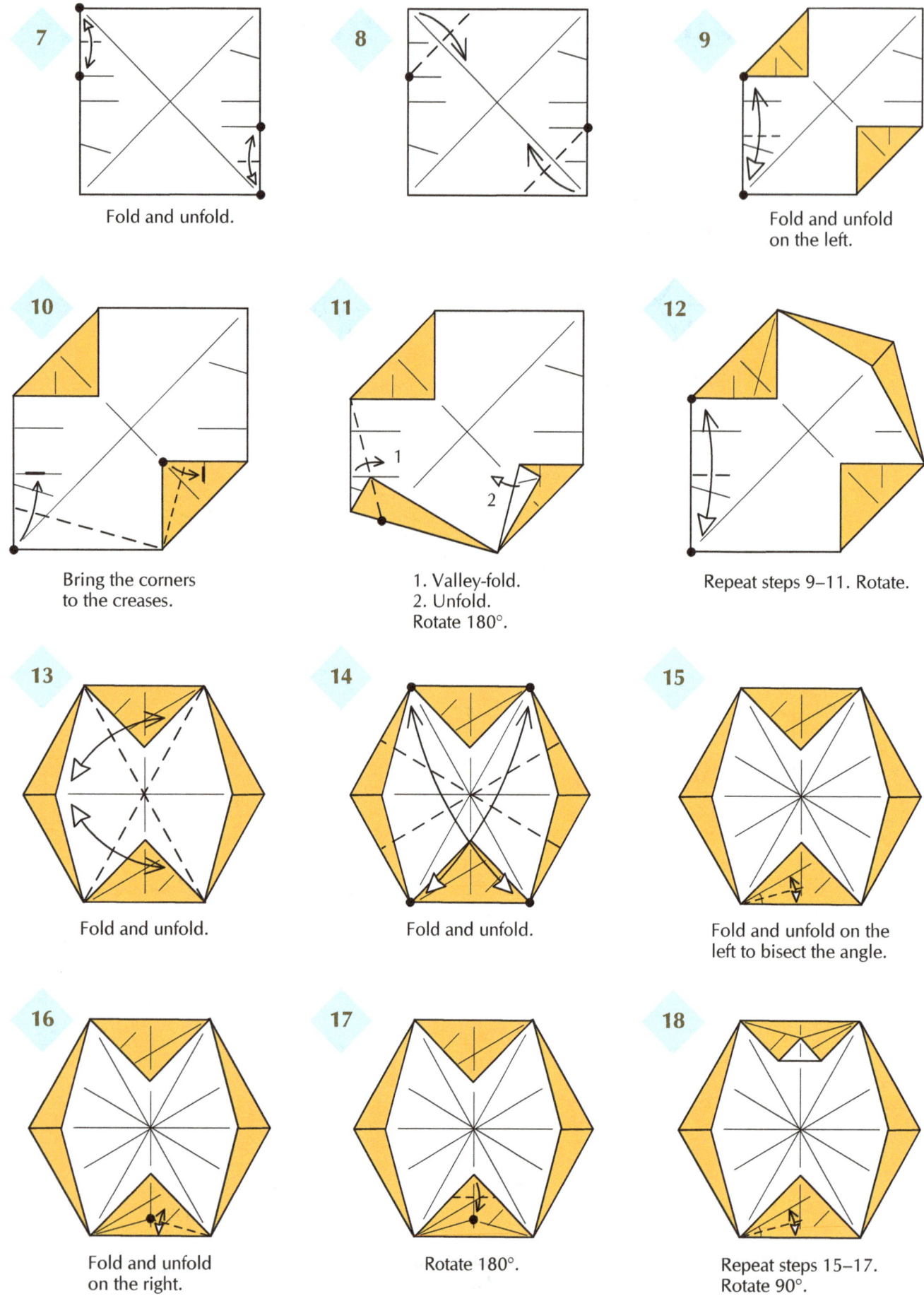

56 *Galaxy of Origami Stars*

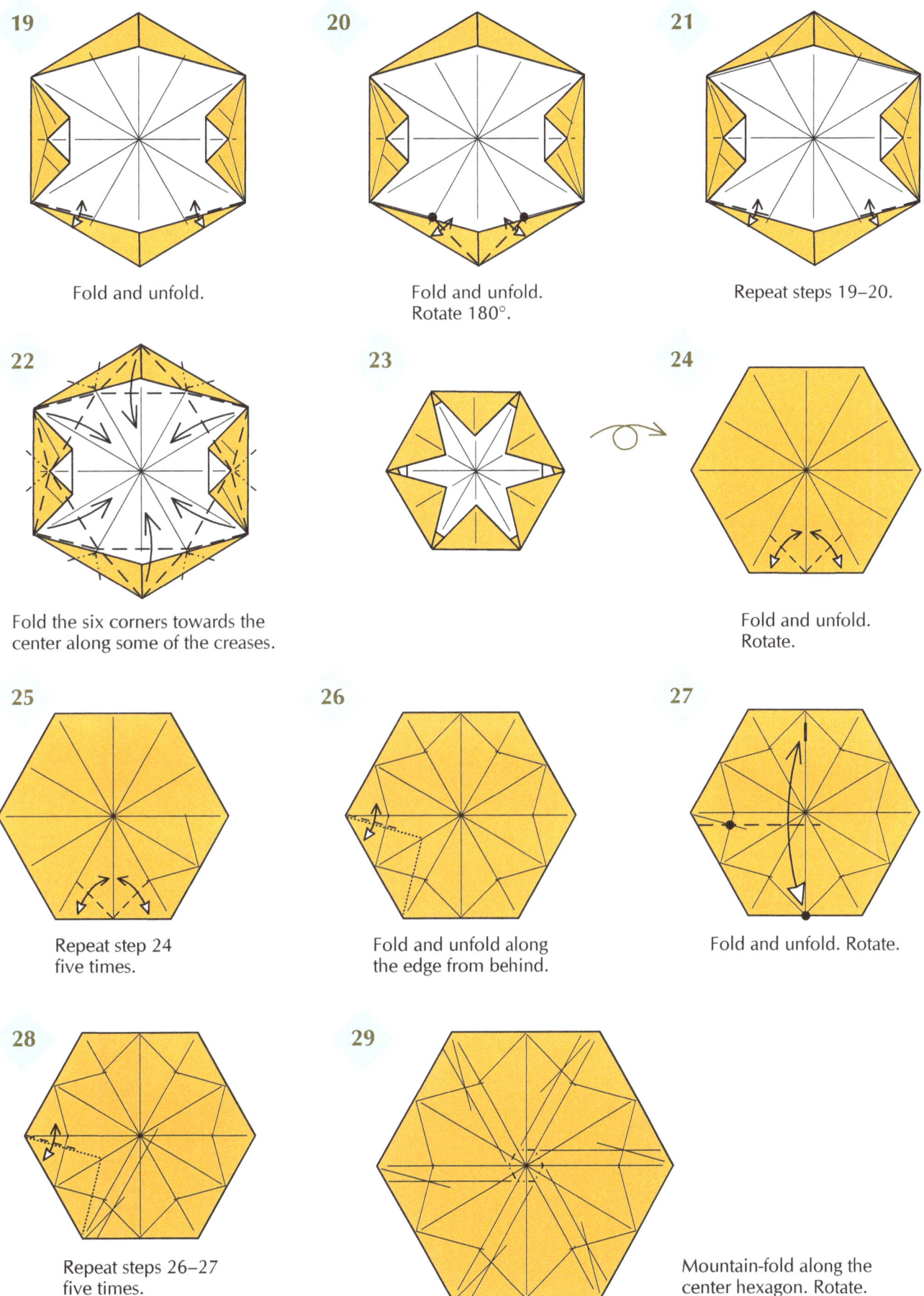

Double Six-Pointed Star 57

30

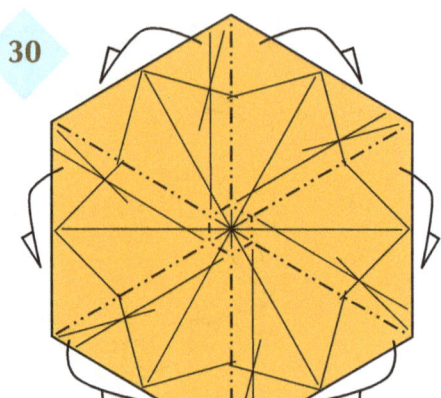

Fold along the creases. Form a hexagon in the center. It will become the top.

31

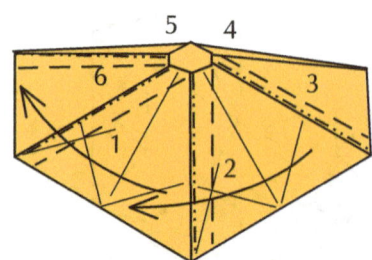

Twist-fold. Fold all around in order. Flatten.

32

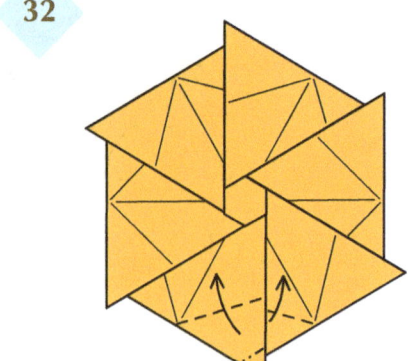

Spread and flatten. Crease sharply. Rotate.

33

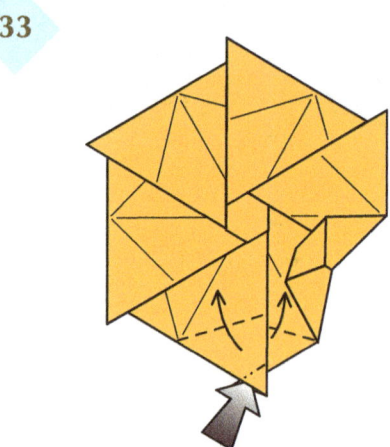

Repeat step 32 five times. Rotate.

34

35

Double Six-Pointed Star

58 *Galaxy of Origami Stars*

Intersecting Triangles

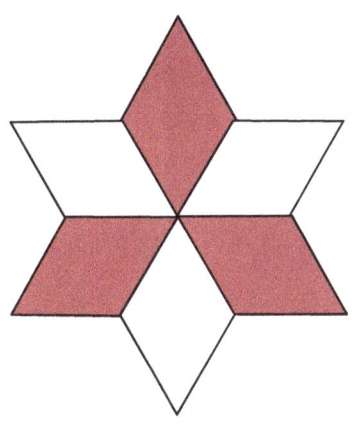

The paper is divided into fifths to fold this star with alternating color pattern. Step 21 shows a colored hexagon with an inscribed white triangle. This figure leads to a star with alternating colors.

1. 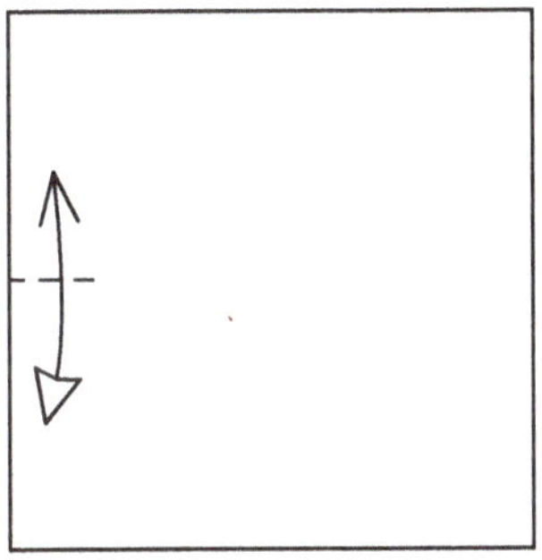 Fold and unfold on the left.

2. Crease on the left.

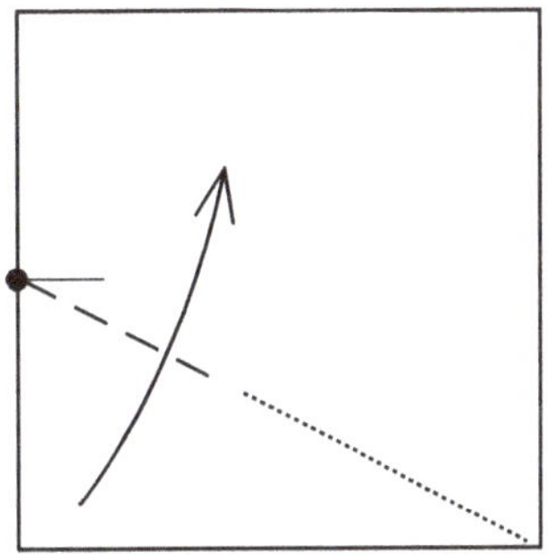

3. The paper is divided into fifths. (1/5, 4/5)

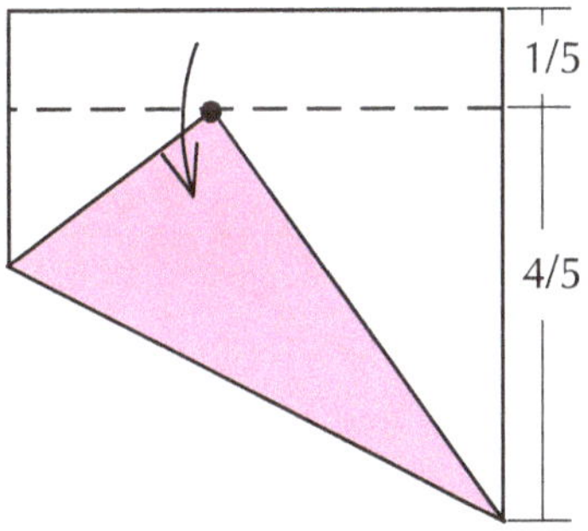

4. Unfold.

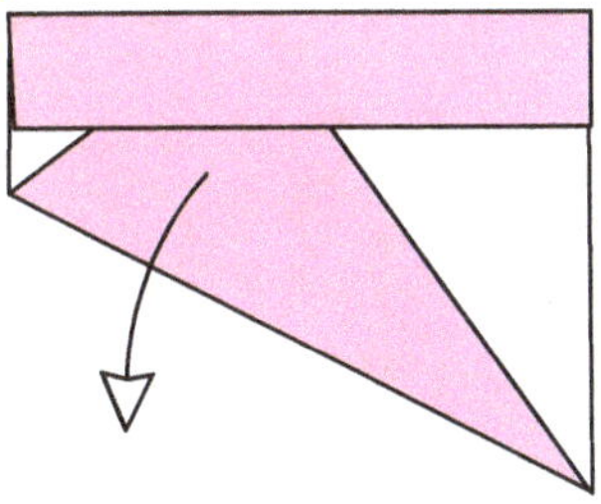

5. Fold and unfold.

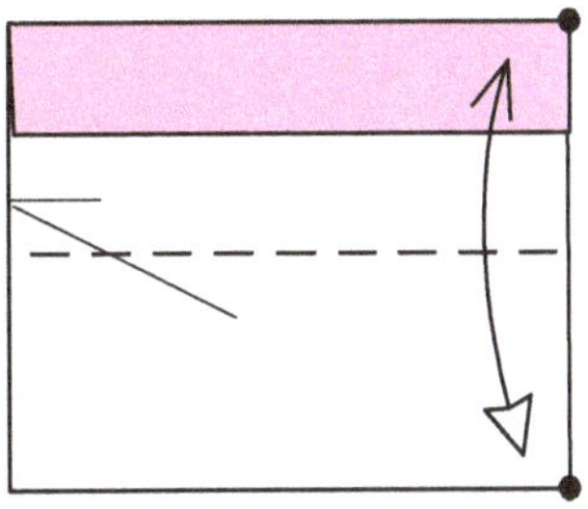

6. Fold to the center and unfold.

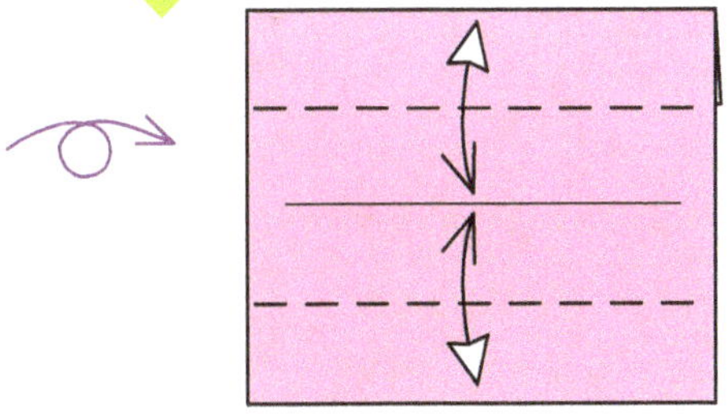

Intersecting Triangles 59

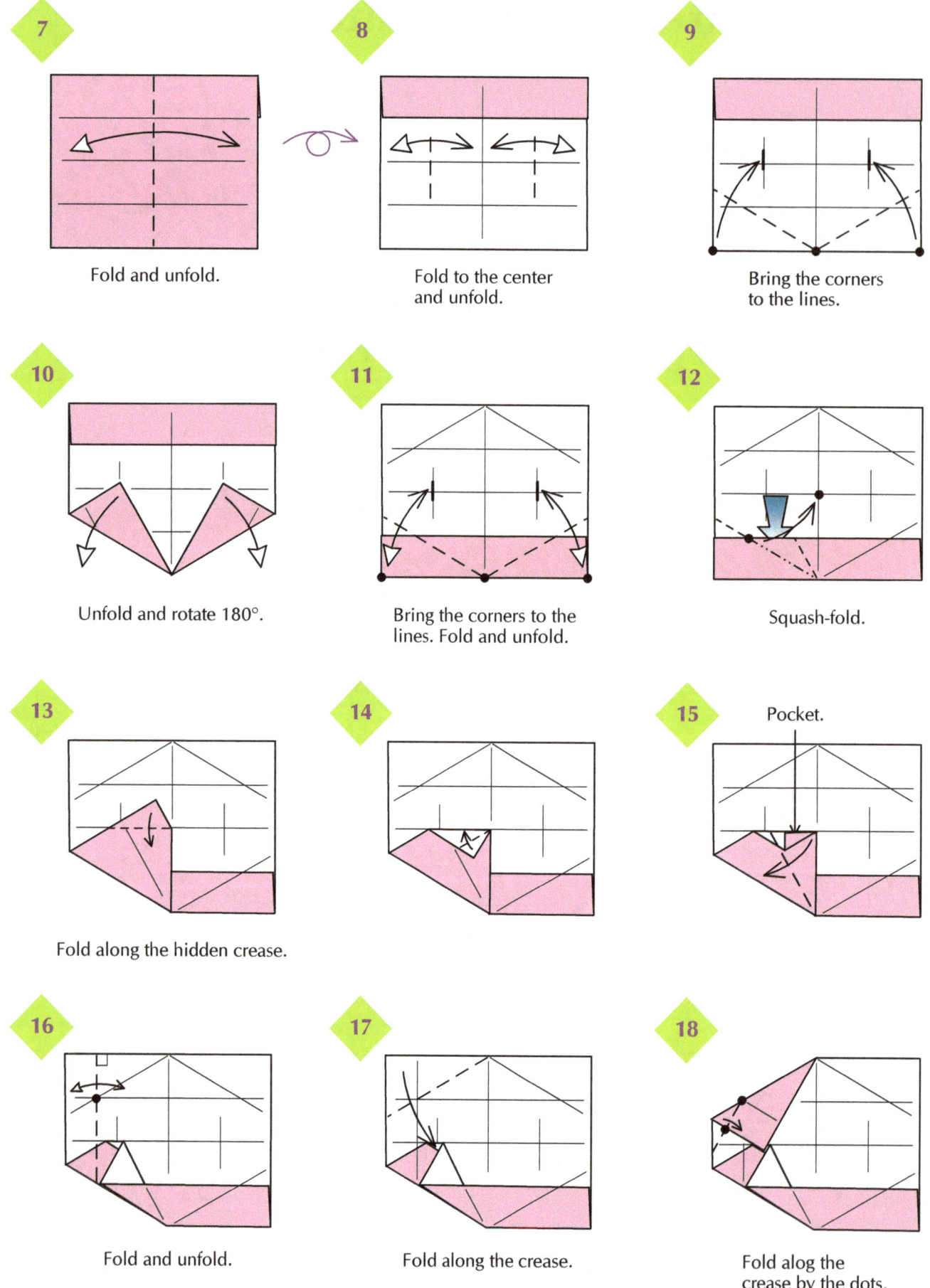

60 *Galaxy of Origami Stars*

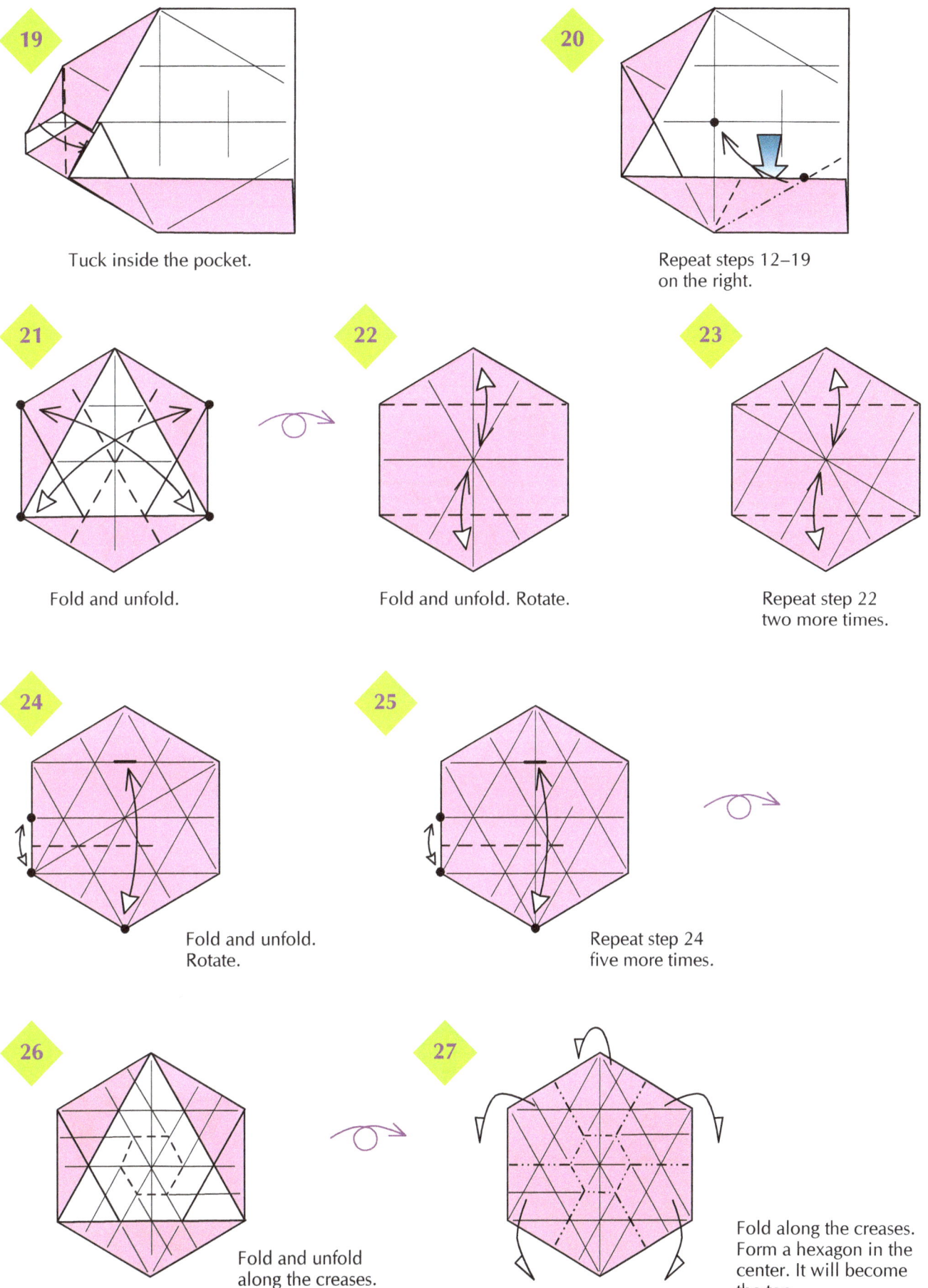

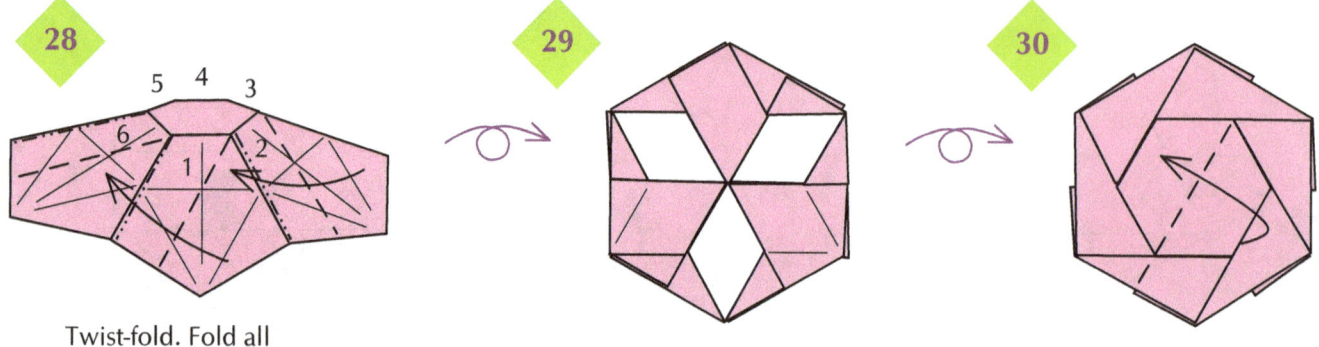

28. Twist-fold. Fold all around in order. Flatten.

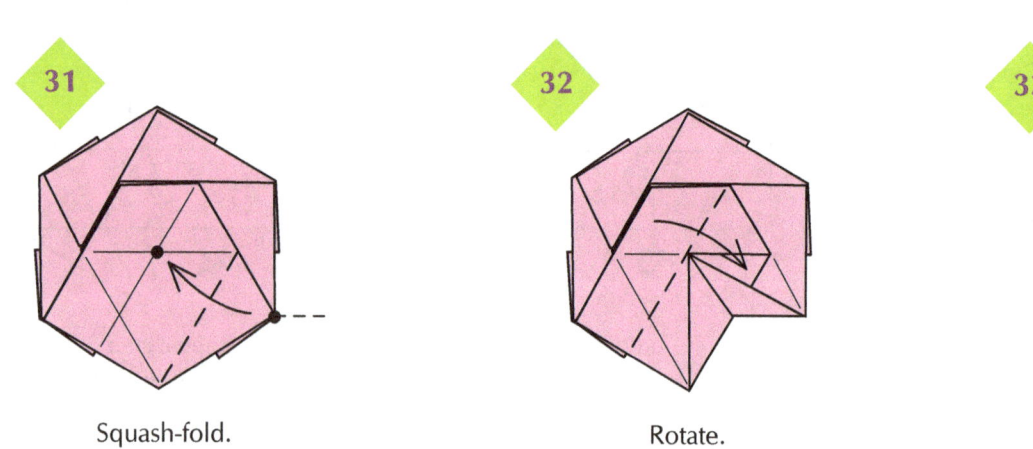

31. Squash-fold.

32. Rotate.

33. Repeat steps 30–32 five more times.

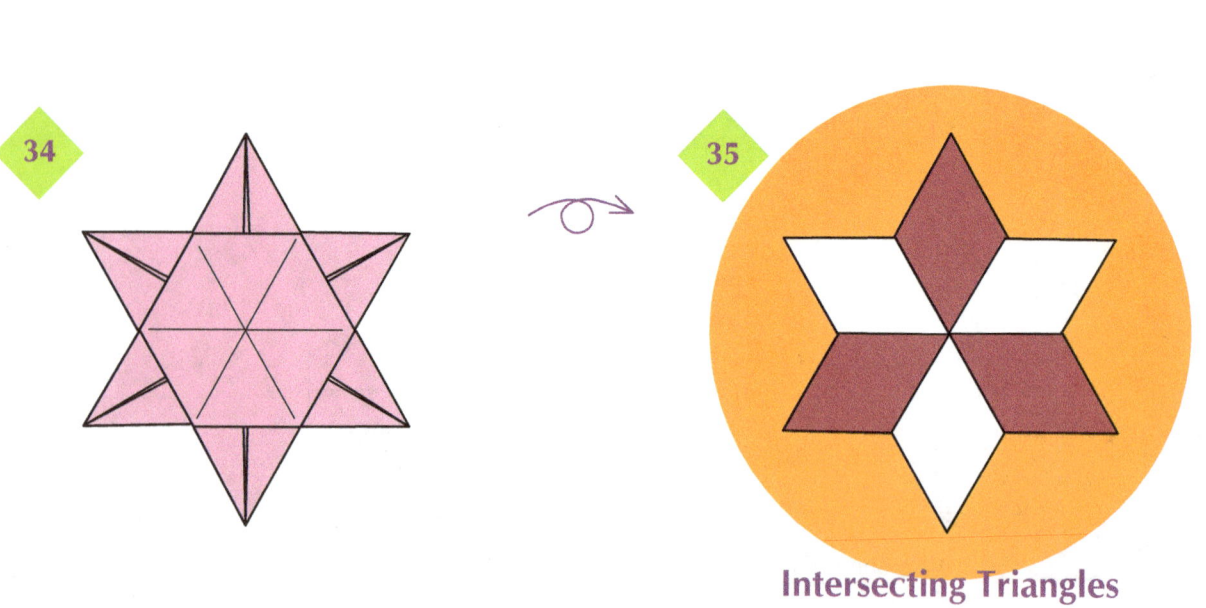

Intersecting Triangles

62 *Galaxy of Origami Stars*

Radiant Six-Pointed Star

Designed by Russell Cashdollar,
modified by John Montroll

The method to create this radiant star is to fold the square into a hexagon, do a twist fold, and make the color changes. Using the specific hexagon shown in step 26, there are no extra lines on the face of the radiant star.

1

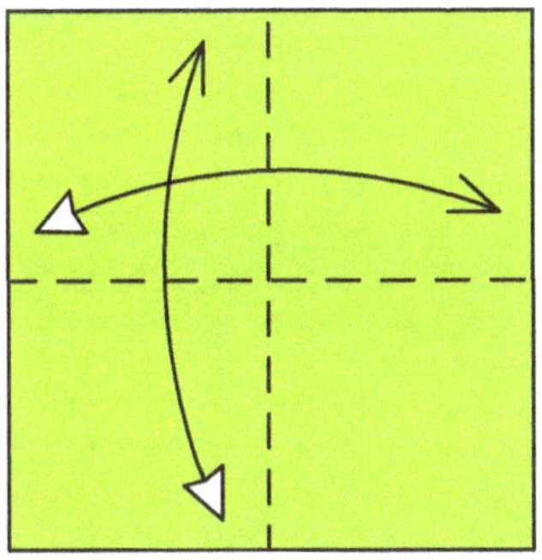

Fold and unfold.

2

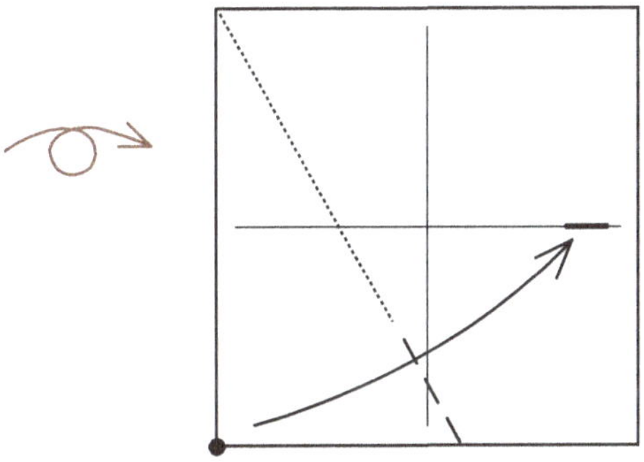

Bring the dot to the line.
Crease on the bottom.

3

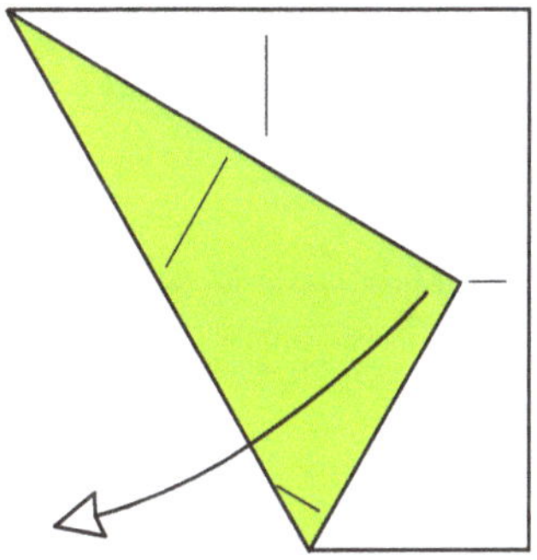

Unfold.

4

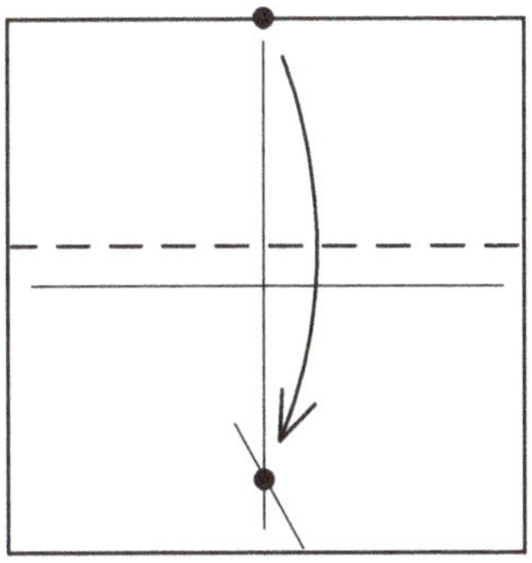

5

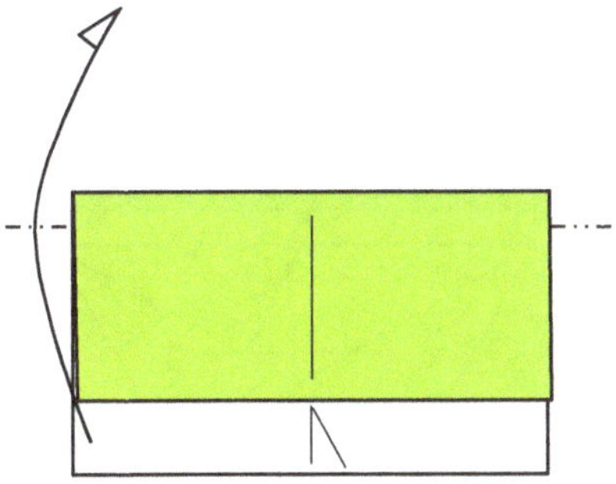

Fold along the crease.

6

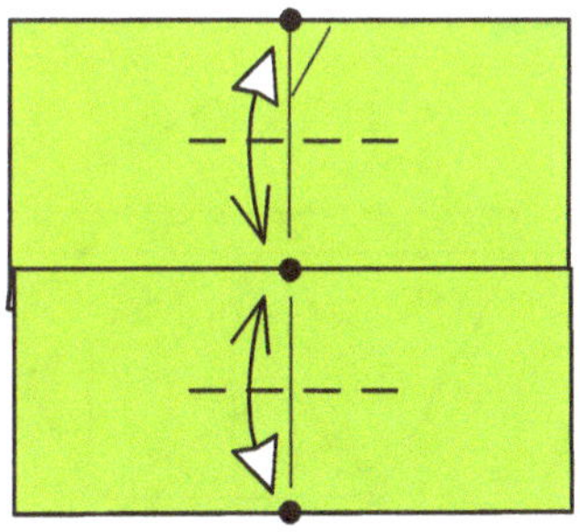

Fold and unfold
in the center.

Radiant Six-Pointed Star   63

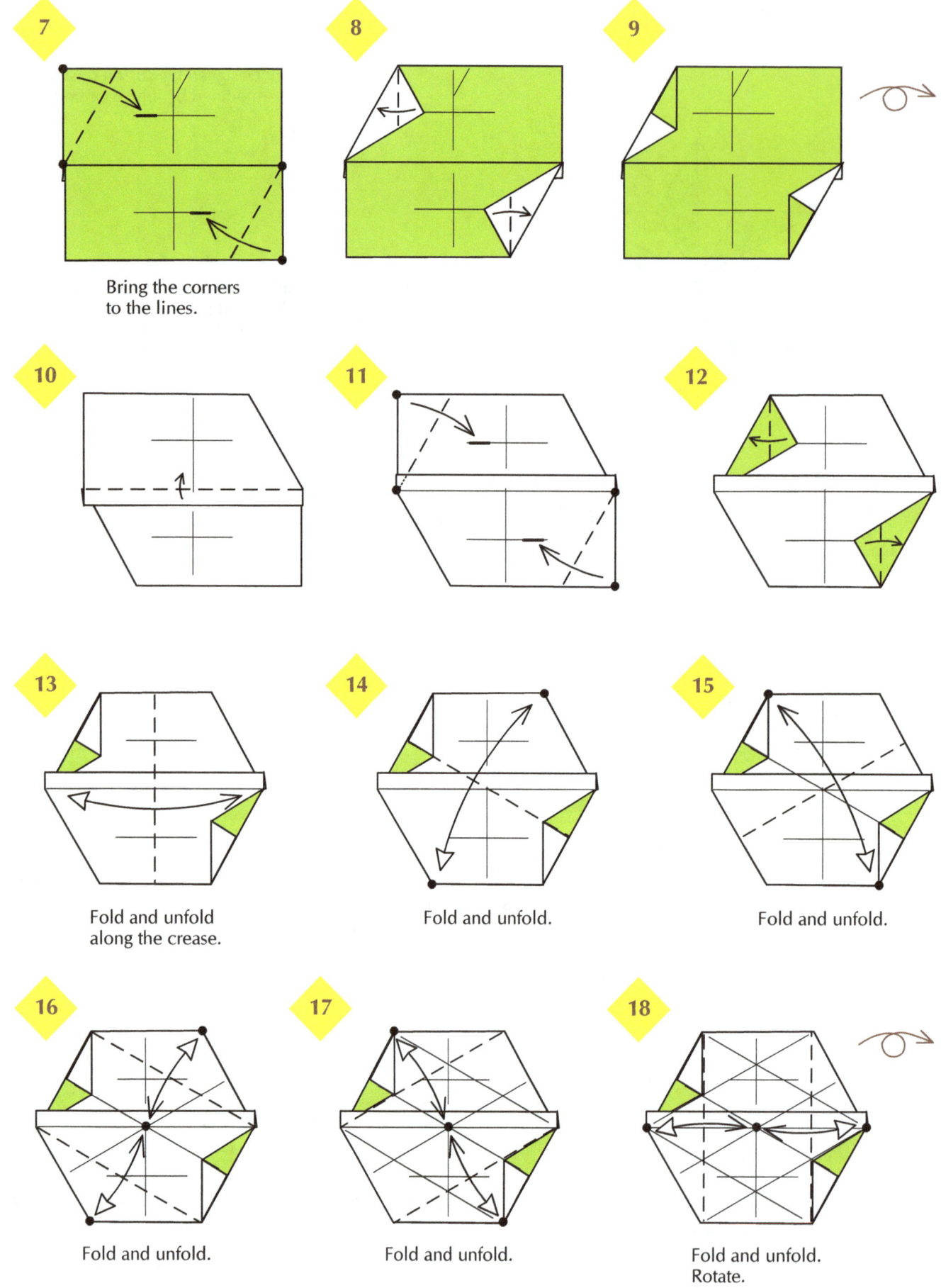

64   Galaxy of Origami Stars

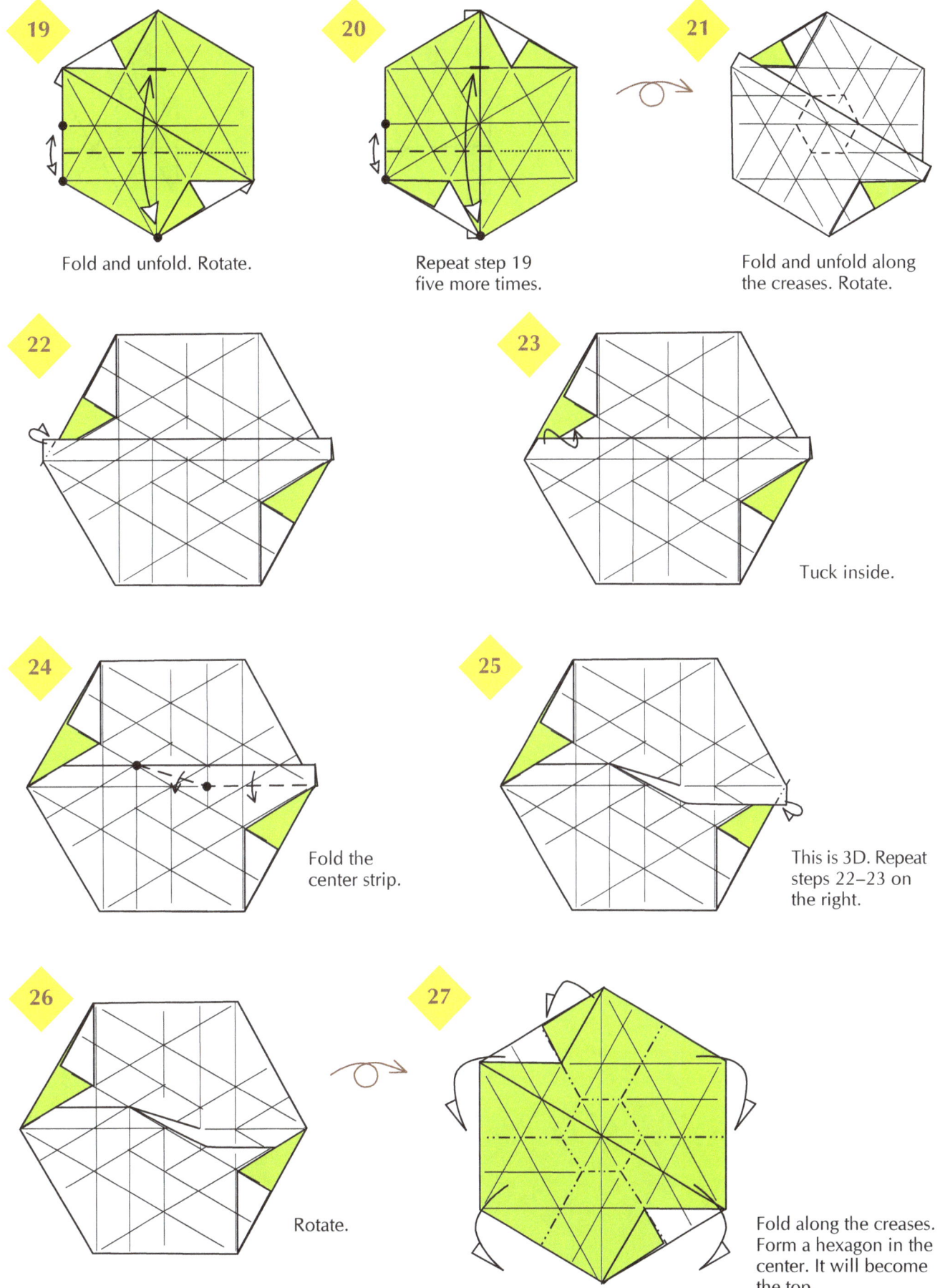

Radiant Six-Pointed Star 65

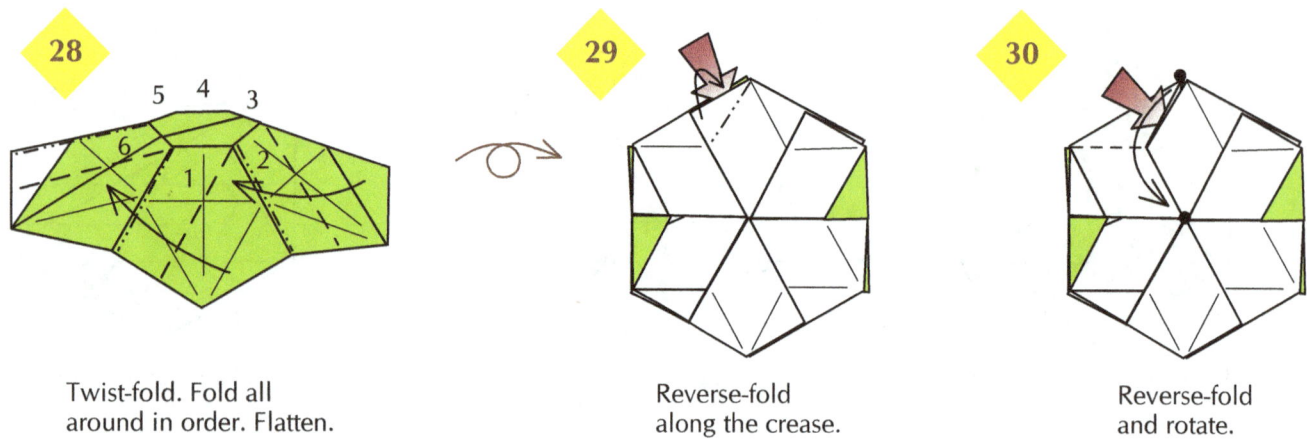

28. Twist-fold. Fold all around in order. Flatten.

29. Reverse-fold along the crease.

30. Reverse-fold and rotate.

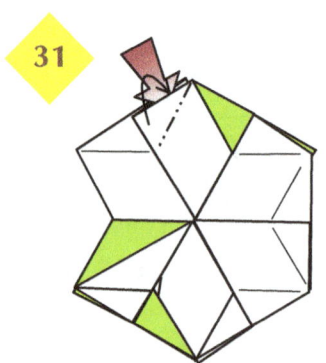

31. Repeat steps 29–30 five more times.

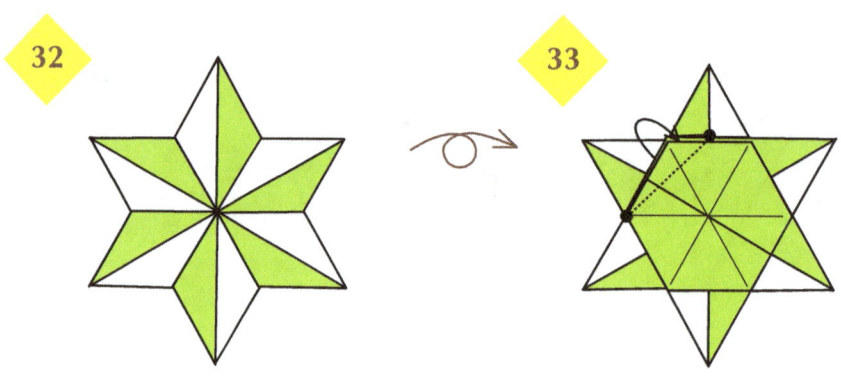

33. Valley-fold on a hidden layer, along the dotted line. Rotate.

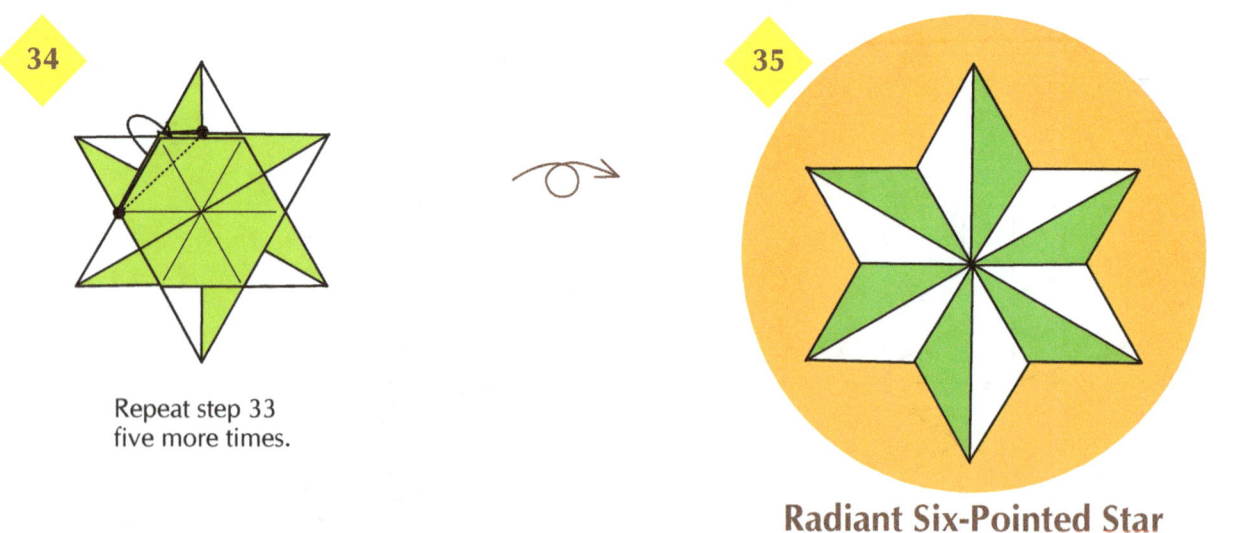

34. Repeat step 33 five more times.

Radiant Six-Pointed Star

66 *Galaxy of Origami Stars*

Propeller

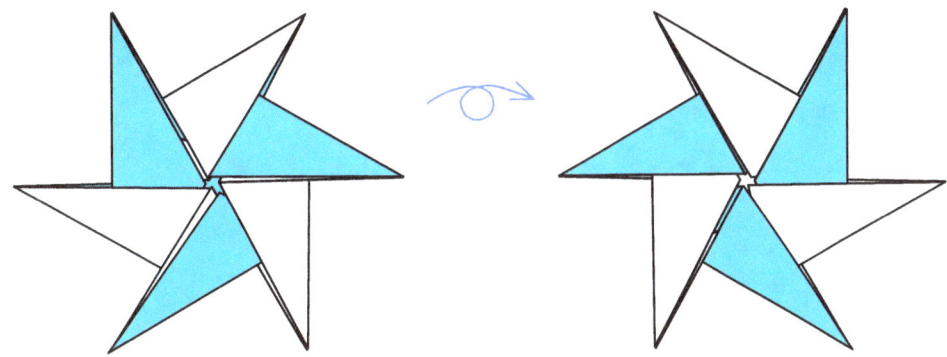

This six-pointed star has the same alternating color pattern on both sides.

1 Fold and unfold. Rotate.

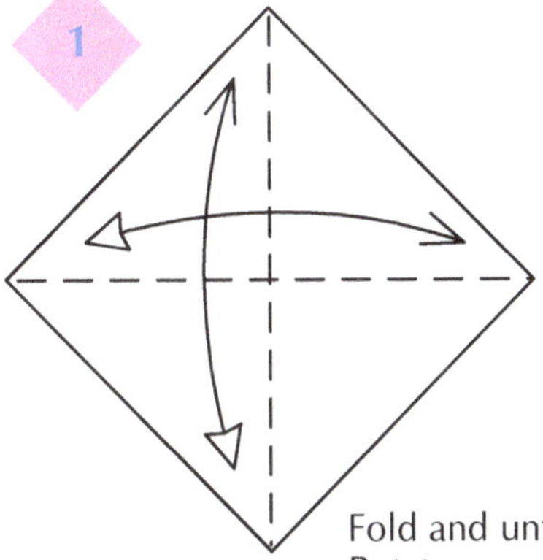

2 Fold and unfold on the edges.

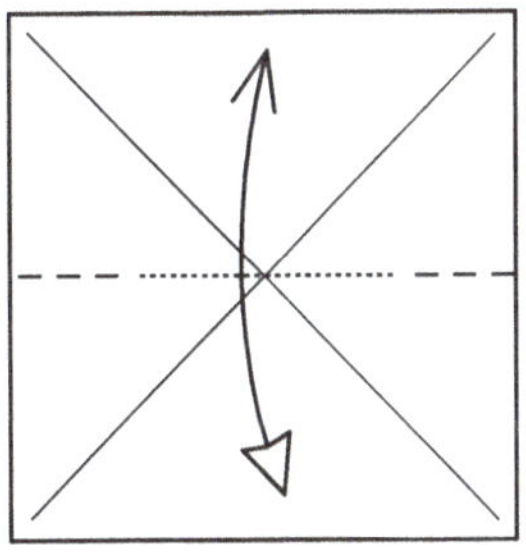

3 Bring the corner to the crease.

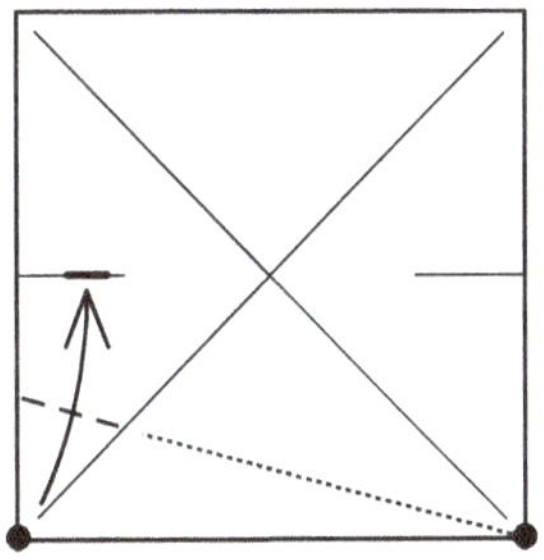

4 Unfold.

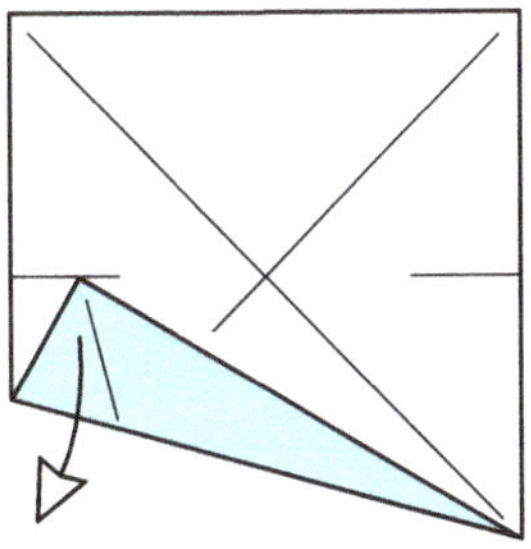

5 Fold and unfold. Rotate 180°.

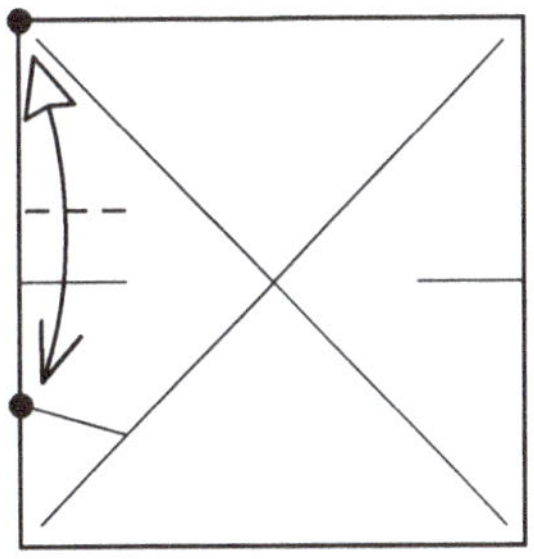

6 Repeat steps 3–5.

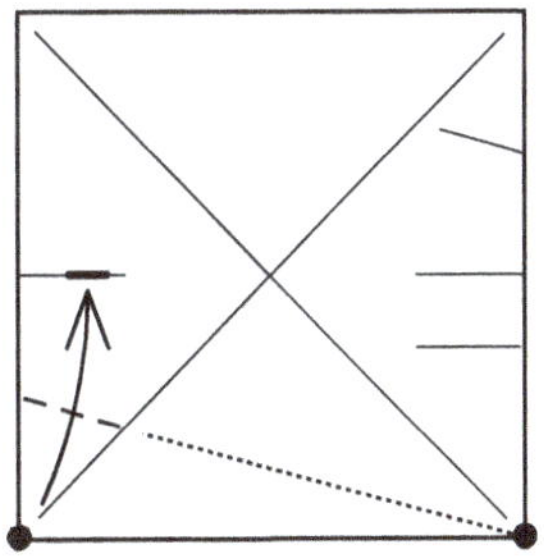

Propeller 67

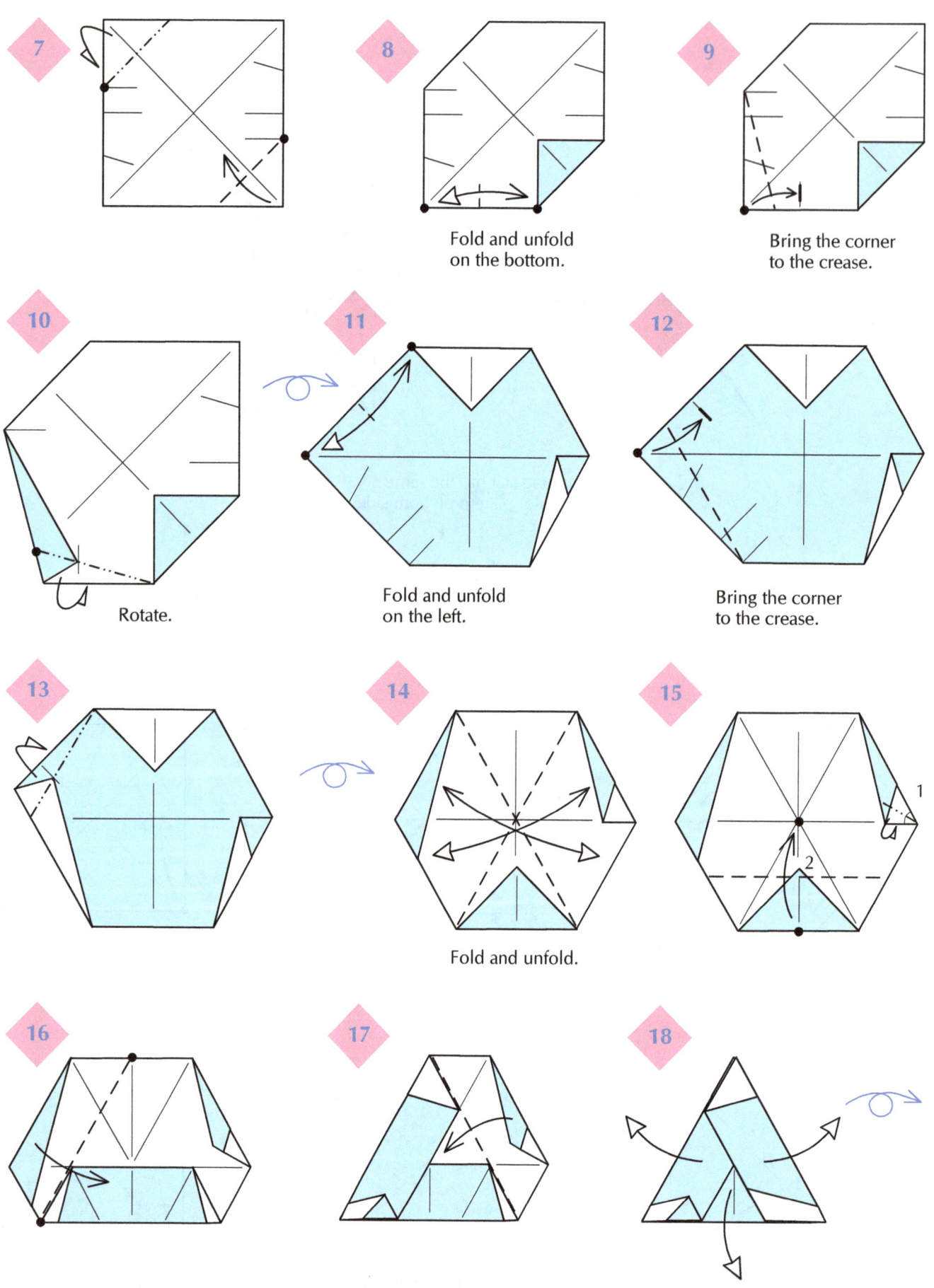

68 *Galaxy of Origami Stars*

Propeller

Seven-Pointed Star

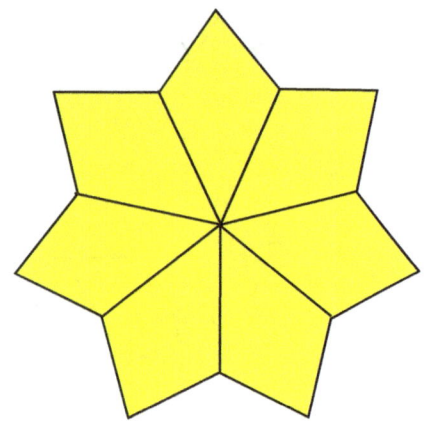

To fold the seven-pointed star, the square is folded into a heptagon and a twist fold is used. This is the only seven-pointed star in this collection but many more can be made. I encourage you to design some.

1

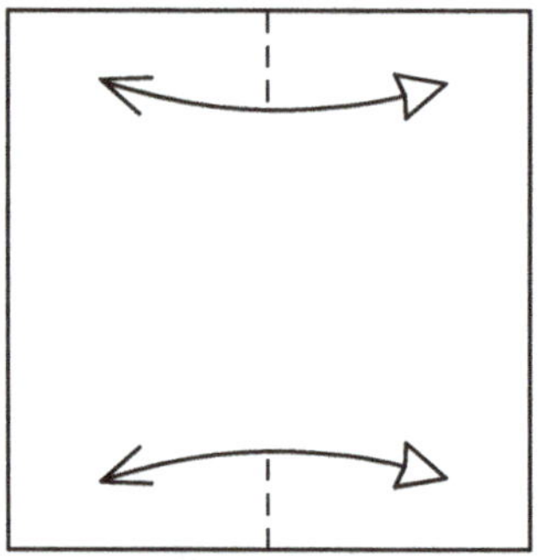

Fold and unfold on the edges.

2

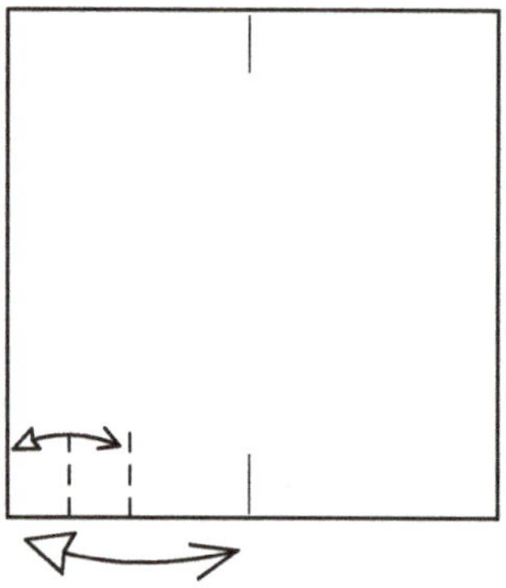

Fold and unfold in half twice, on the bottom.

3

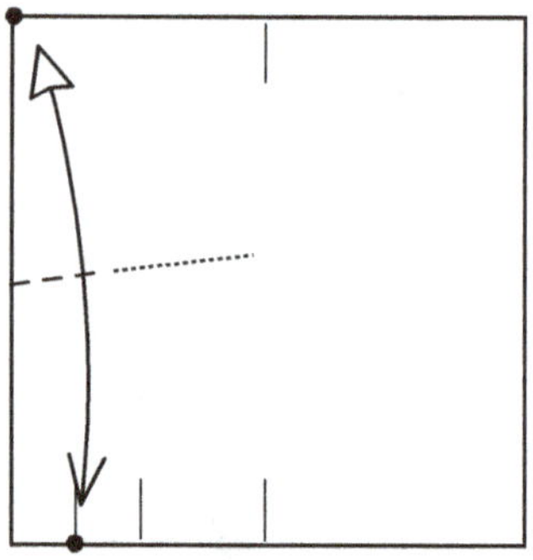

Fold and unfold on the left.

4

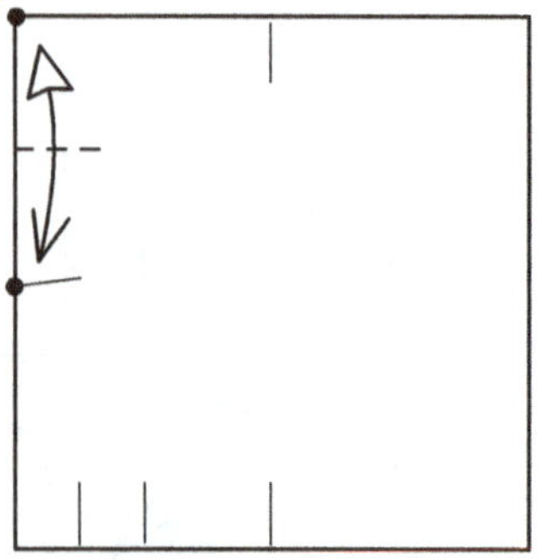

Fold and unfold on the left.

5

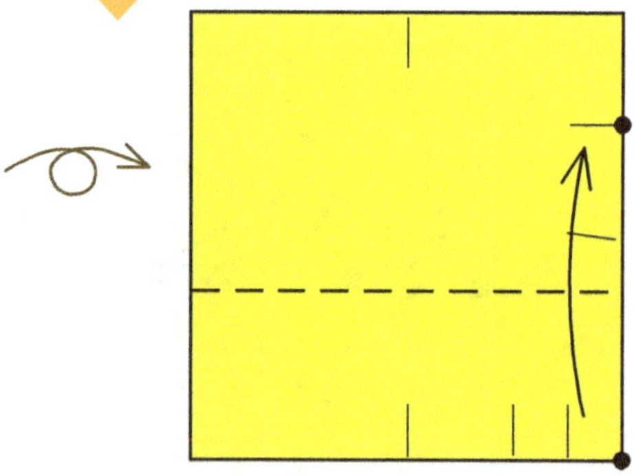

6

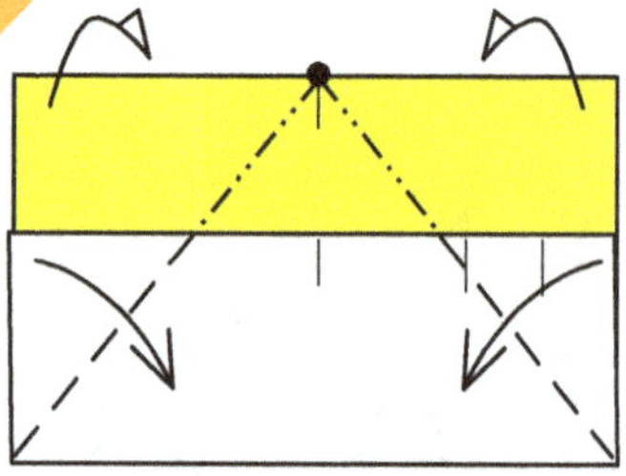

70 *Galaxy of Origami Stars*

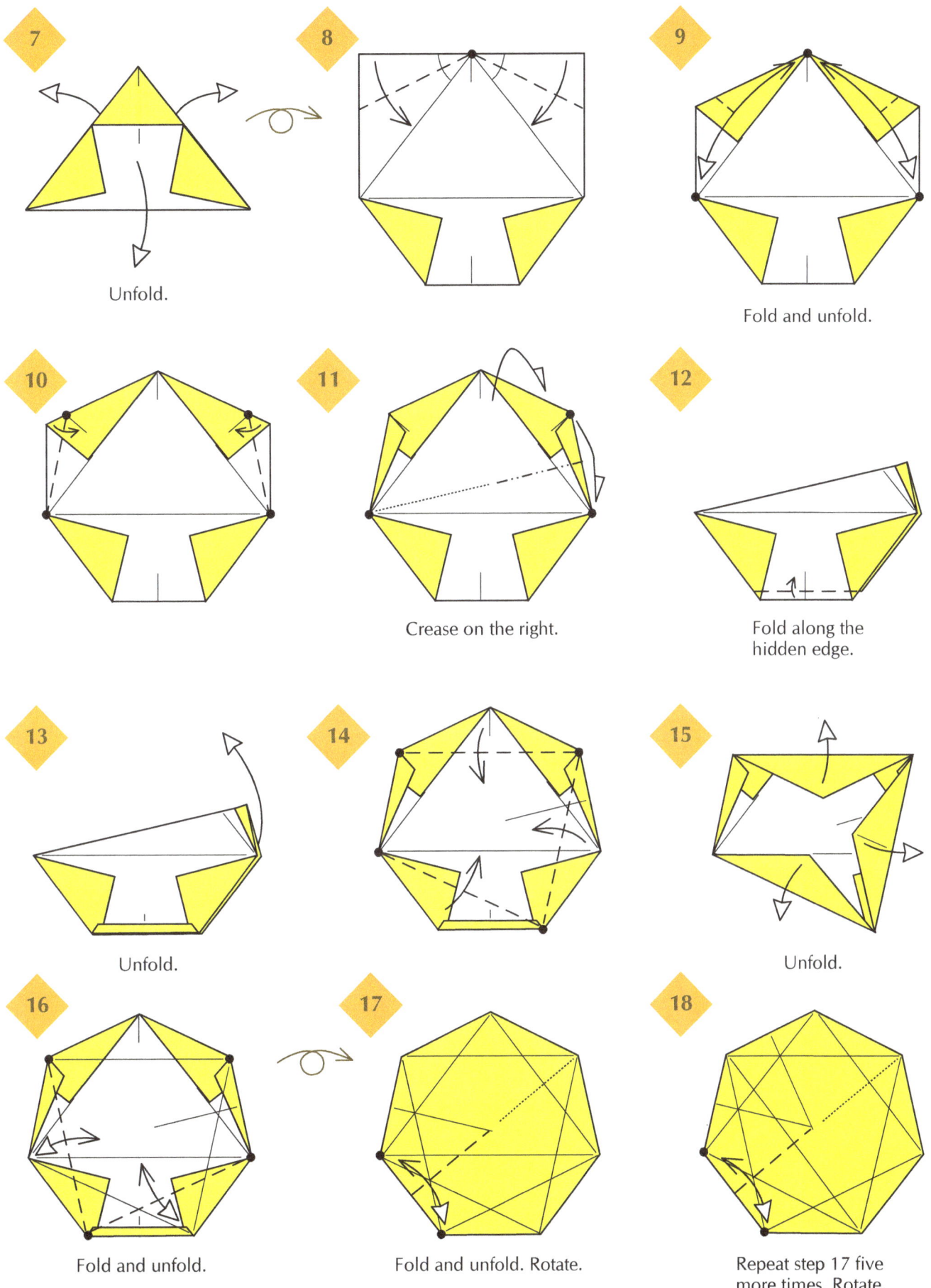

Seven-Pointed Star 71

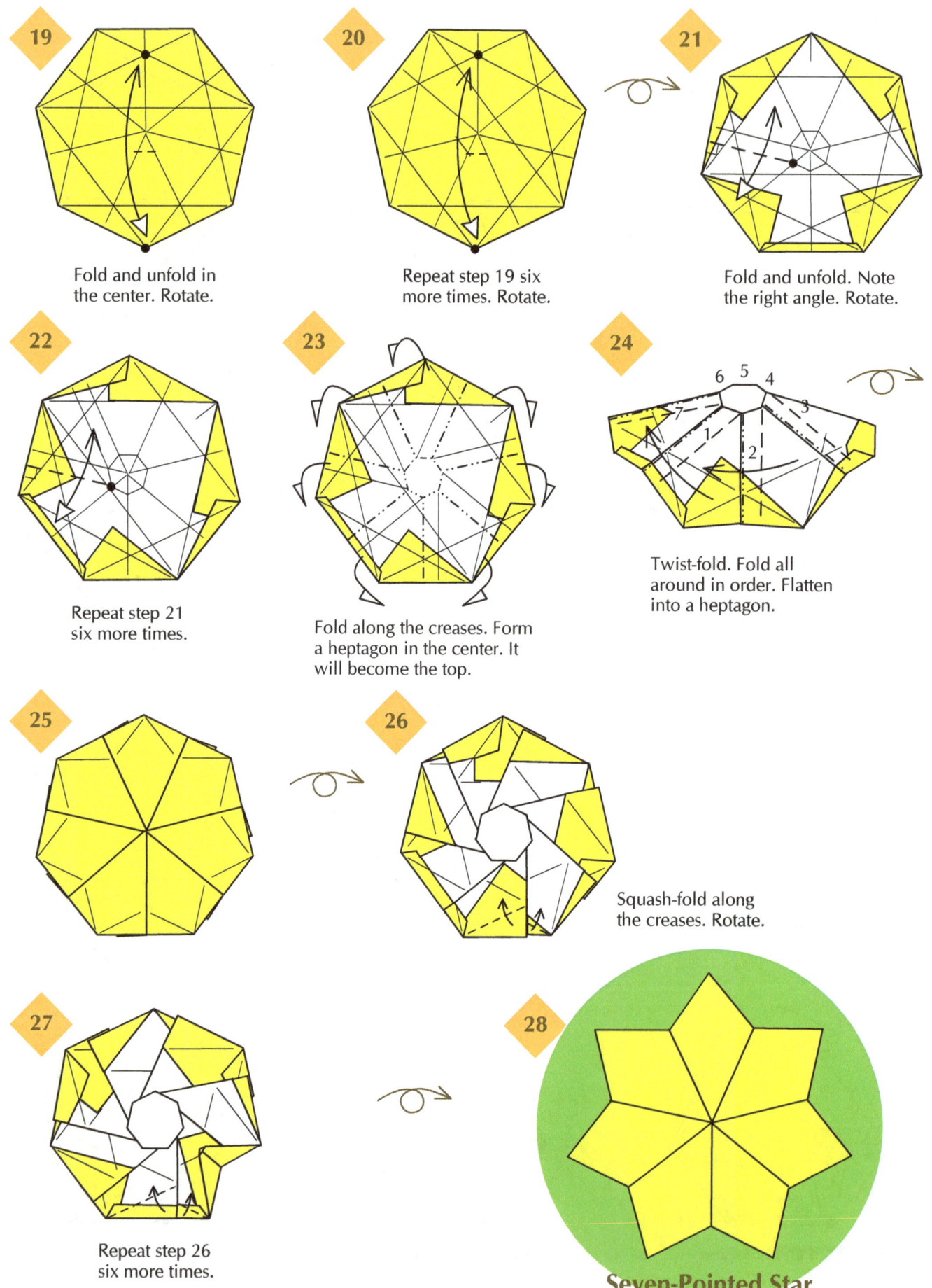

Layered Eight-Pointed Star

This eight-pointed star uses a square twist fold.

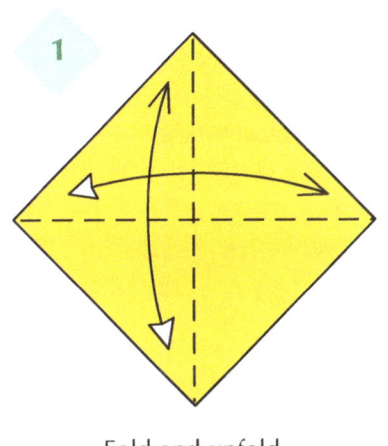

Fold and unfold.

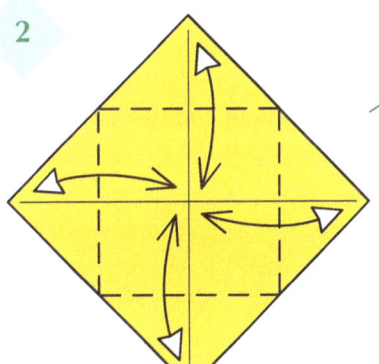

Fold to the center and unfold.

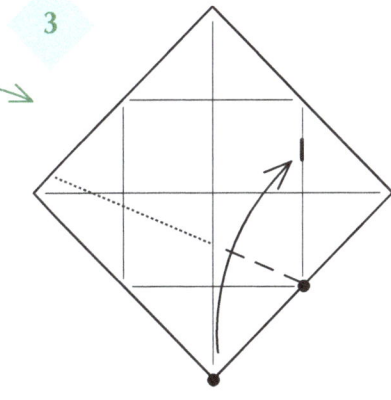

Bring the lower dot to the line and crease on the right.

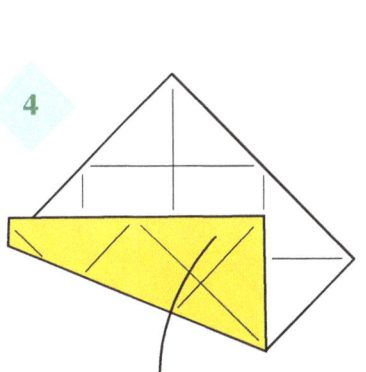

Unfold.

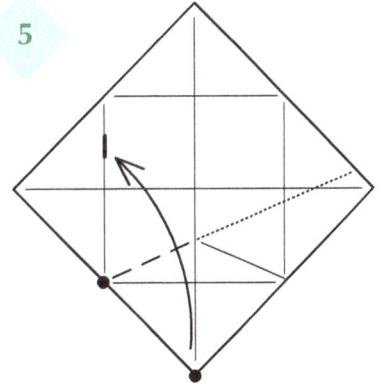

Repeat steps 3–4 in the opposite direction. Rotate 90°.

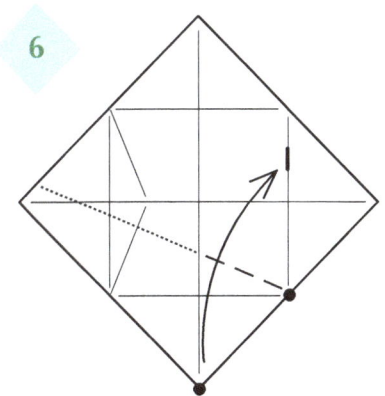

Repeat steps 3–5 three more times.

Layered Eight-Pointed Star 73

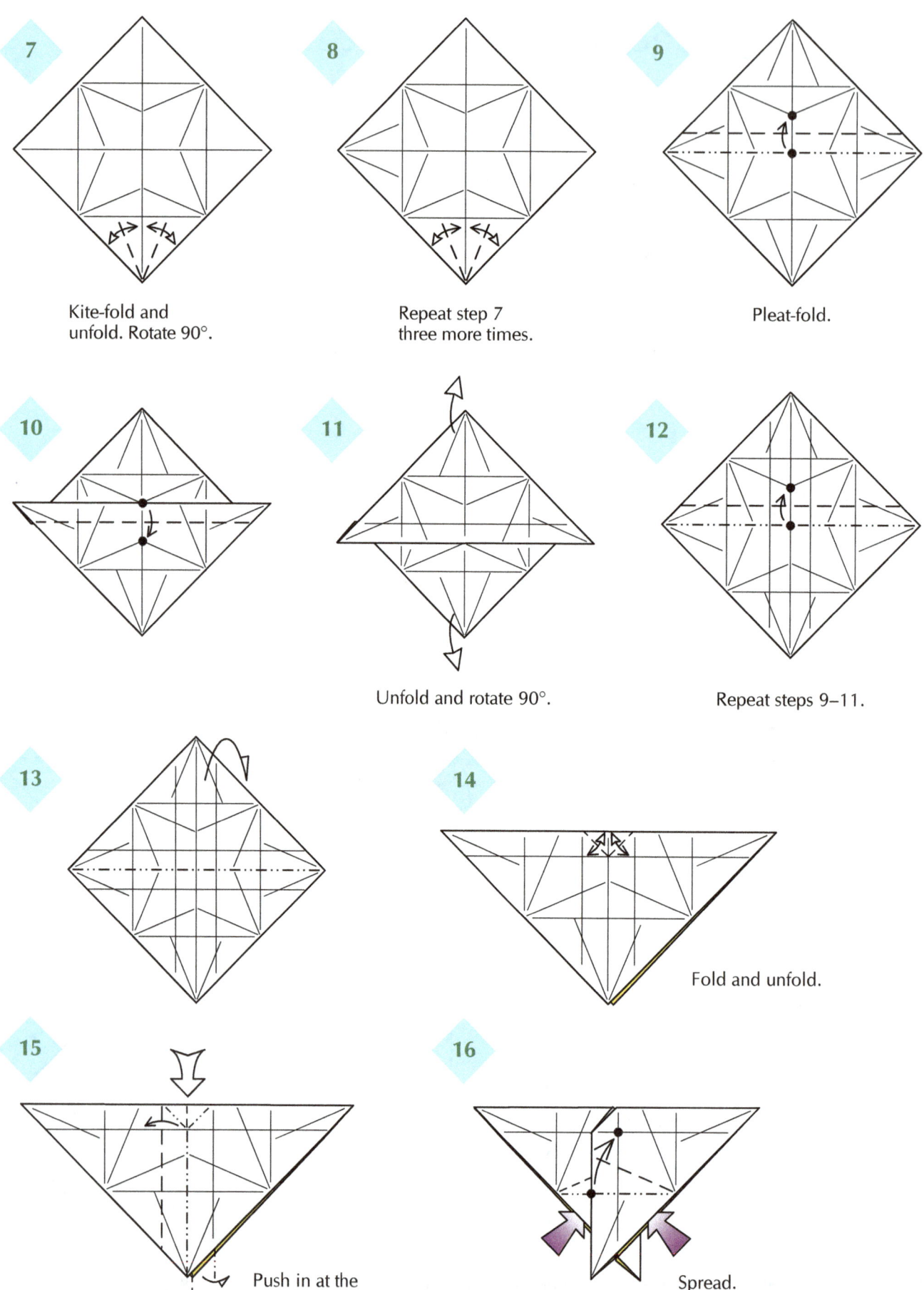

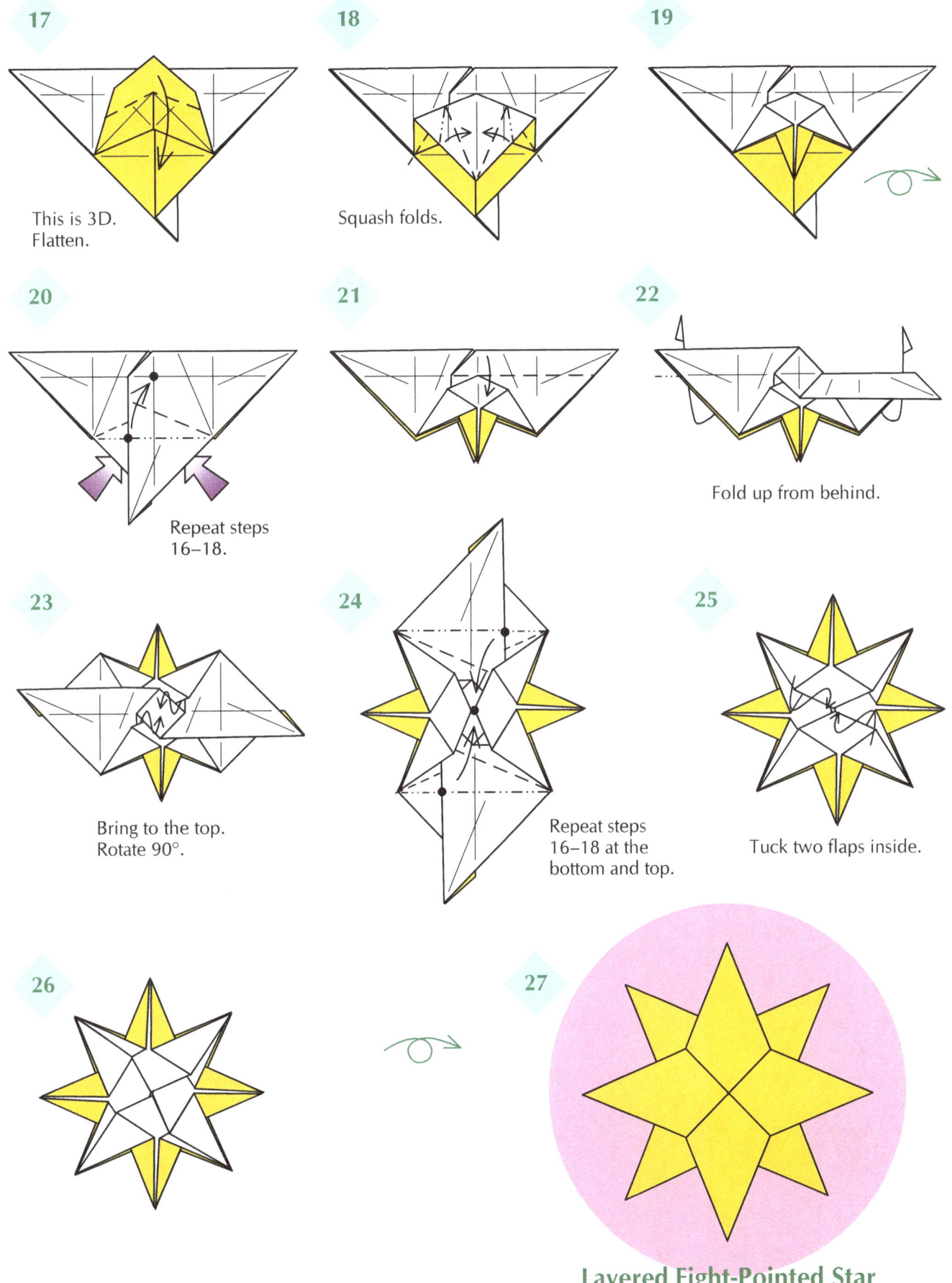

Eight-Pointed Star

This solid colored star begins by folding the square into an octagon followed by an octagonal twist fold.

1 Fold and unfold.

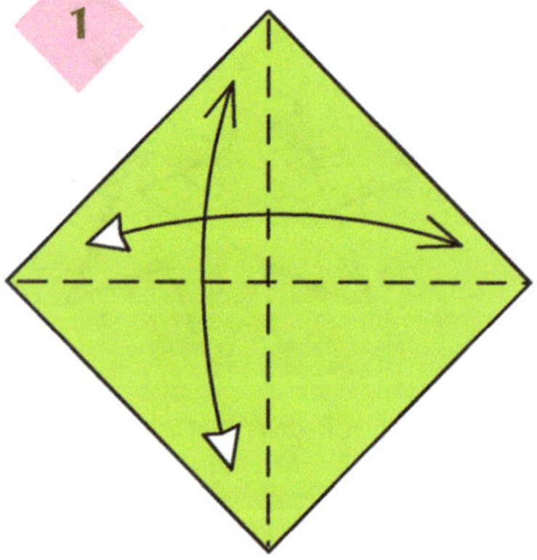

2 Fold and unfold.

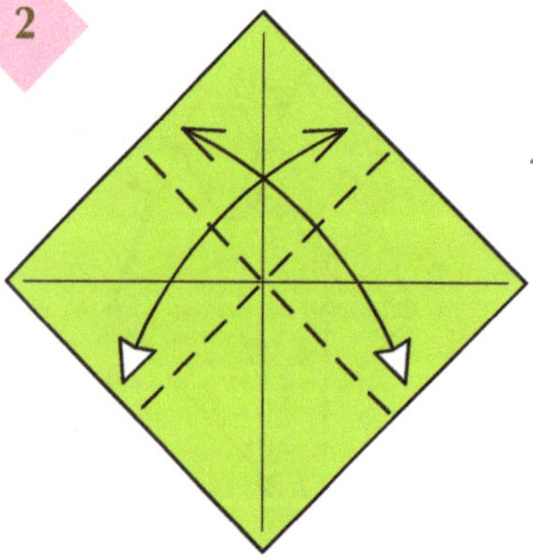

3 Crease by the diagonal.

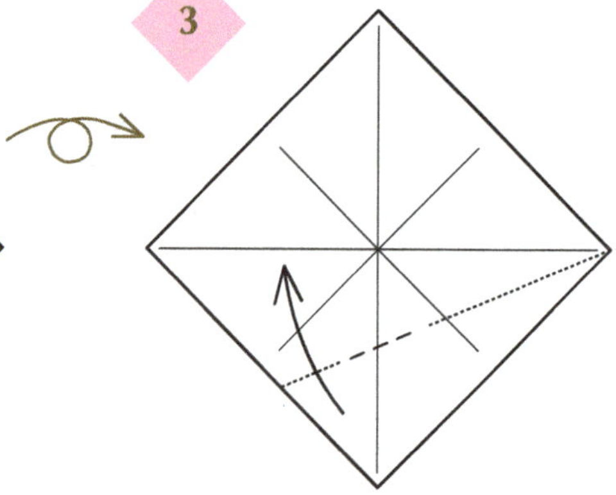

4 Unfold and rotate 90°.

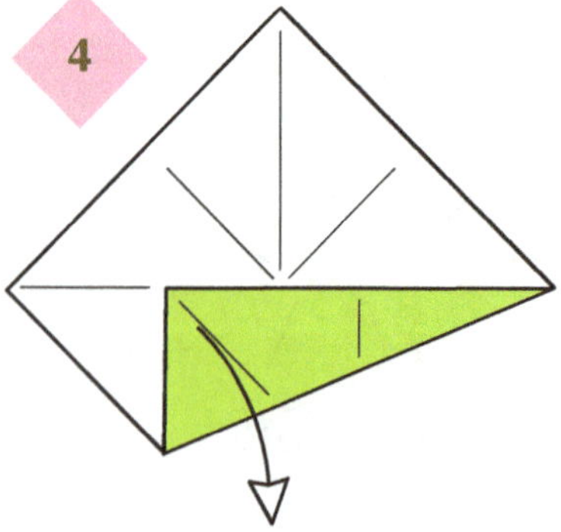

5 Repeat steps 3–4 three more times.

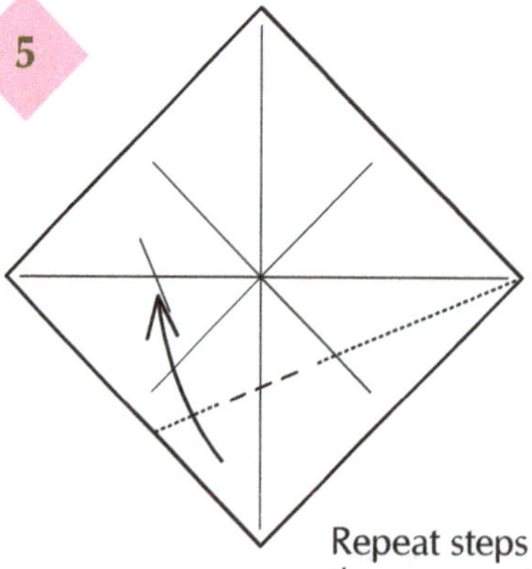

6

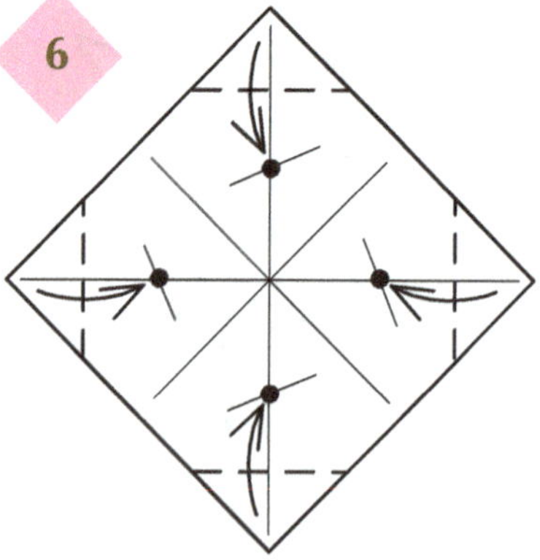

76   *Galaxy of Origami Stars*

7 Fold and unfold. Rotate.

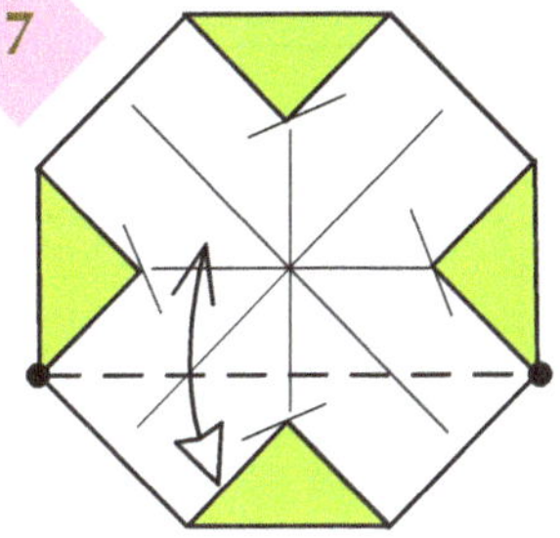

8 Fold and unfold. Rotate.

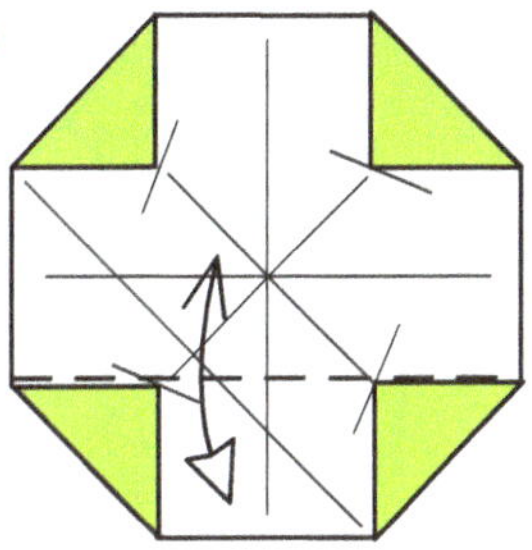

9 Repeat steps 7–8 three more times.

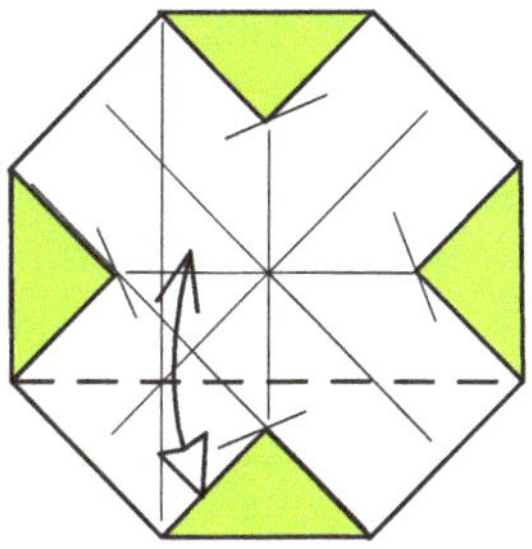

10 Fold and unfold. Rotate.

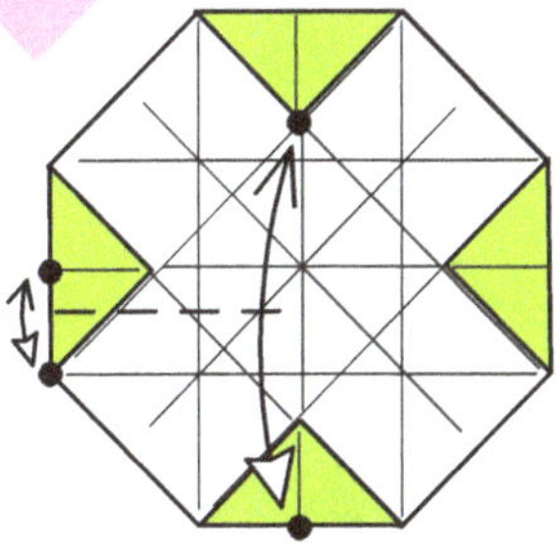

11 Fold and unfold. Rotate.

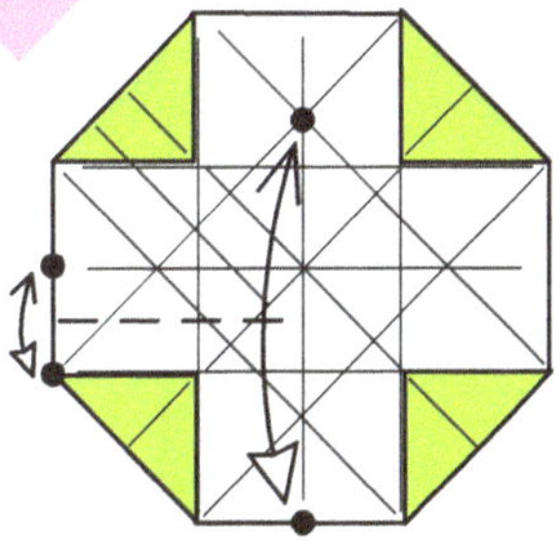

12 Repeat steps 10–11 three more times.

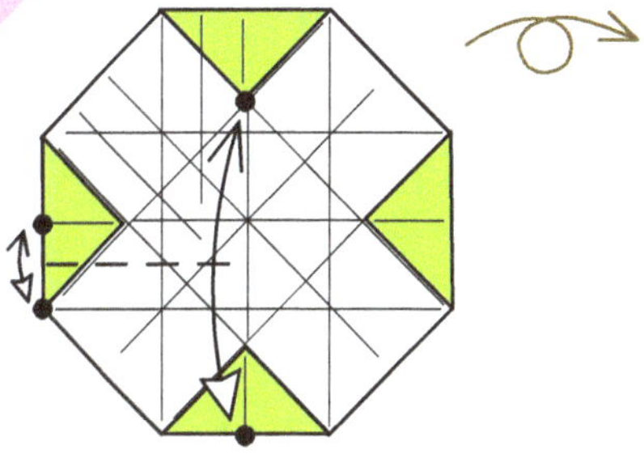

13 Crease in the center.

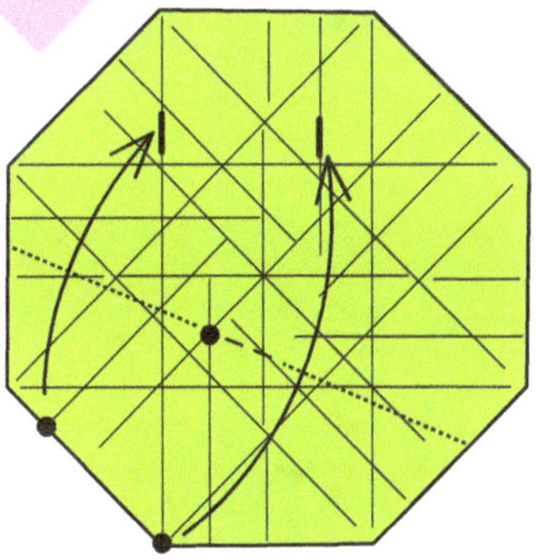

14 Unfold and rotate.

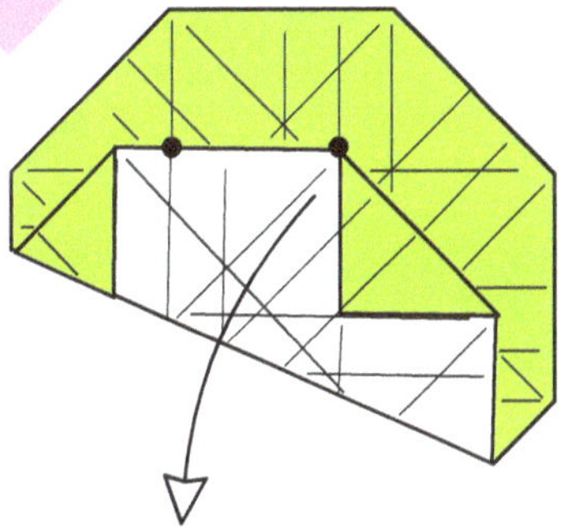

15 Repeat steps 13–14 seven more times.

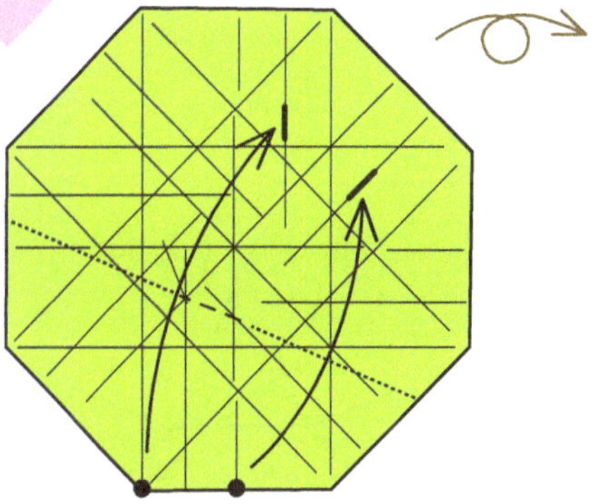

16 Fold along the creases. Form an octagon in the center. It will become the top.

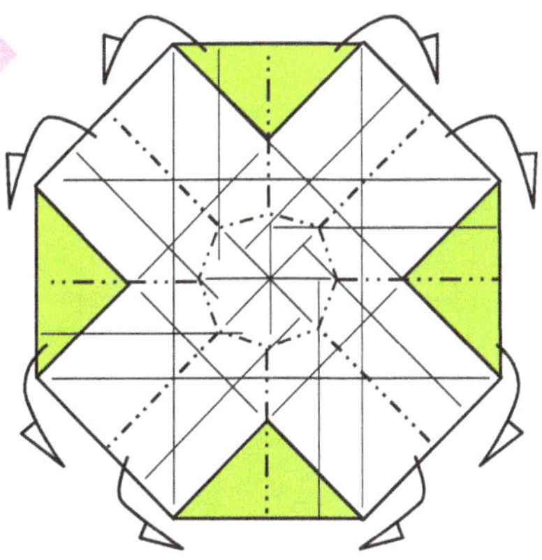

17 Twist-fold. Fold all around in order. Flatten.

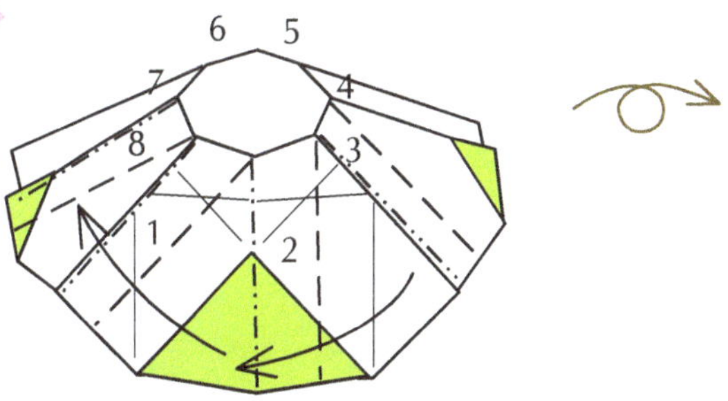

Eight-Pointed Star 77

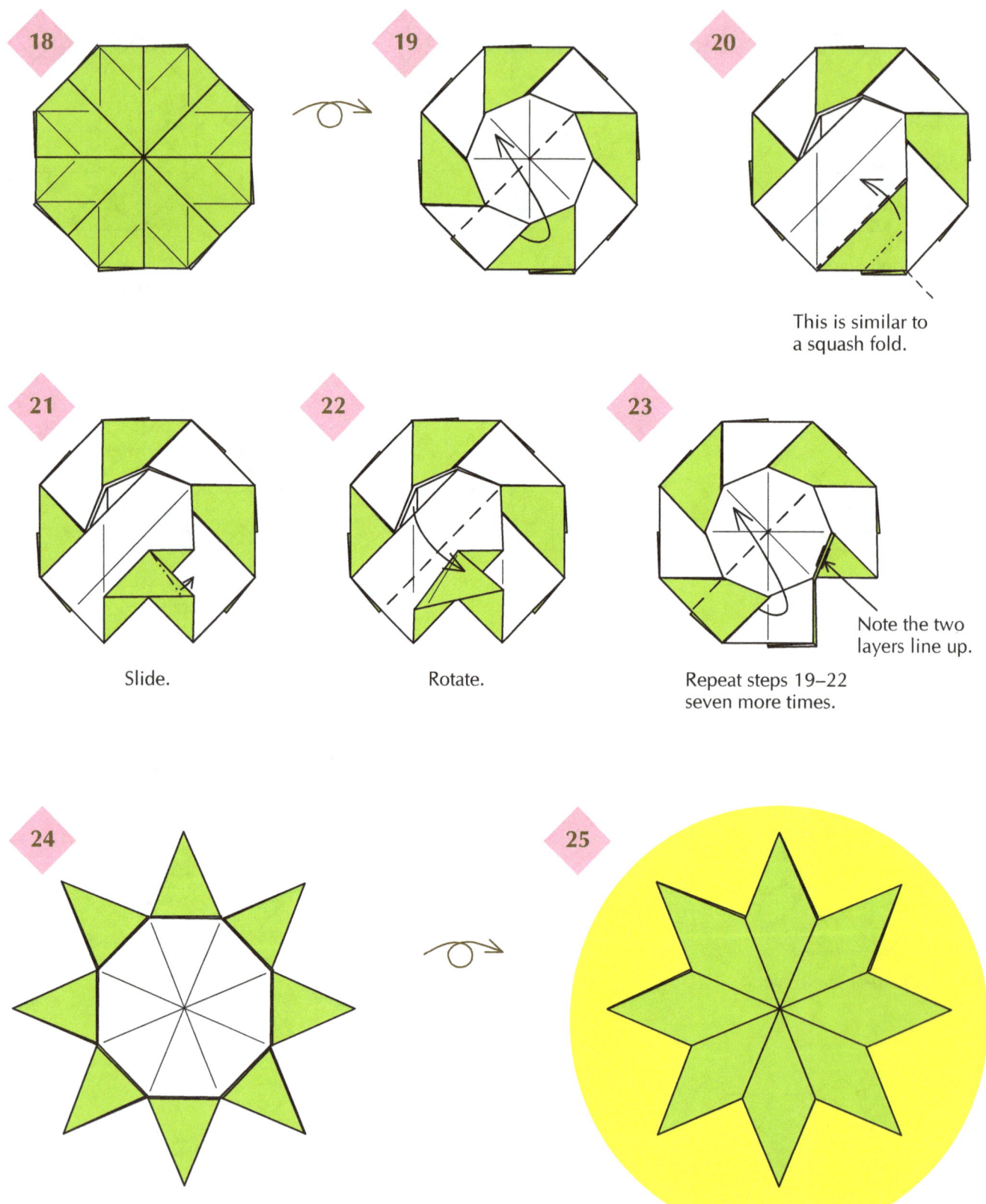

Double Eight-Pointed Star

To fold this double star, the square is folded into an octagon which is folded into a smaller octagon. A twist fold is used.

1. Fold and unfold.

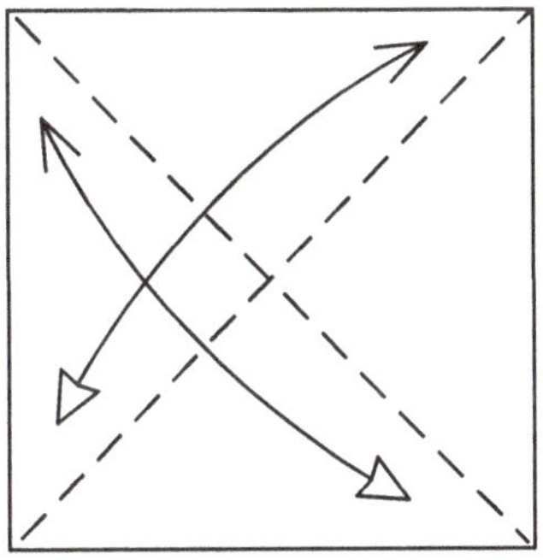

2.

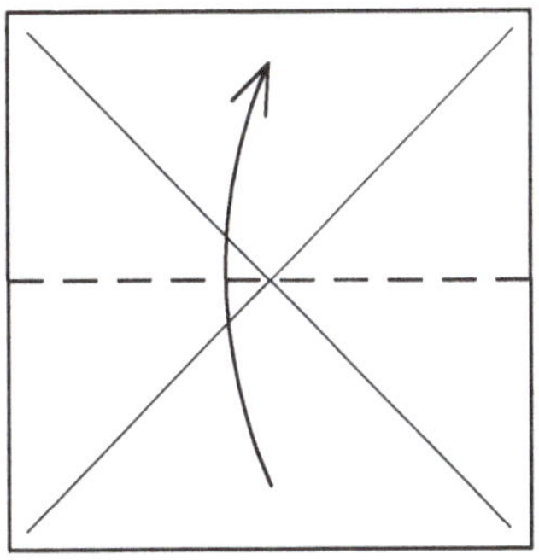

3.

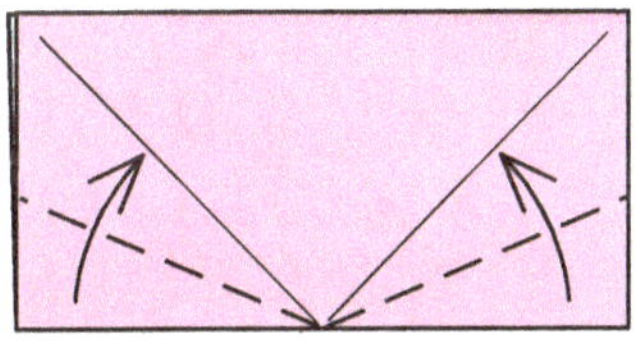

4. 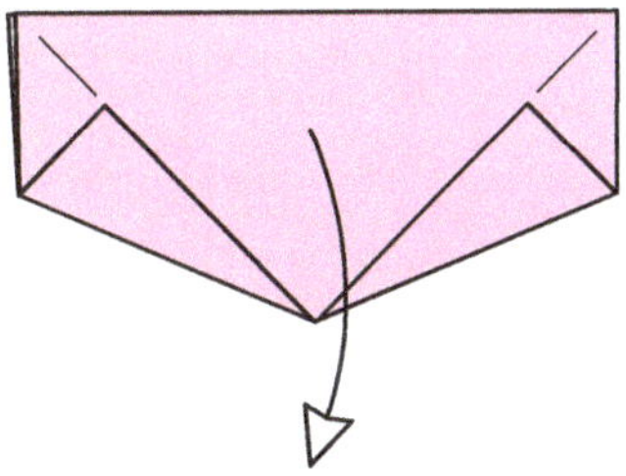 Unfold everything and rotate.

5. Repeat steps 2–4.

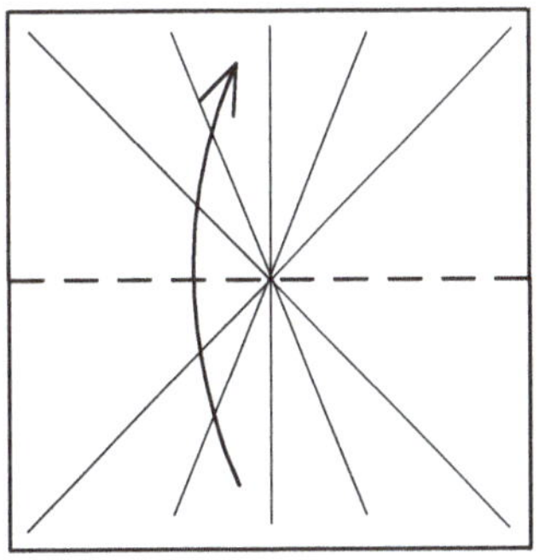

6.

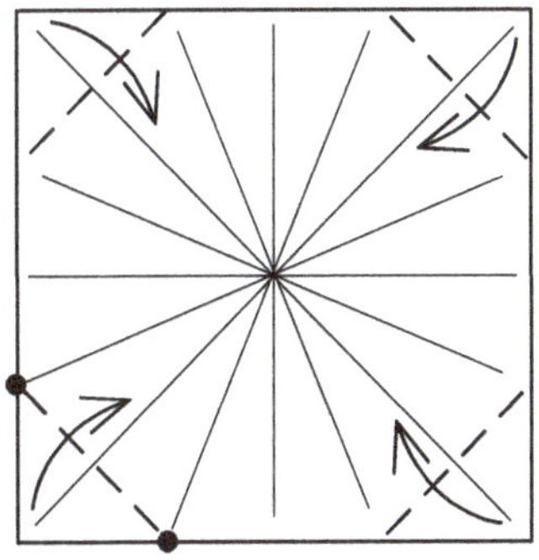

Double Eight-Pointed Star 79

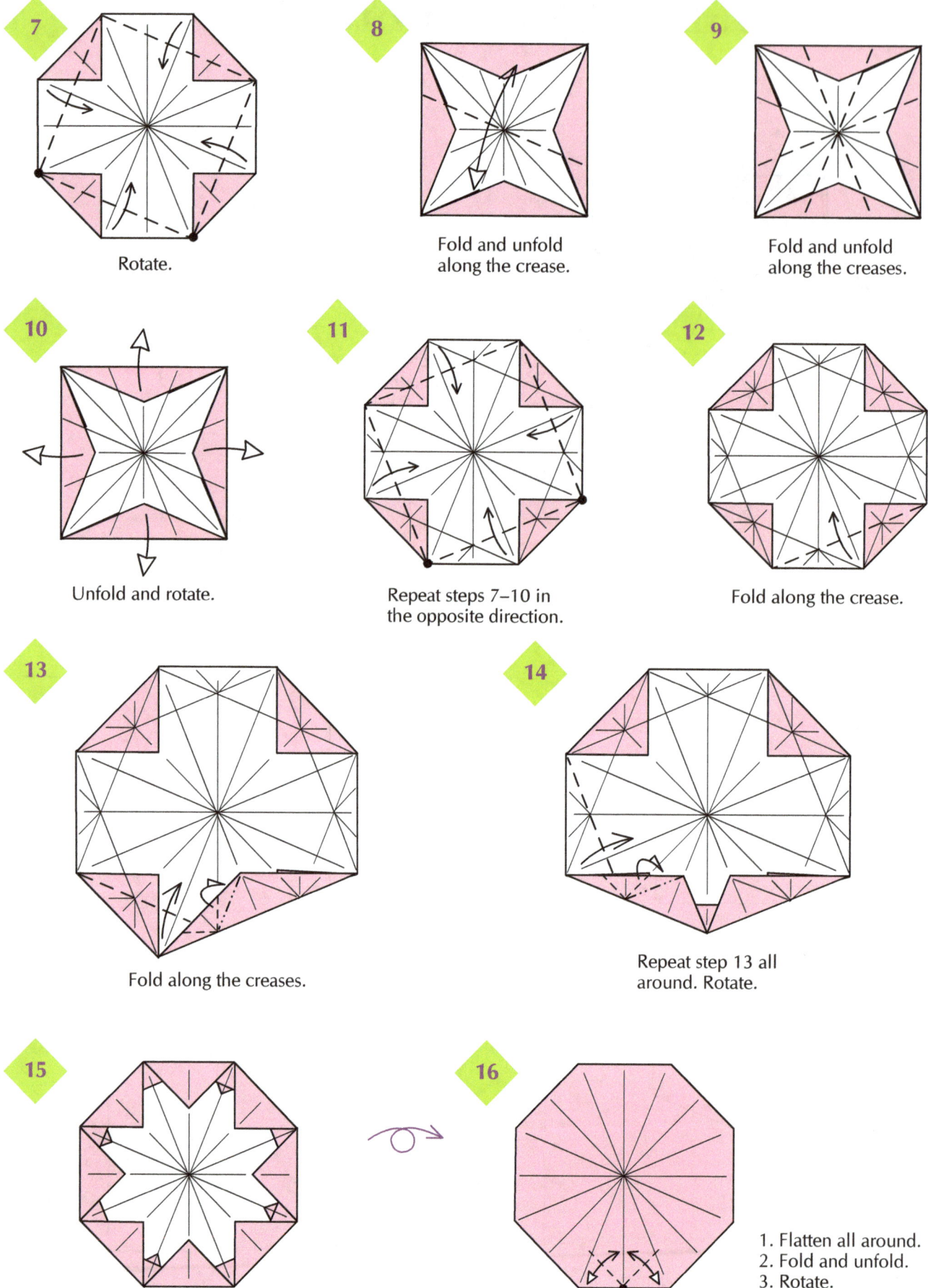

80 *Galaxy of Origami Stars*

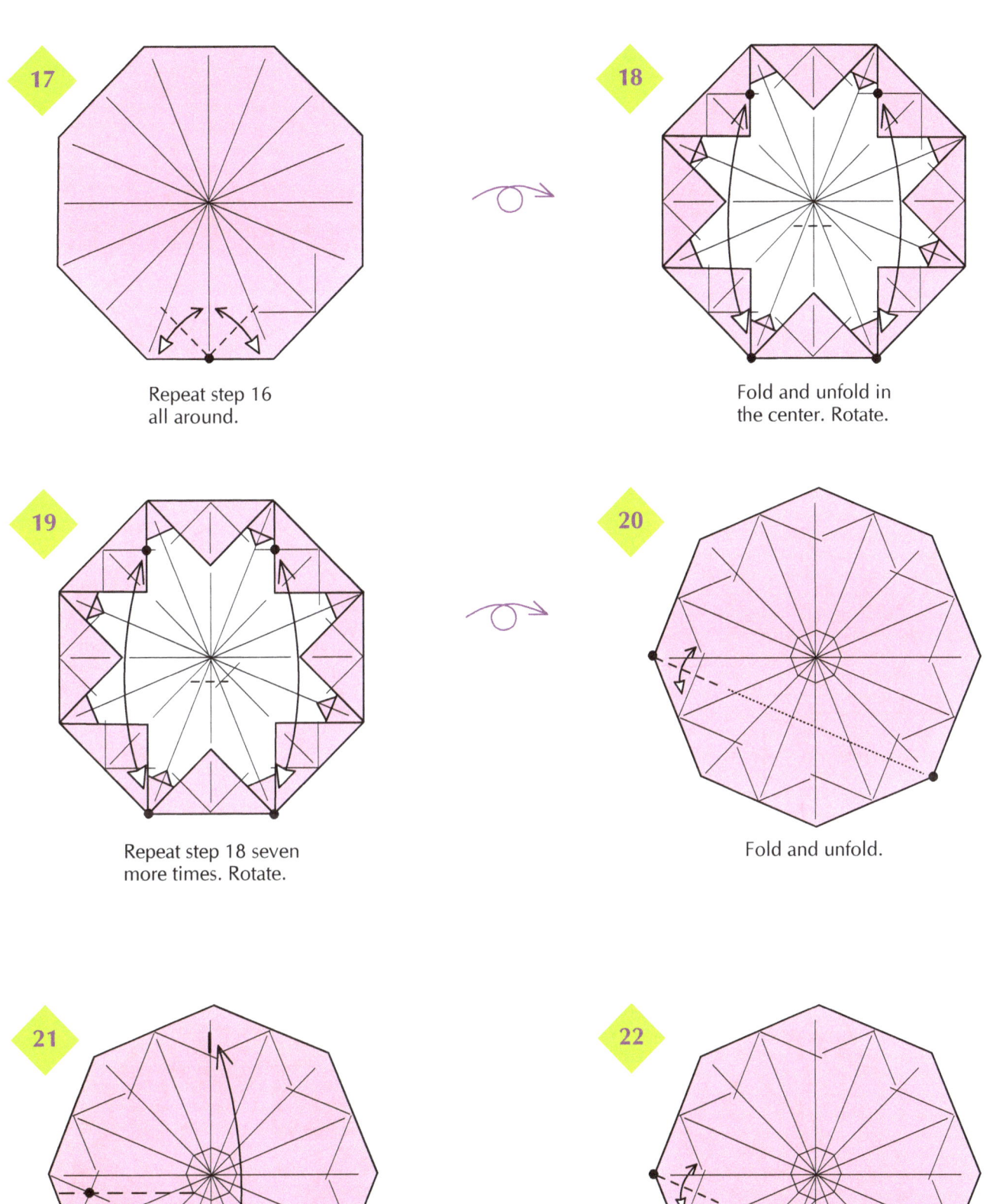

Double Eight-Pointed Star 81

23

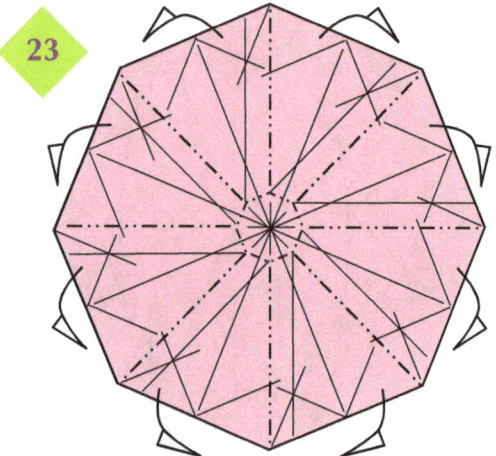

Fold along the creases. Form an octagon in the center. It will become the top.

24

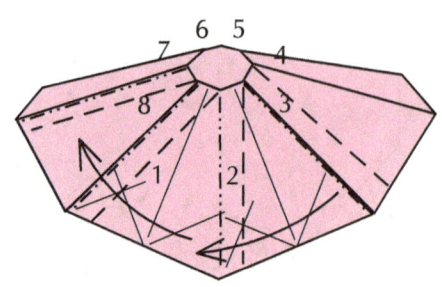

Twist-fold. Fold all around in order. Flatten.

25

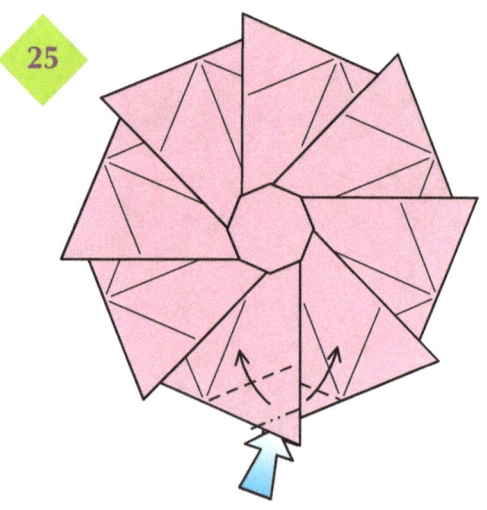

Spread and flatten. Crease sharply. Rotate.

26

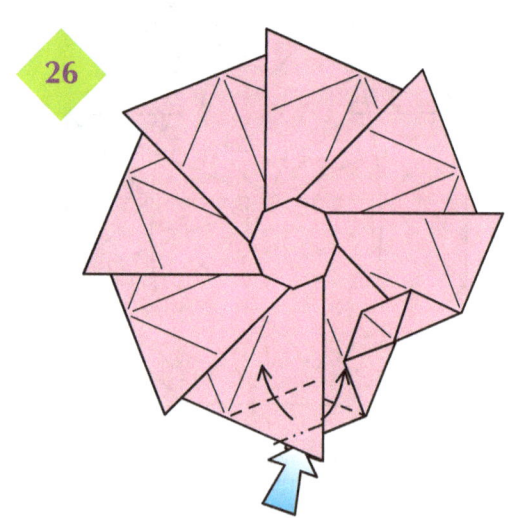

Repeat step 25 seven more times. Rotate.

27

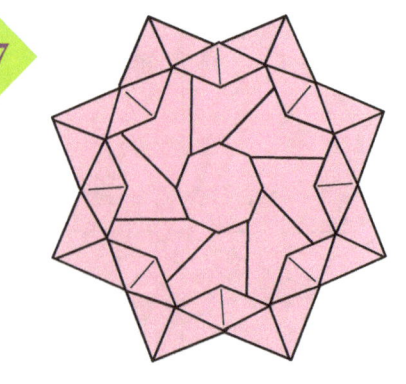

28

Double Eight-Pointed Star

82 *Galaxy of Origami Stars*

Two-Toned Eight-Pointed Star

The square is divided into thirds. Then an octagon is formed with both sides of the paper showing (step 15). This allows for the points to alternate in color after a twist fold.

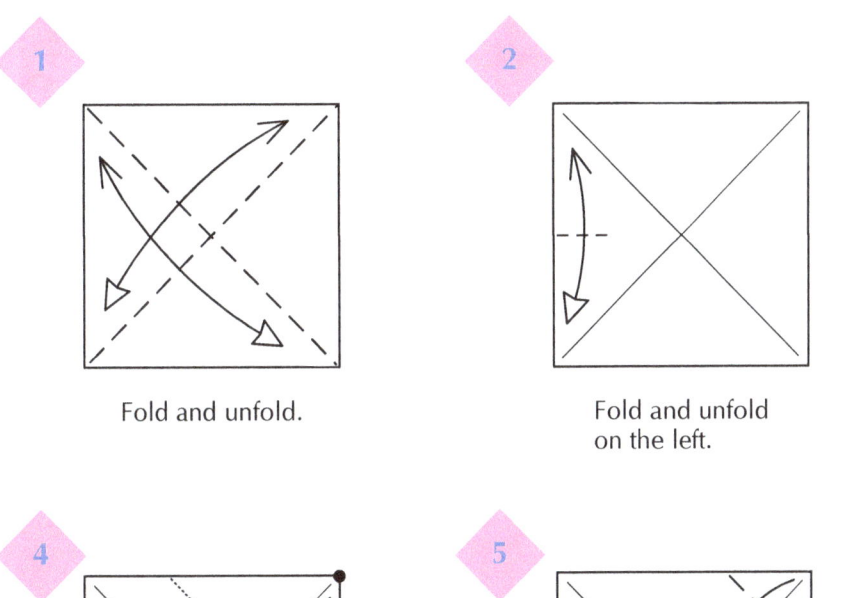

1. Fold and unfold.

2. Fold and unfold on the left.

3. Fold and unfold by the diagonal.

4.
 1. Fold to the dot.
 2. Fold and unfold by the diagonal.

5.

6. Fold and unfold on the edges.

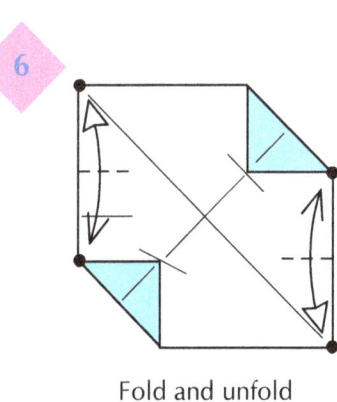

Two-Toned Eight-Pointed Star 83

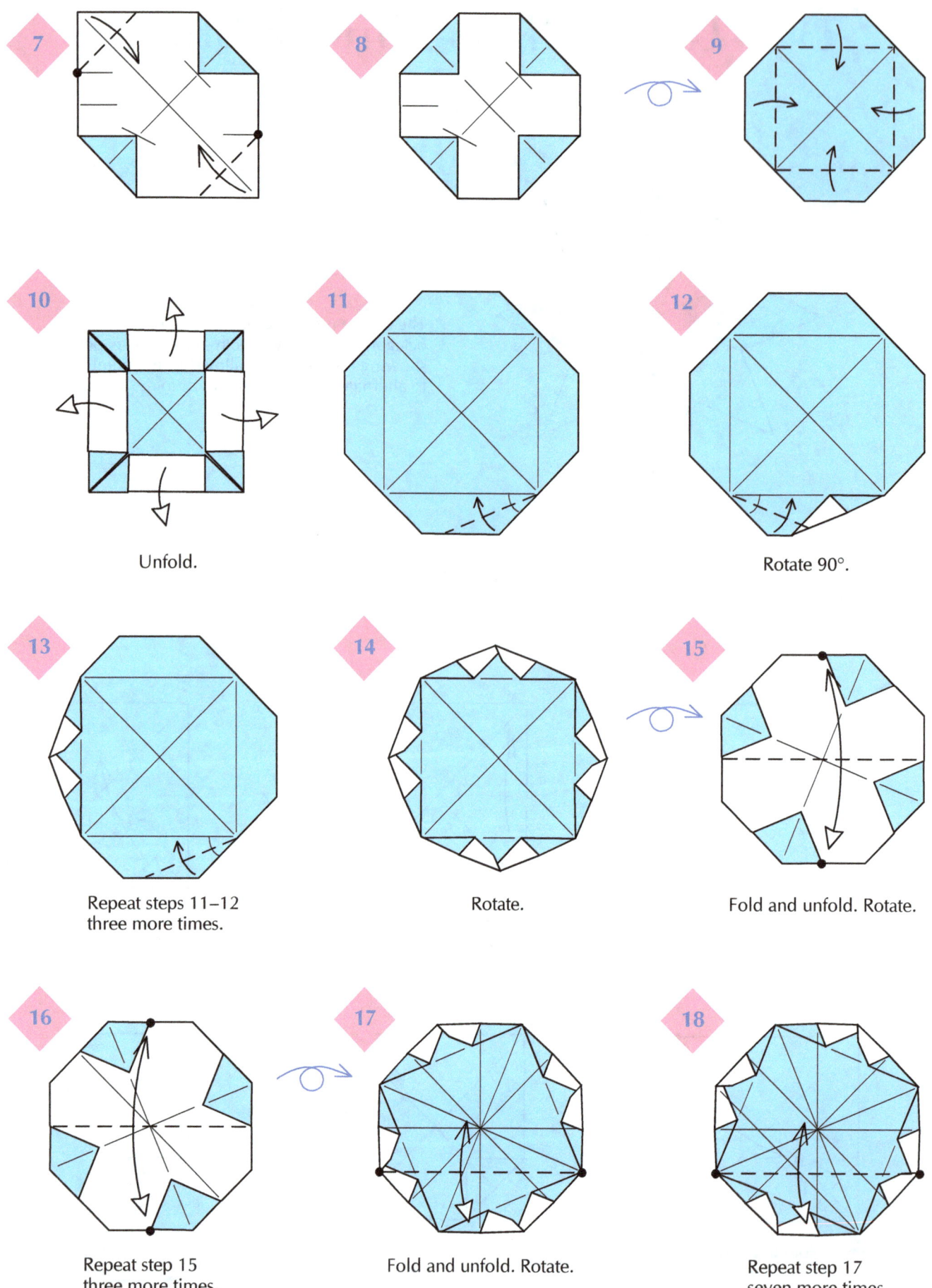

Unfold.

Rotate 90°.

Repeat steps 11–12 three more times.

Rotate.

Fold and unfold. Rotate.

Repeat step 15 three more times.

Fold and unfold. Rotate.

Repeat step 17 seven more times.

84 *Galaxy of Origami Stars*

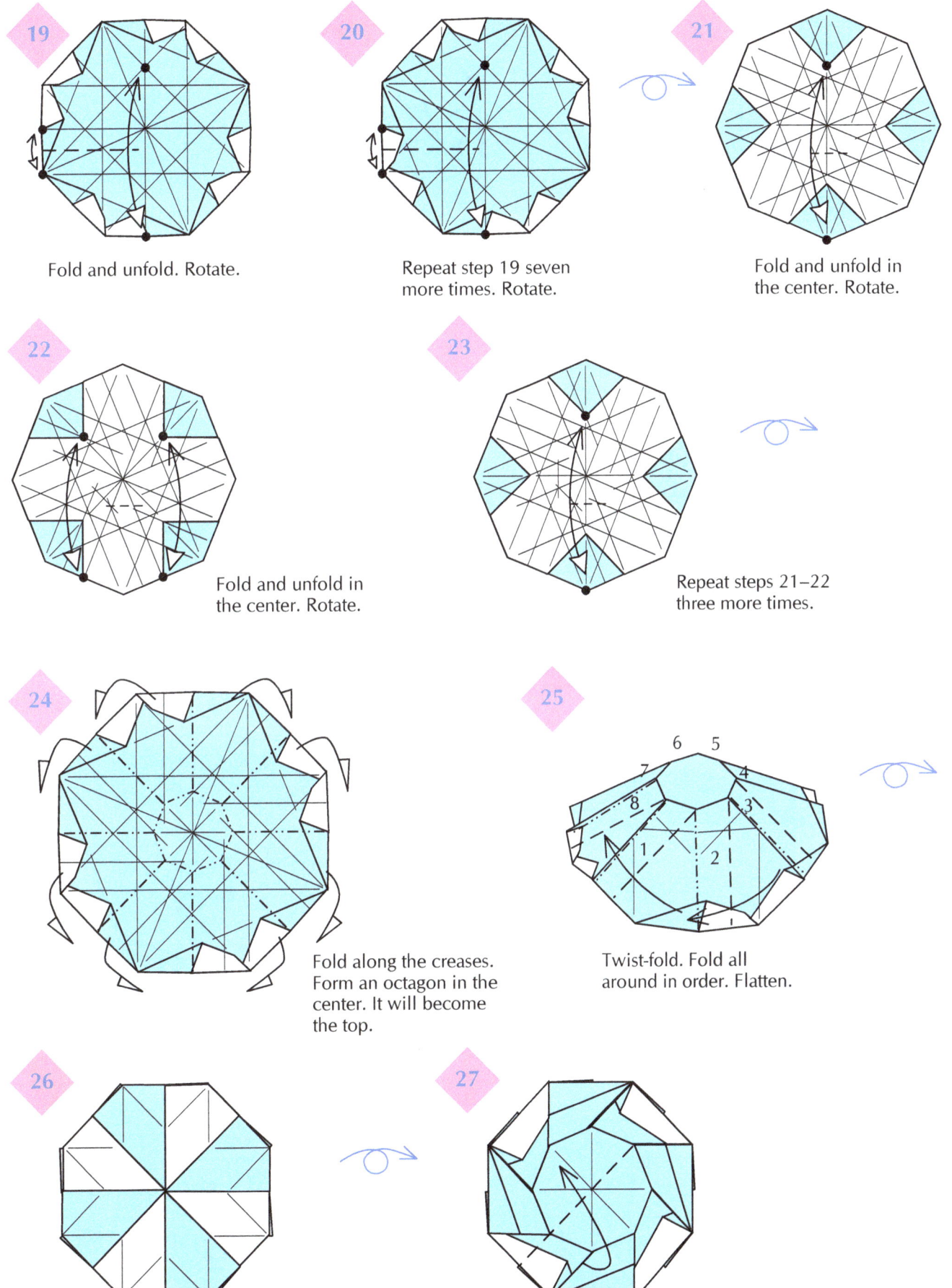

Two-Toned Eight-Pointed Star

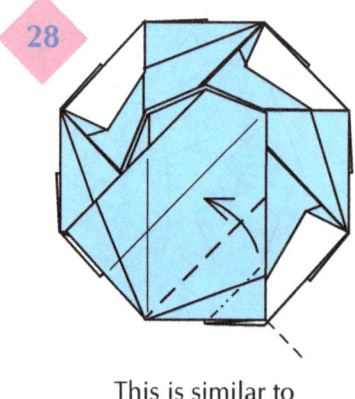

This is similar to a squash fold.

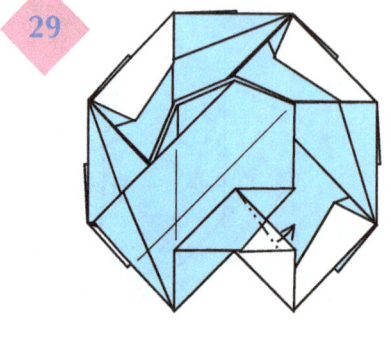

Slide.

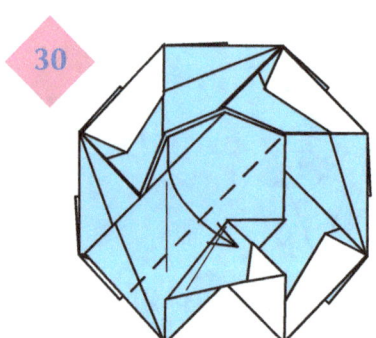

Rotate.

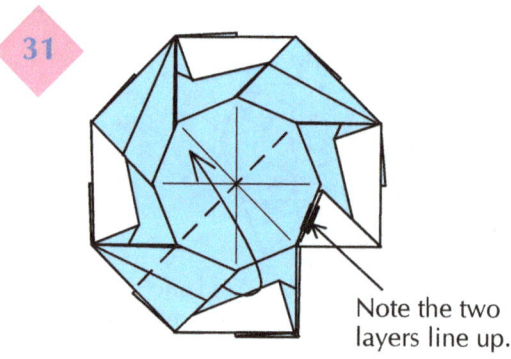

Note the two layers line up.

Repeat steps 27–30 seven more times.

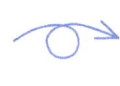

Two-Toned Eight-Pointed Star

86 *Galaxy of Origami Stars*

Radiant Eight-Pointed Star

Designed by Russell Cashdollar

This radiant star begins with an octagon and uses a twist fold. An important landmark for the fold in step 15 allows for the right amount of paper for the color changes in steps 21 and beyond.

1. Fold and unfold.

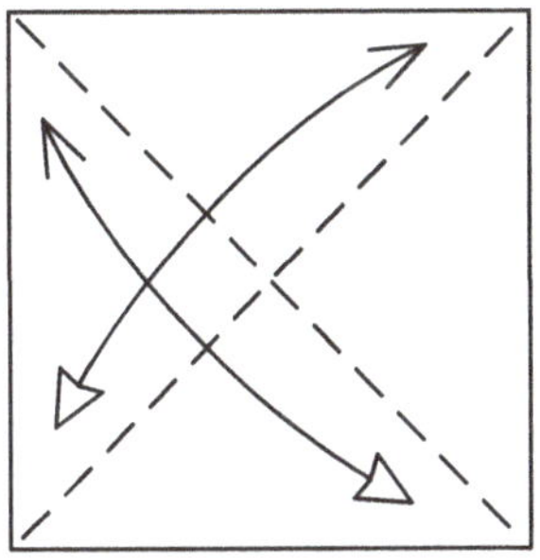

2.

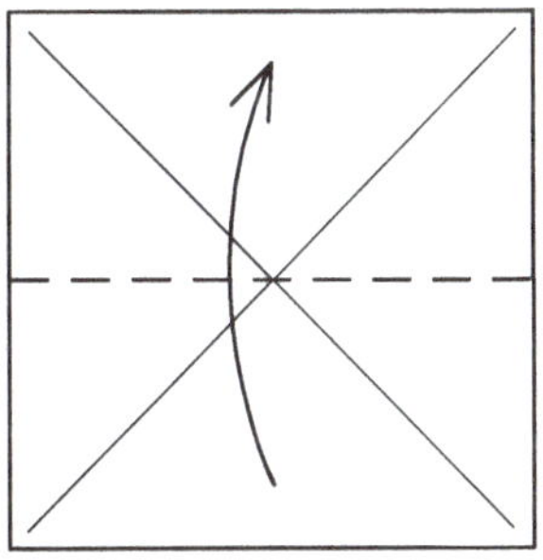

3.

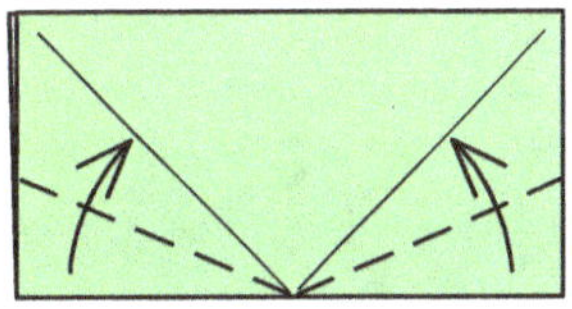

4. 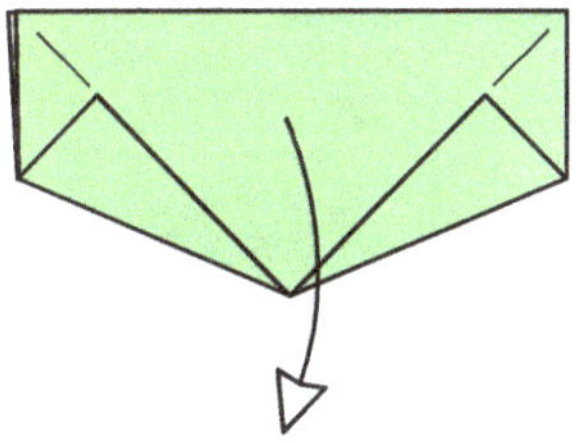 Unfold everything and rotate.

5. Repeat steps 2–4.

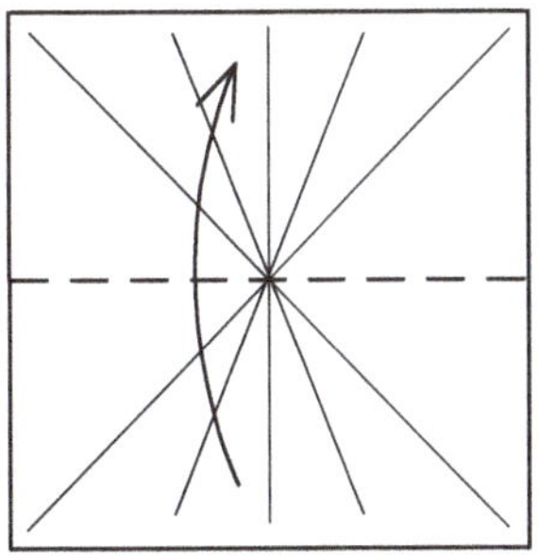

6. Rotate.

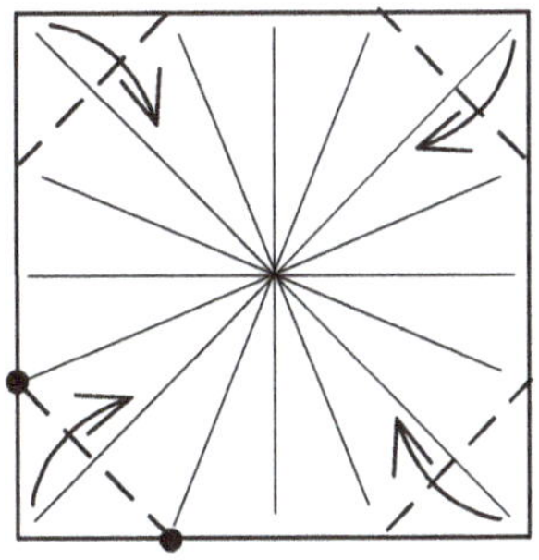

7.

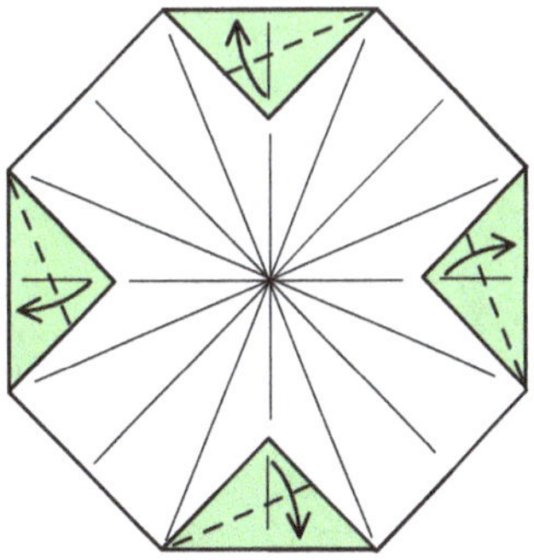

8. 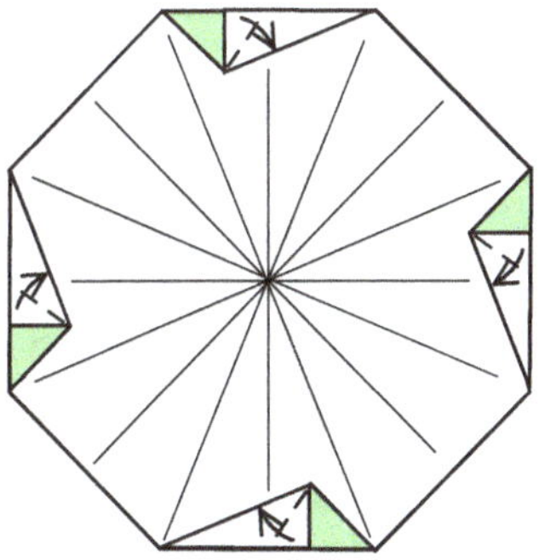 Rotate.

Radiant Eight-Pointed Star 87

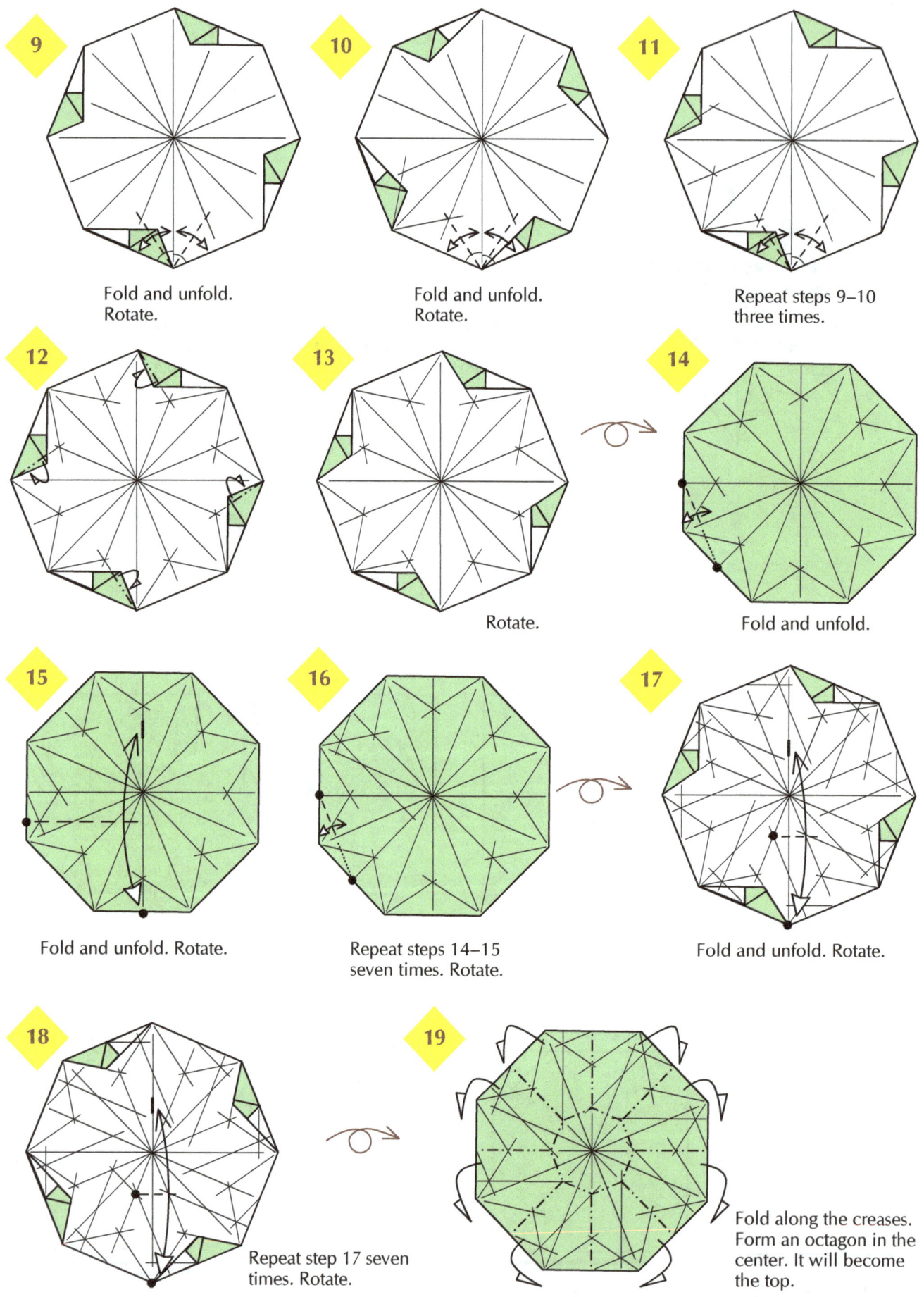

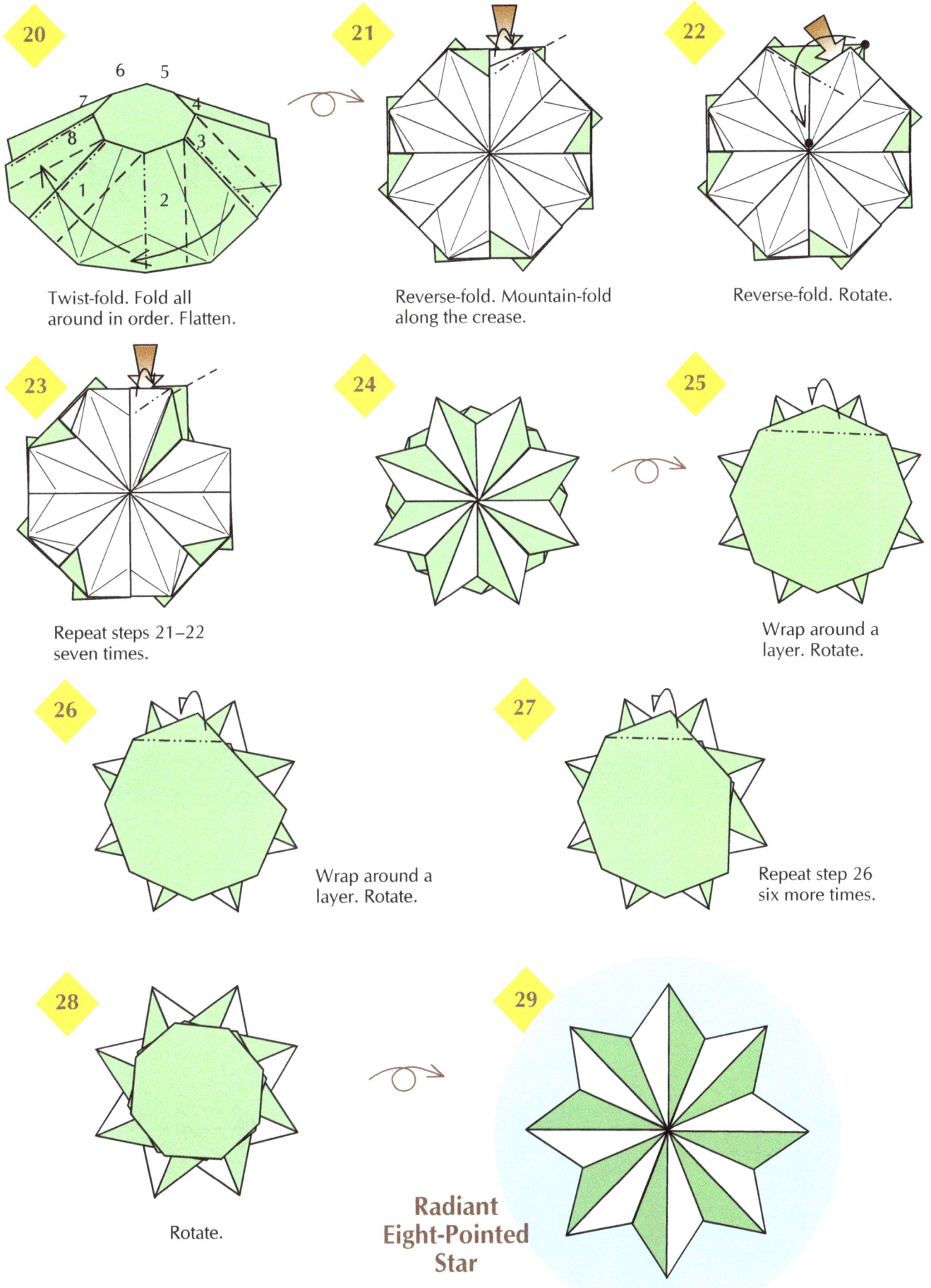

Radiant Eight-Pointed Star

Magic Star

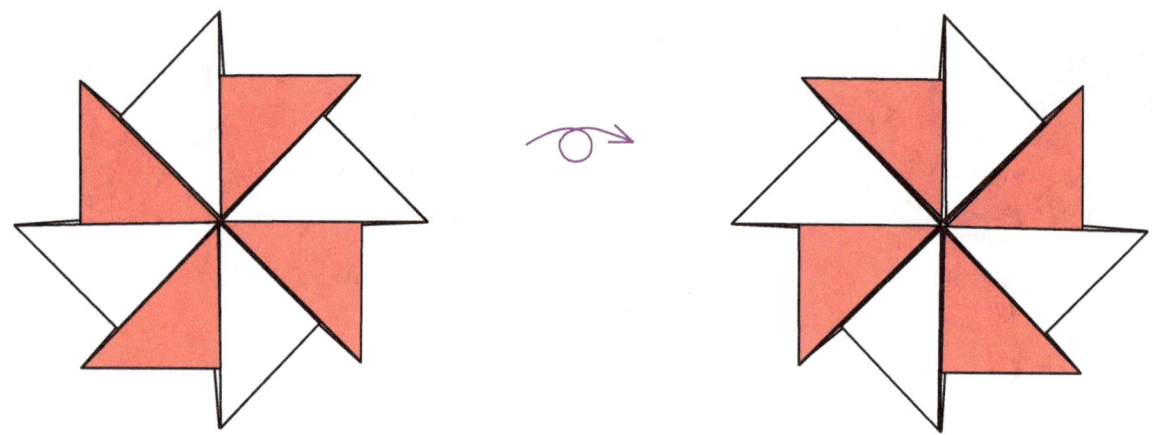

This star has the same pattern on both sides with alternating colors. Though from one sheet, it appears to be a modular work from eight sheets. After an octagon is formed, a sequence of folds circle around. The model is turned over and the next sequence of folds circle around.

1 Fold and unfold.

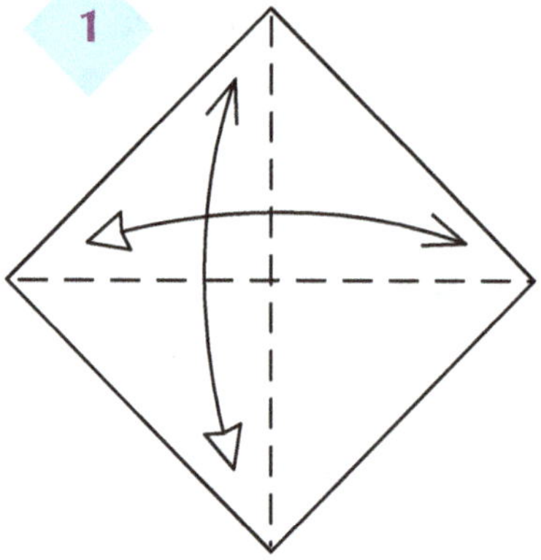

2 Fold and unfold.

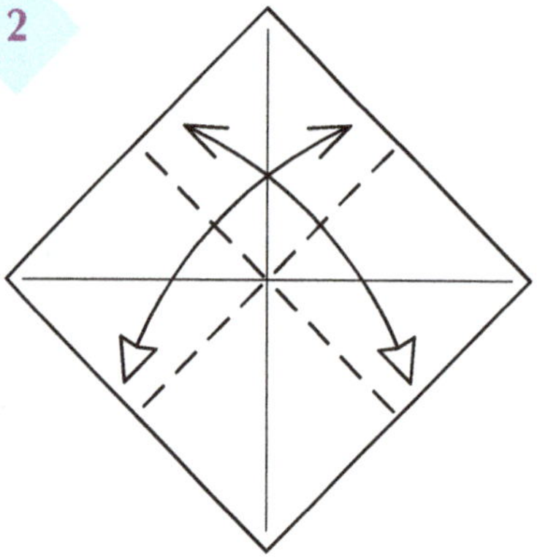

3 Crease between the dots.

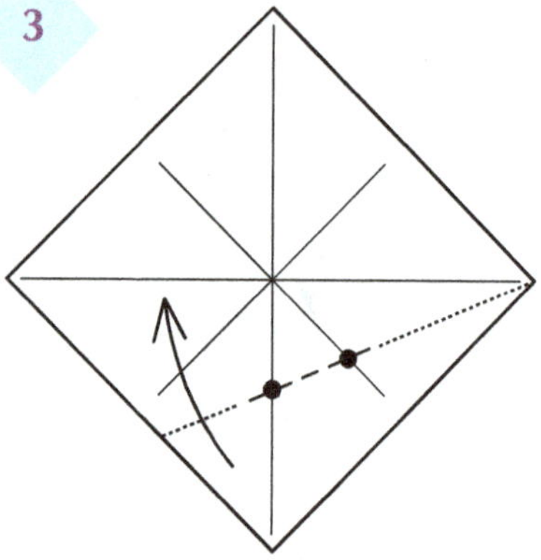

4 Unfold and rotate 90°.

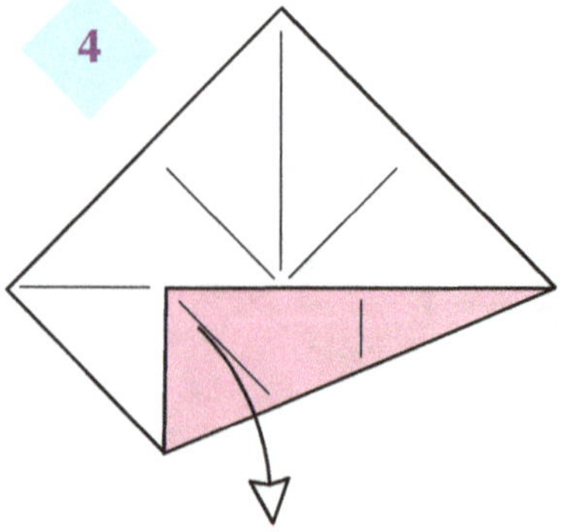

5 Repeat steps 3–4 three more times.

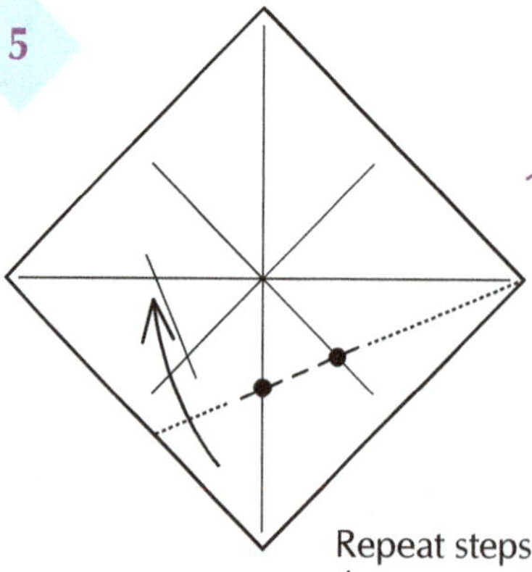

6

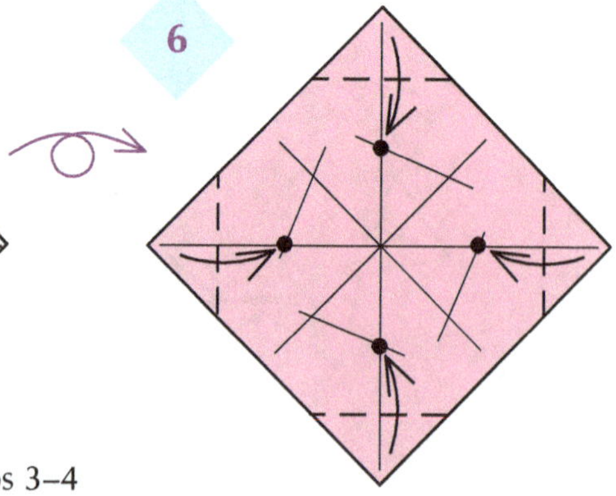

90 *Galaxy of Origami Stars*

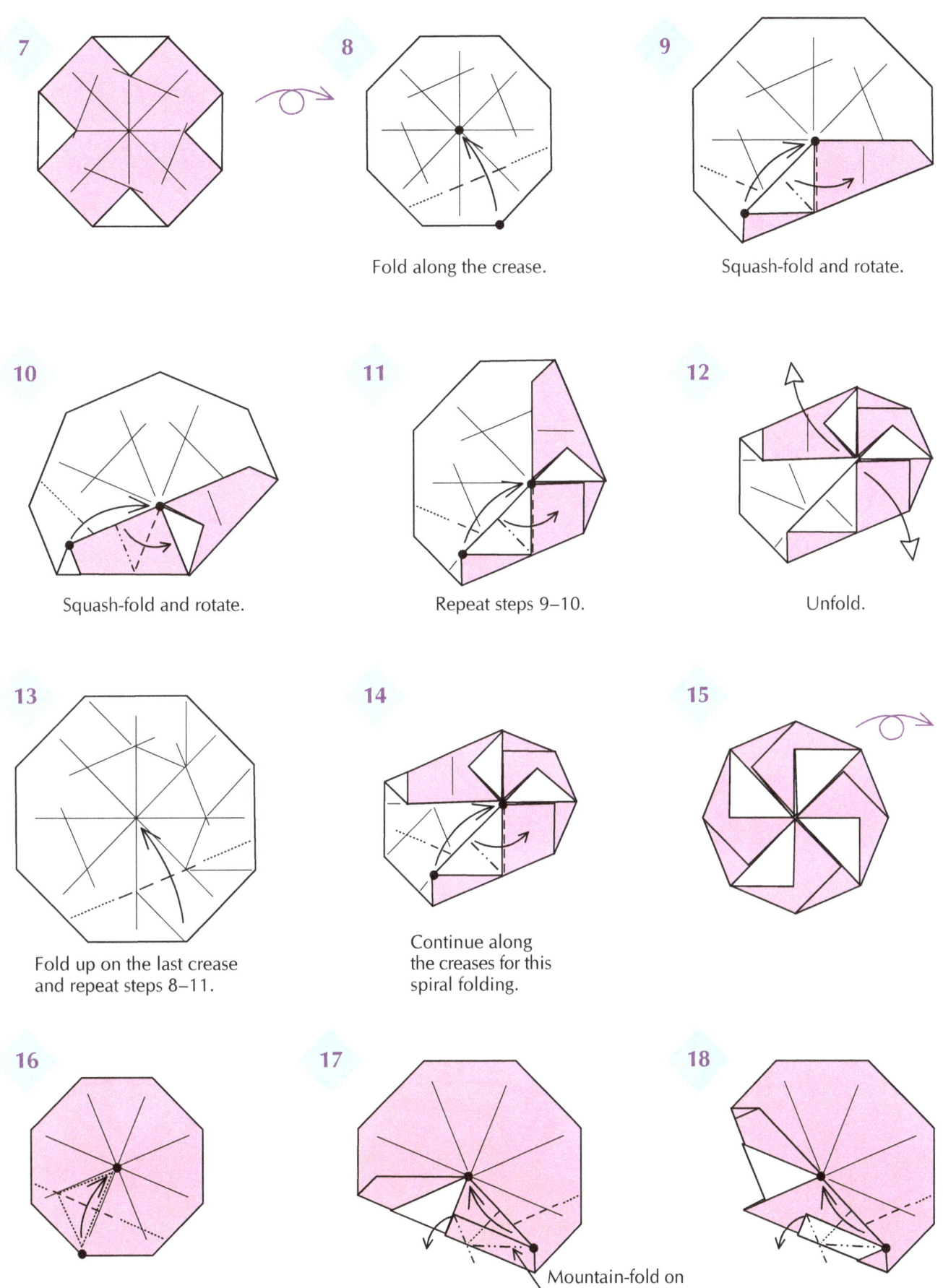

Magic Star 91

19

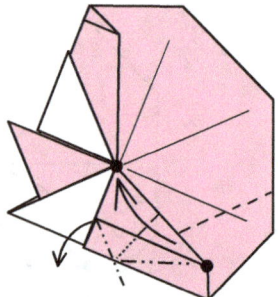

Repeat steps 17–18.

20

Unfold.

21

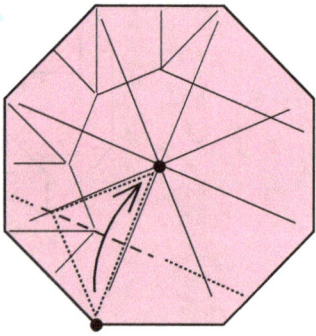

Fold up on the last crease and repeat steps 16–19.

22

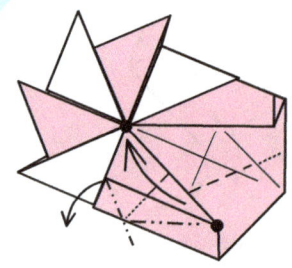

Continue along the creases for this spiral folding.

23

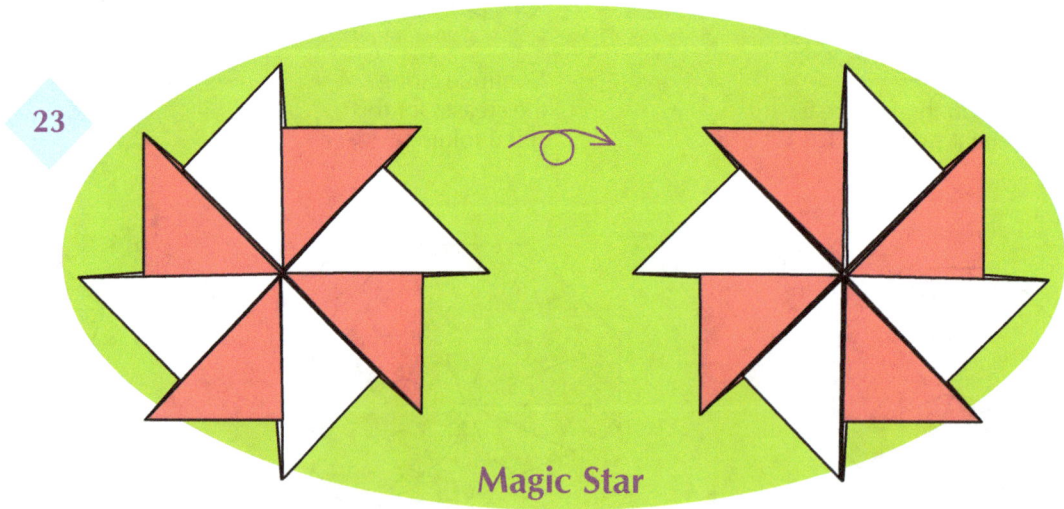

Magic Star

92 *Galaxy of Origami Stars*

Water Wheel

The water wheel is a variation of the magic star.

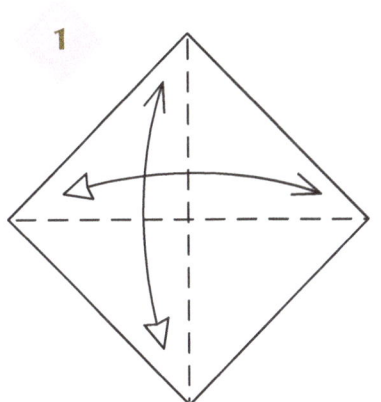

1. Fold and unfold.

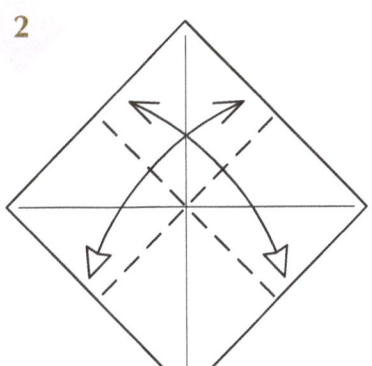

2. Fold and unfold.

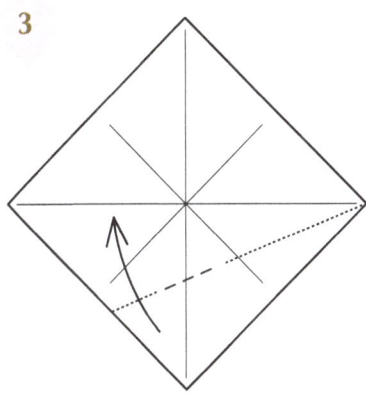

3. Crease by the diagonal.

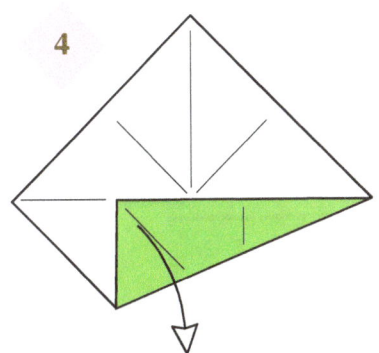

4. Unfold and rotate 90°.

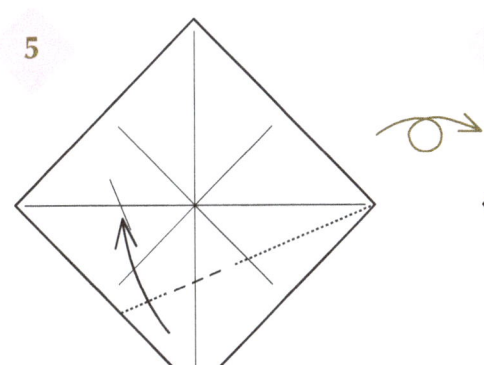

5. Repeat steps 3–4 three more times.

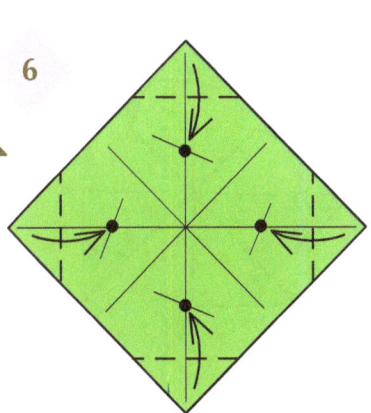

Water Wheel 93

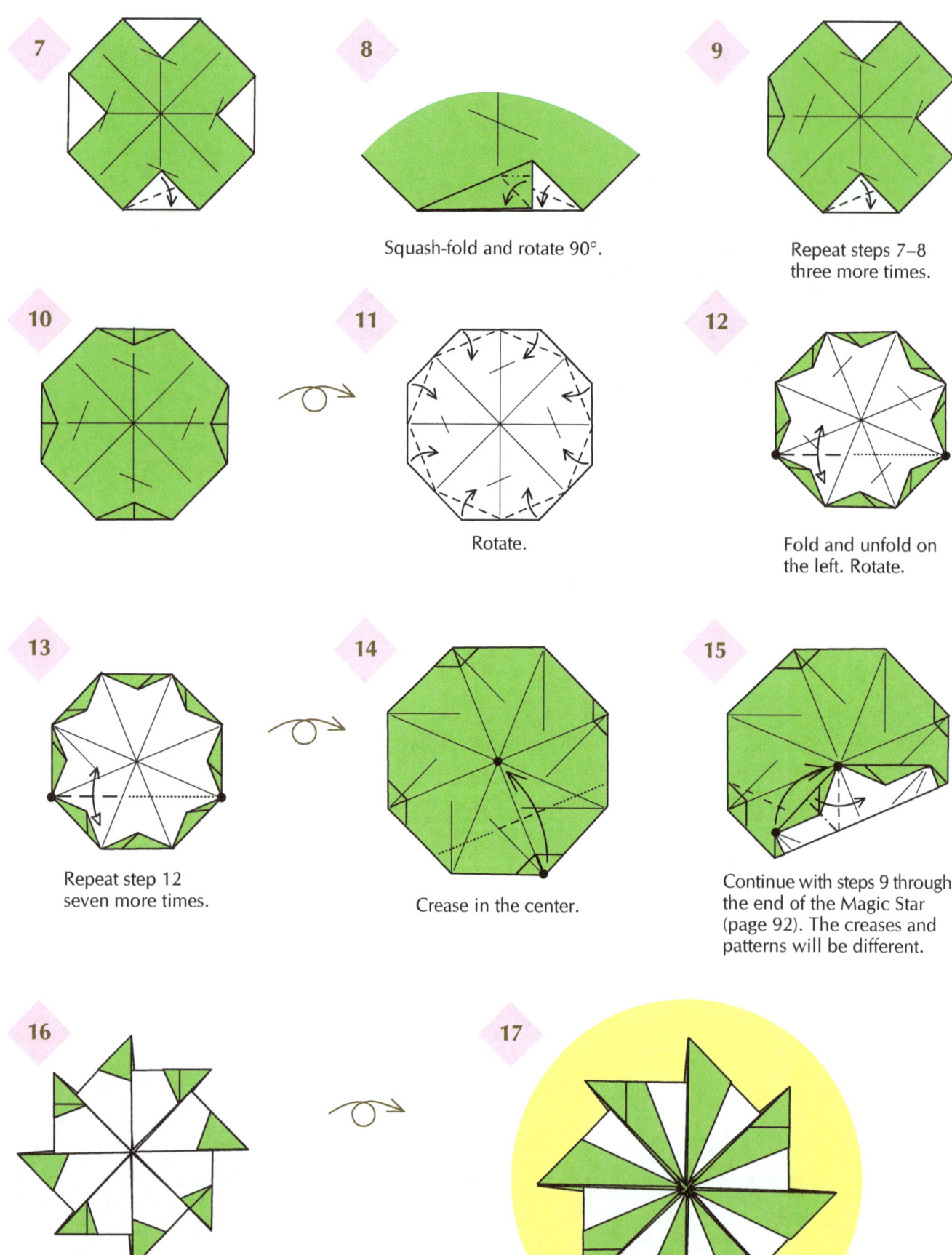

94 *Galaxy of Origami Stars*

Ohio Star

Named for a quilt pattern, this star uses a square twist fold.

1. Fold and unfold.

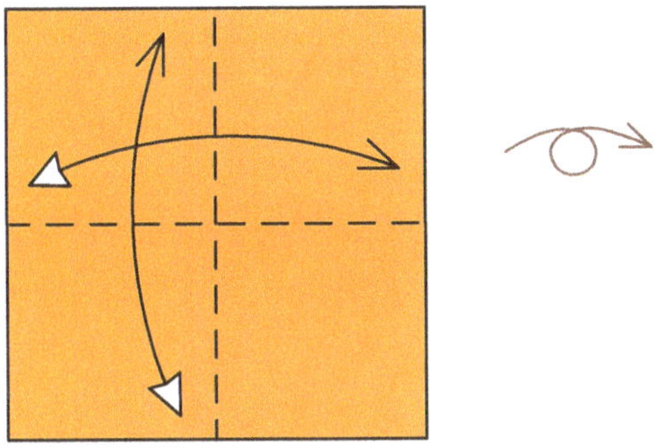

2. Fold and unfold. Rotate 90°.

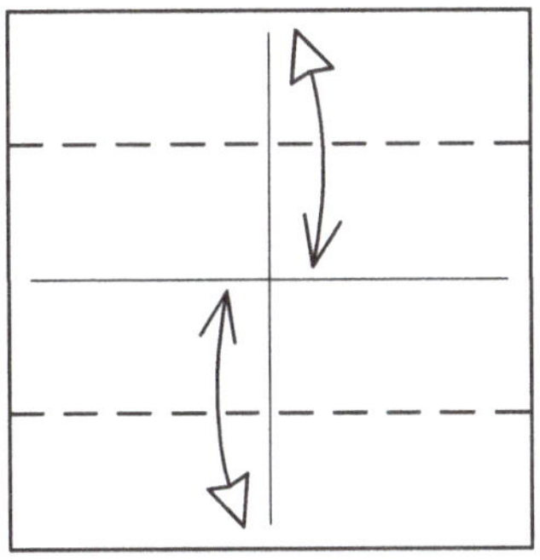

3. Fold and unfold.

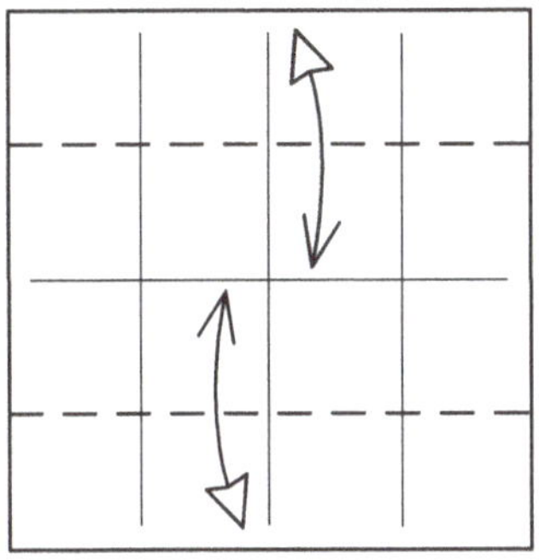

4. Fold and unfold. Rotate 90°.

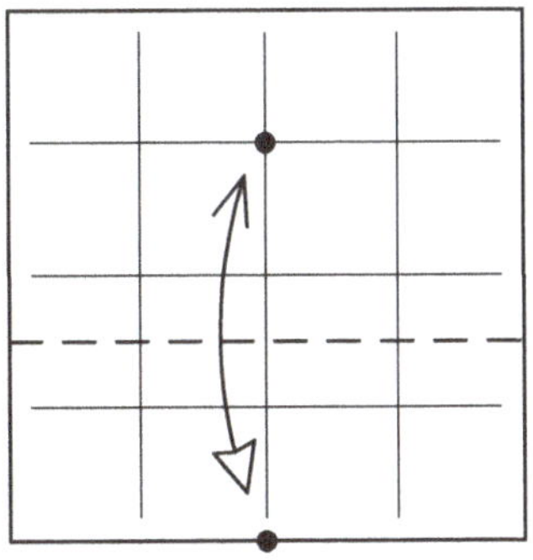

5. Repeat step 4 three more times.

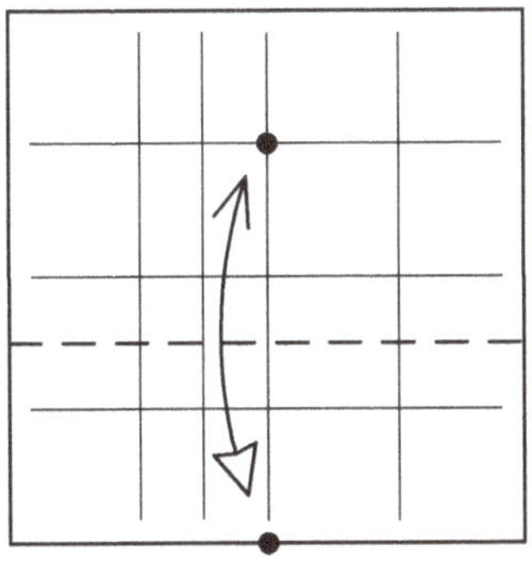

6.

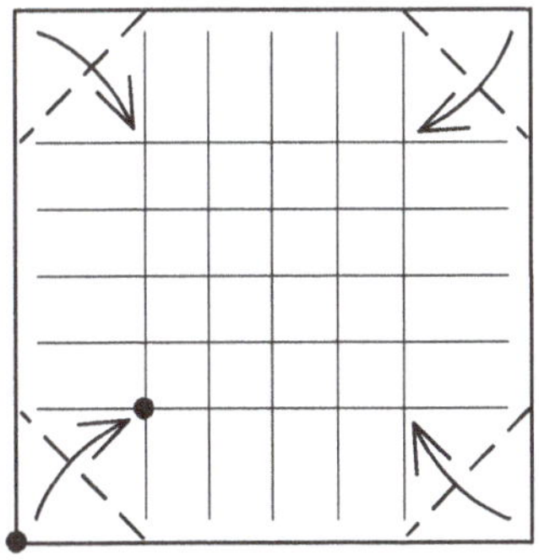

Ohio Star 95

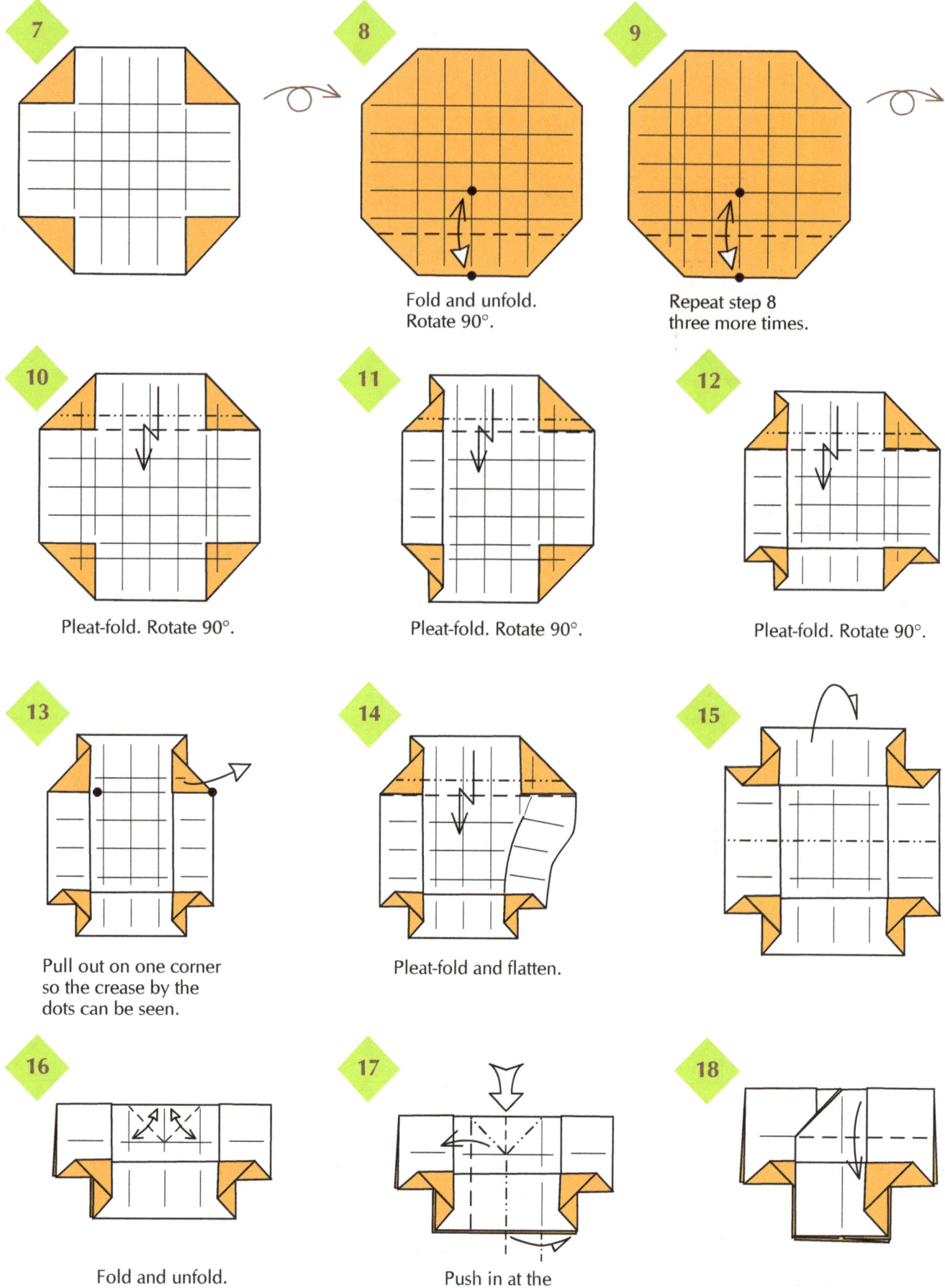

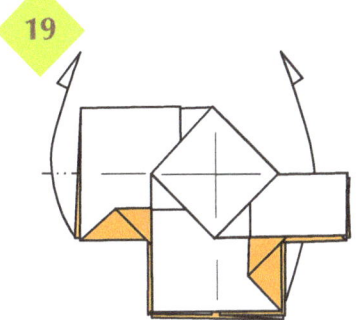

Fold up from behind.

This is similar to a squash fold. Rotate 90°.

Repeat step 20 three more times.

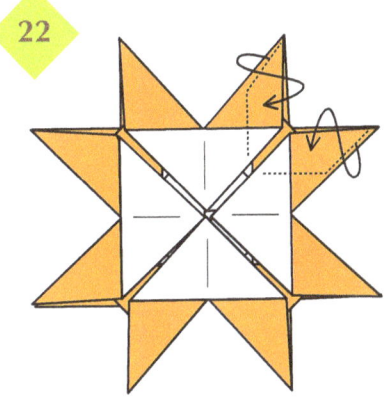

Bring the hidden paper to the front.

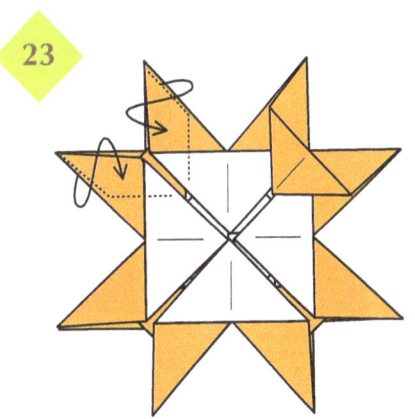

Repeat step 22 three more times.

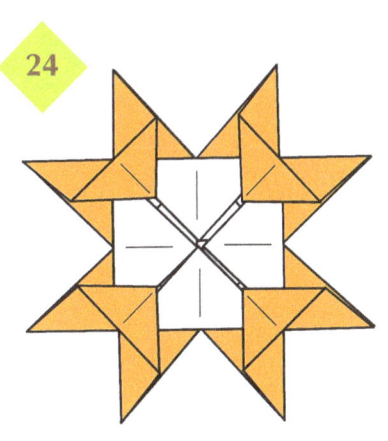

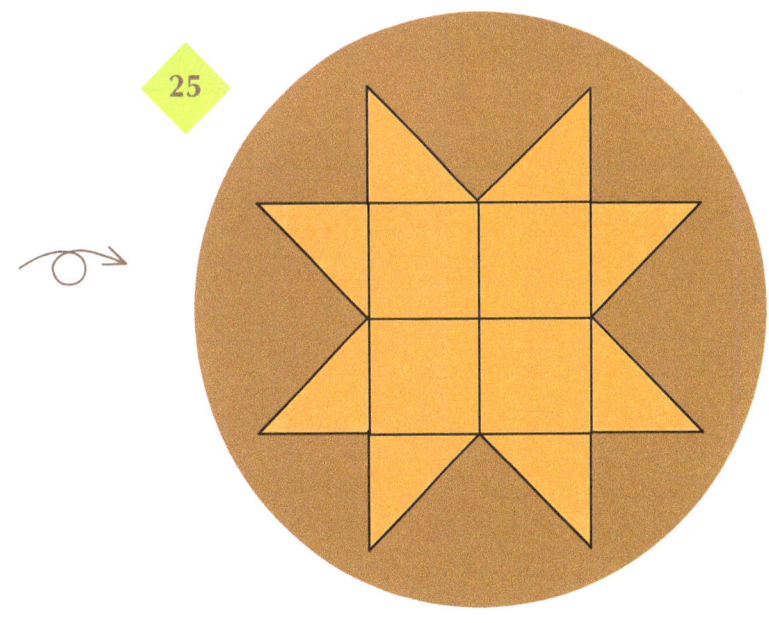

Ohio Star

Ohio Star 97

Woven Star

This twelve-pointed star appears to have woven strips. It uses a square twist fold. The paper is divided into twelfths.

1 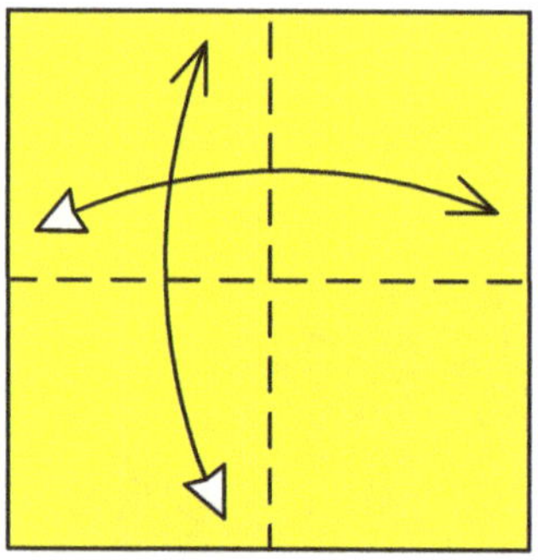 Fold and unfold.

2 Fold and unfold. Rotate 90°.

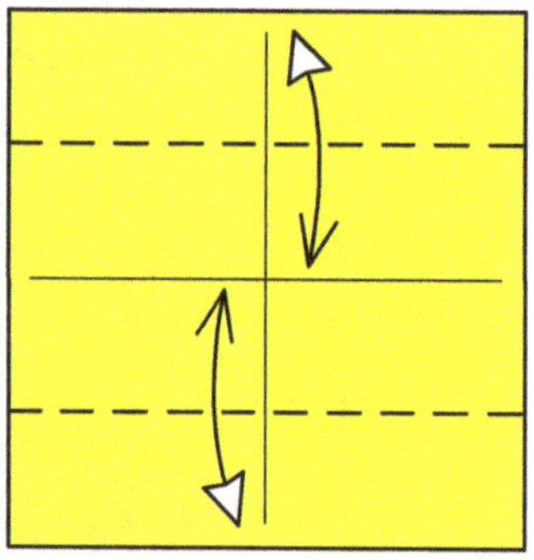

3 Fold and unfold.

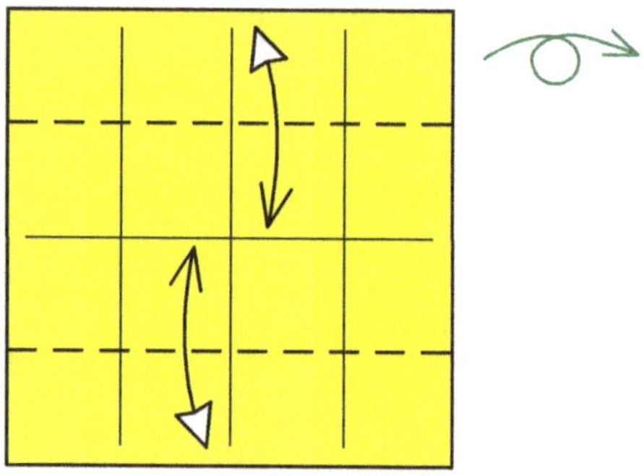

4 Fold and unfold.

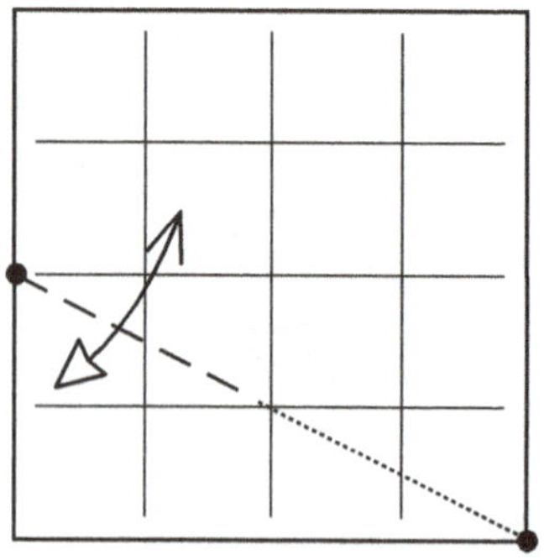

5 Fold and unfold on the diagonal. Crease by the intersection.

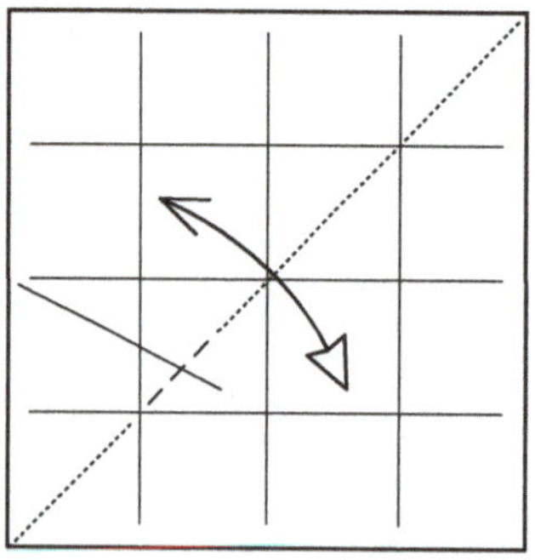

6 Fold and unfold.

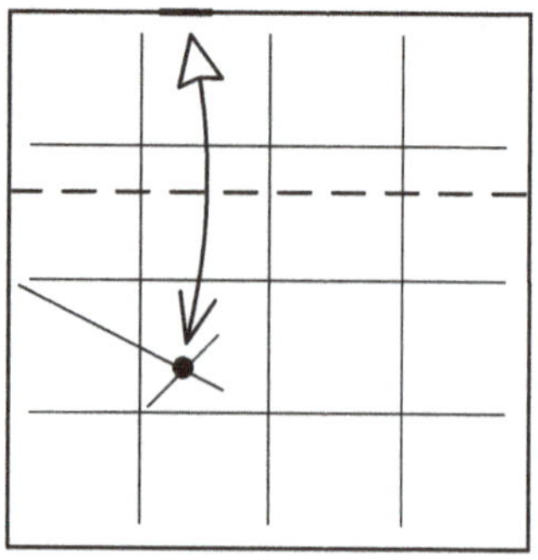

98   Galaxy of Origami Stars

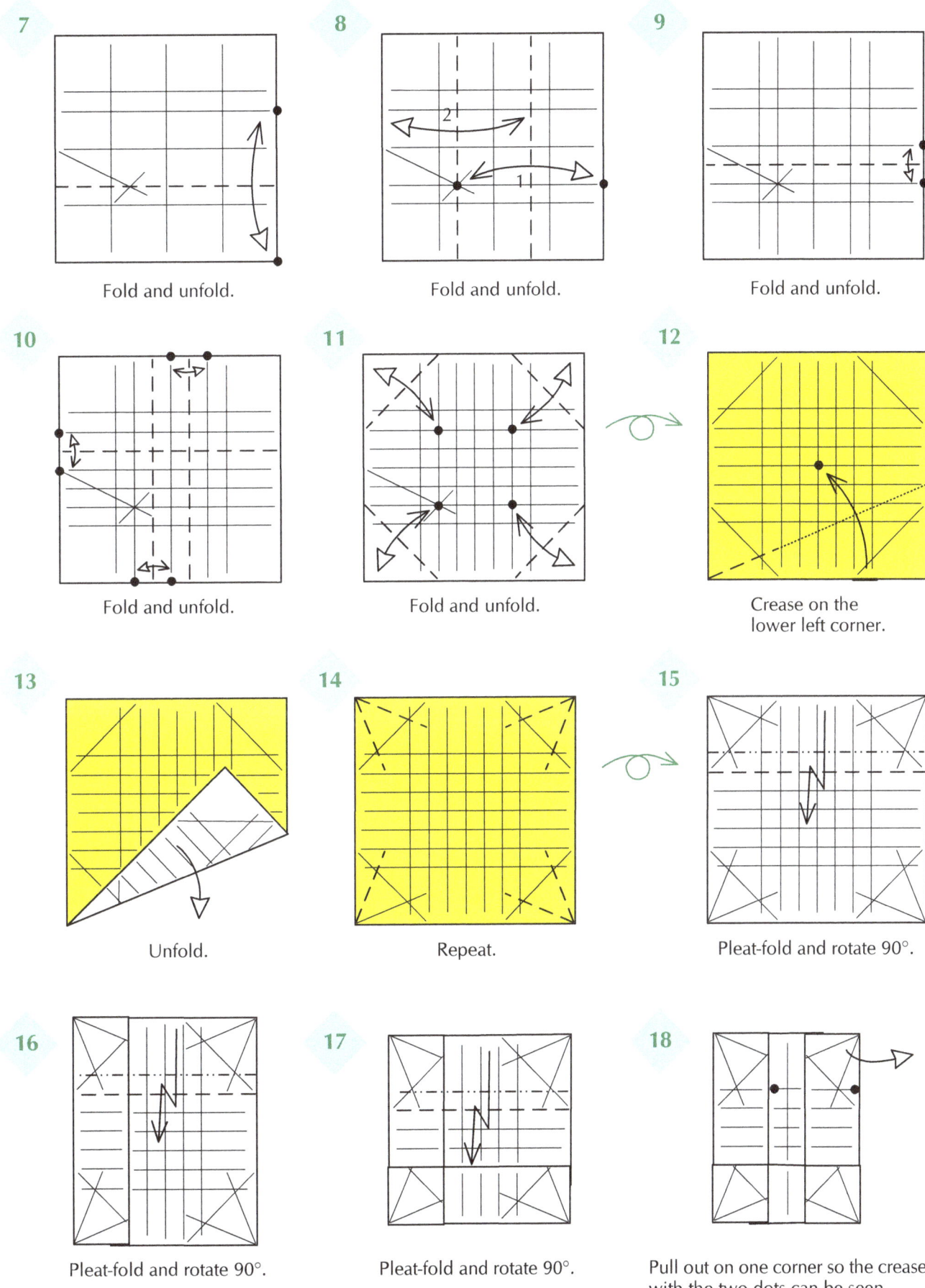

Woven Star 99

19

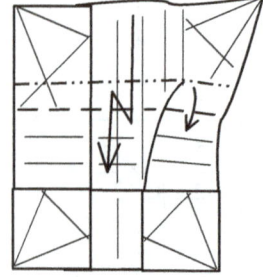

Pleat-fold and flatten. Rotate.

20

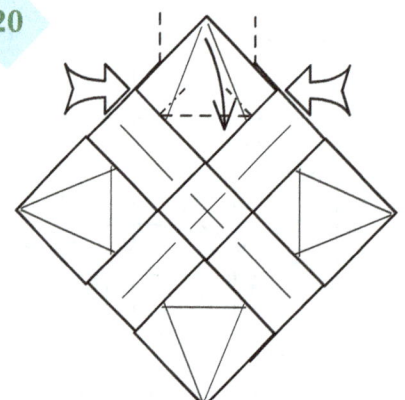

Valley-fold along the creases for this petal fold.

21

This is 3D with the dot above. Flatten.

22

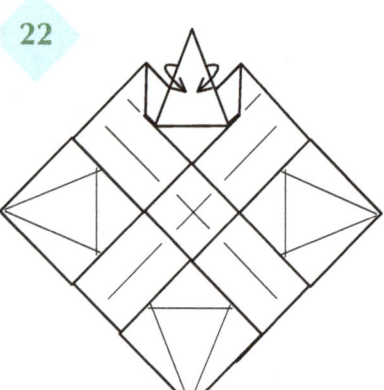

Wrap around. Rotate 90°.

23

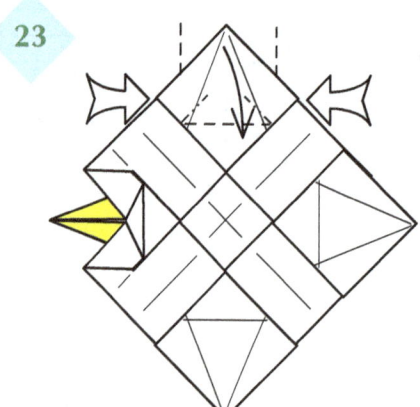

Repeat steps 20–22 three more times. Rotate.

24

25

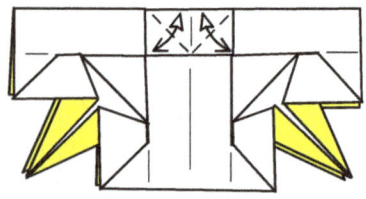

Fold and unfold.

26

Push in at the top and flatten.

27

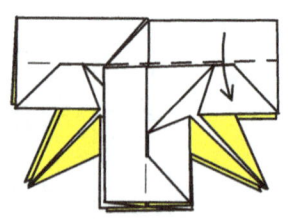

100   *Galaxy of Origami Stars*

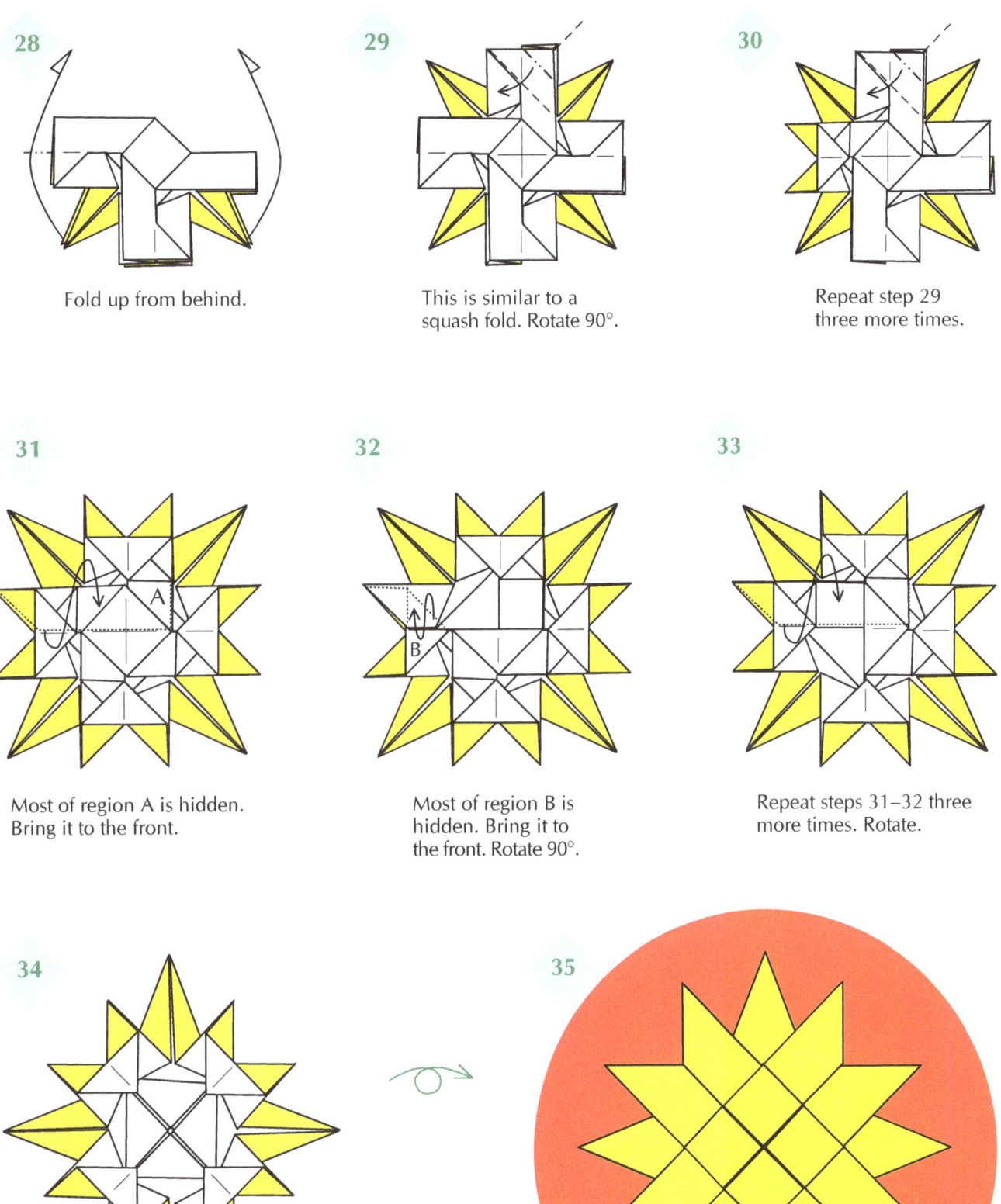

Woven Star

Woven Star 101

Tall Stellated Tetrahedron

Designed by Russell Cashdollar

This three-dimensional star has four points. The apex angle on each face is 45°. The model closes with a three-way twist lock.

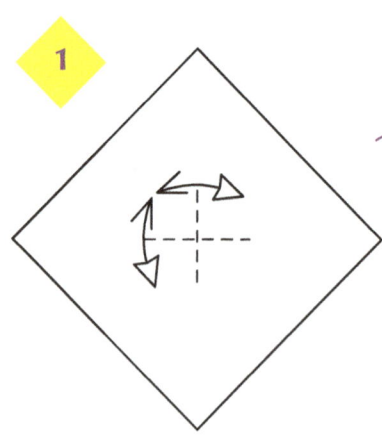

1. Fold and unfold along the diagonals, creasing in the center.

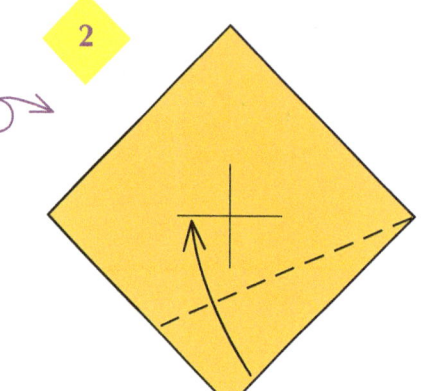

2.

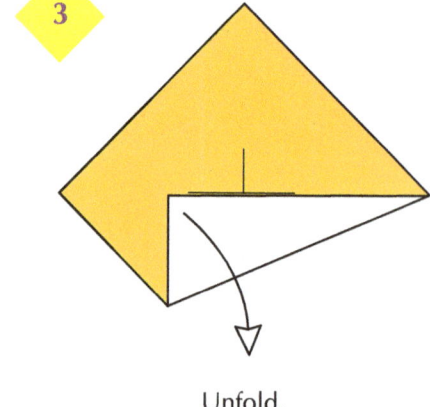

3. Unfold.

4. Fold and unfold three more times.

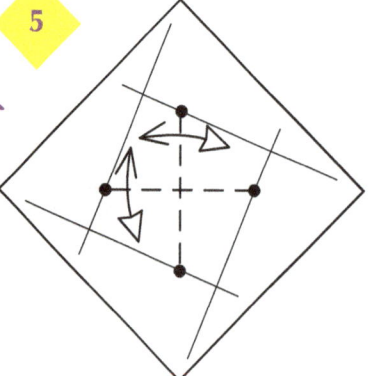

5. Fold and unfold, extending the lines to the creases.

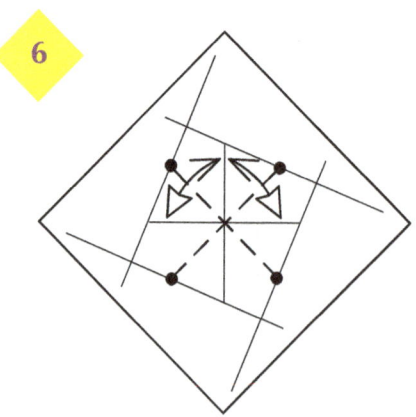

6. Fold and unfold. Rotate.

102 *Galaxy of Origami Stars*

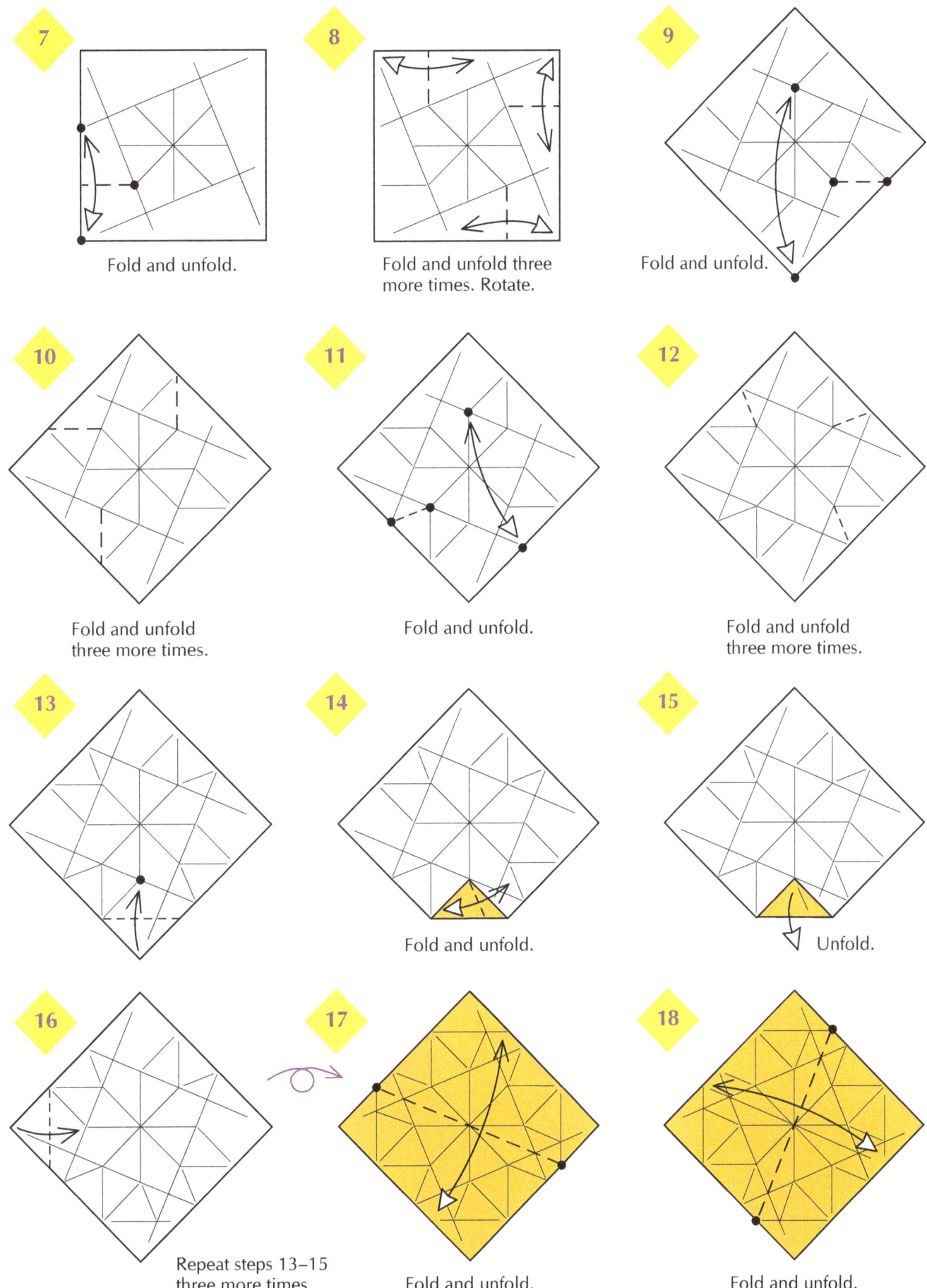

Tall Stellated Tetrahedron 103

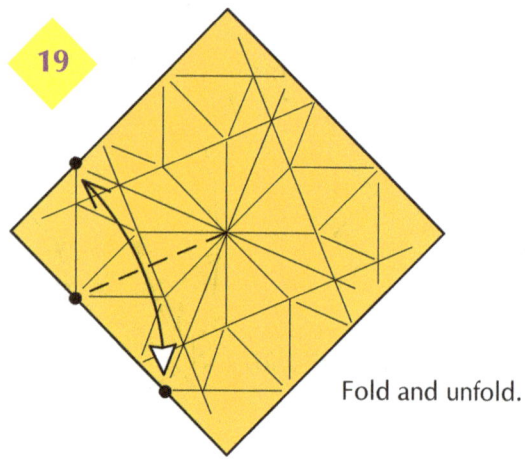

Fold and unfold.

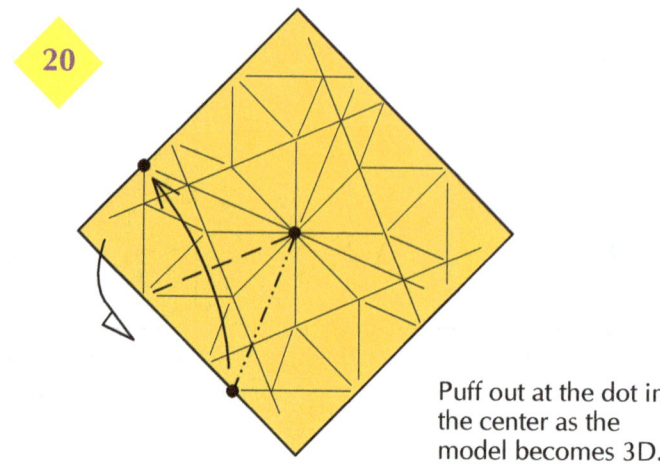

Puff out at the dot in the center as the model becomes 3D.

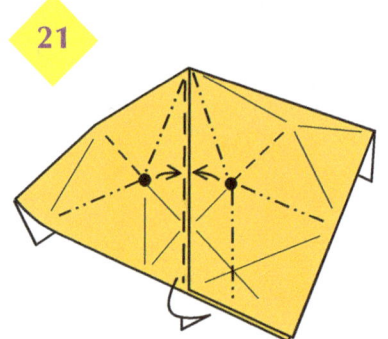

Puff out at the dots and bring them together.

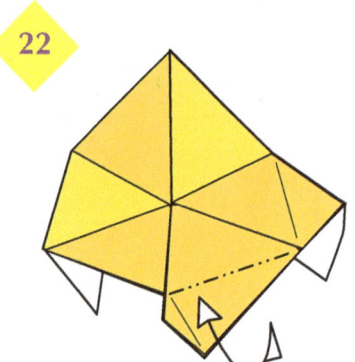

Fold and unfold.

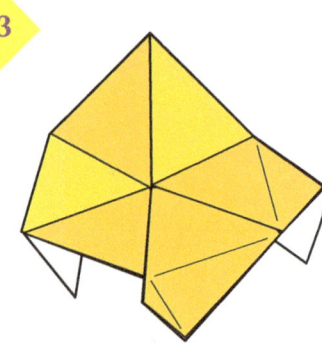

Repeat steps 21–22 two more times going around.

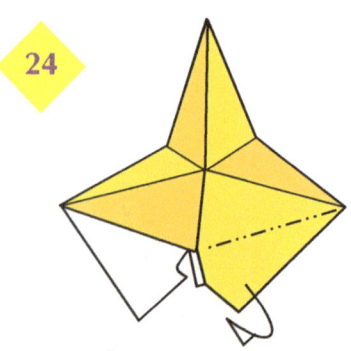

Tuck inside. Repeat twice and interlock the three flaps to lock to model.

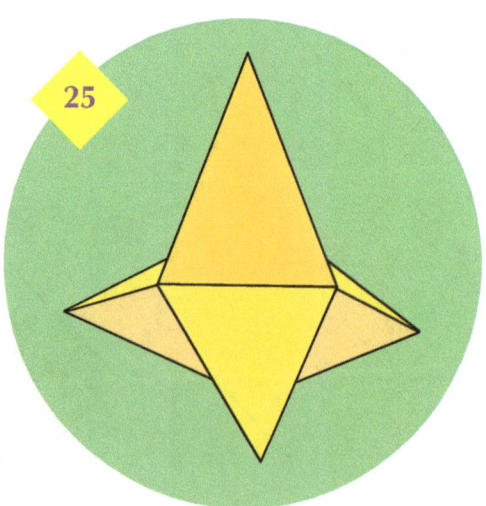

Tall Stellated Tetrahedron

104 *Galaxy of Origami Stars*

Squat Stellated Tetrahedron

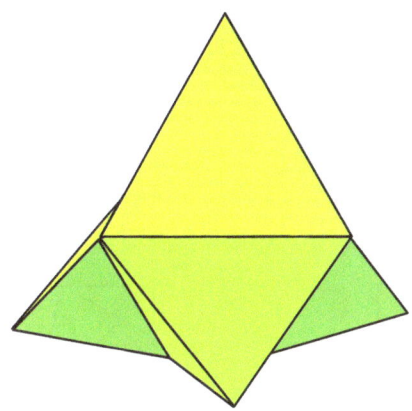

This model resembles four tetrahedra, each on the faces of a central tetrahedron. It closes with a three-way twist lock.

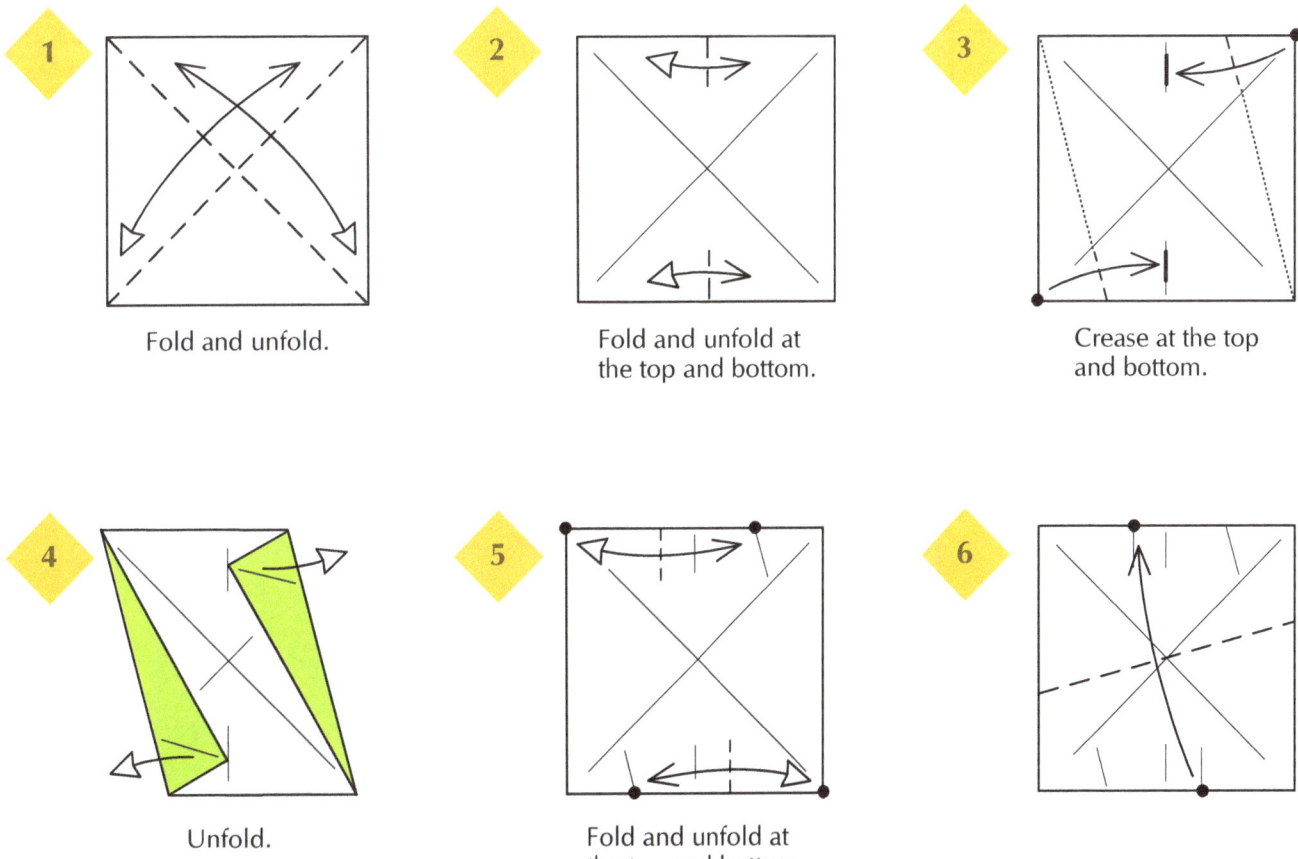

1. Fold and unfold.
2. Fold and unfold at the top and bottom.
3. Crease at the top and bottom.
4. Unfold.
5. Fold and unfold at the top and bottom.

Squat Stellated Tetrahedron 105

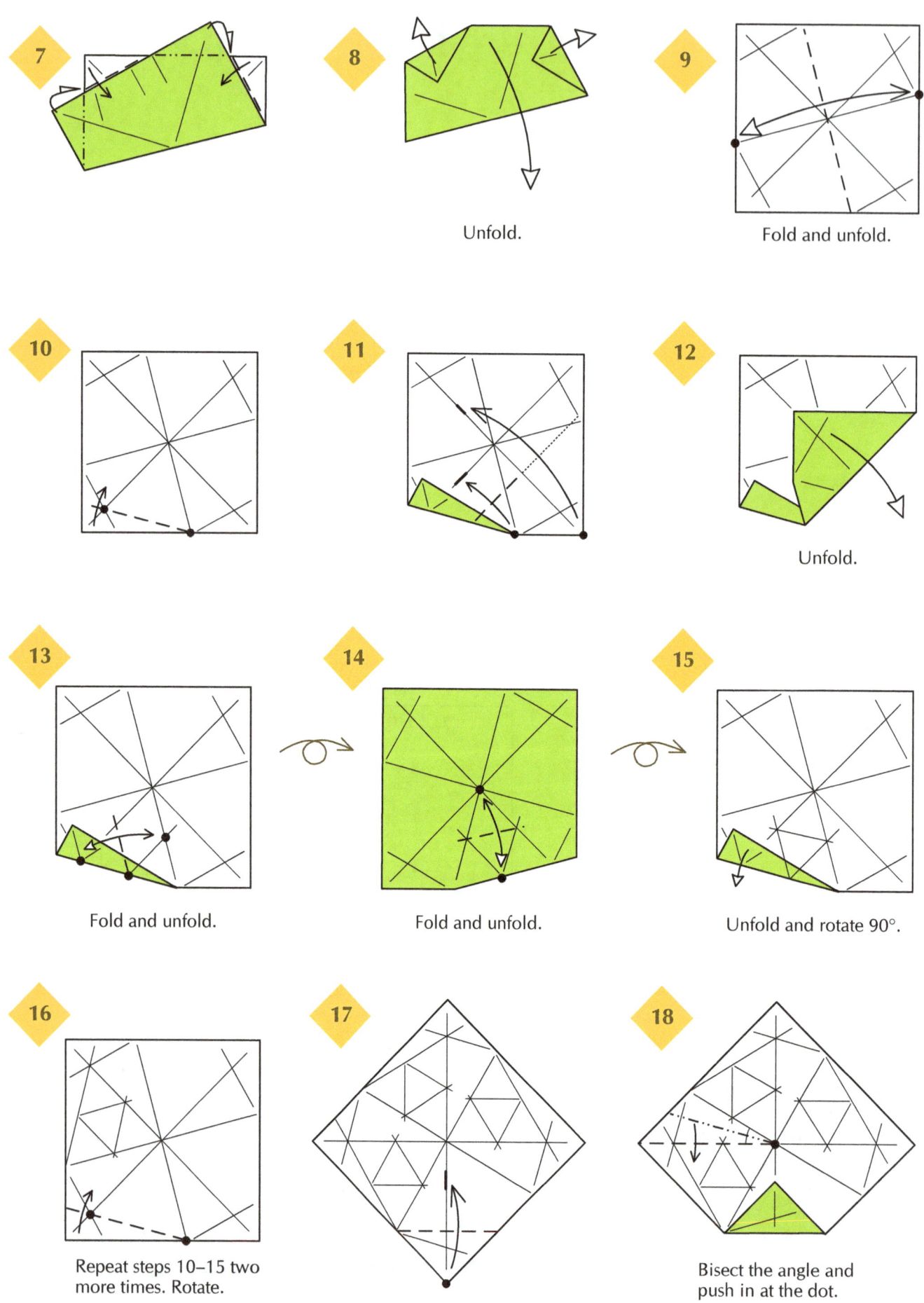

106 *Galaxy of Origami Stars*

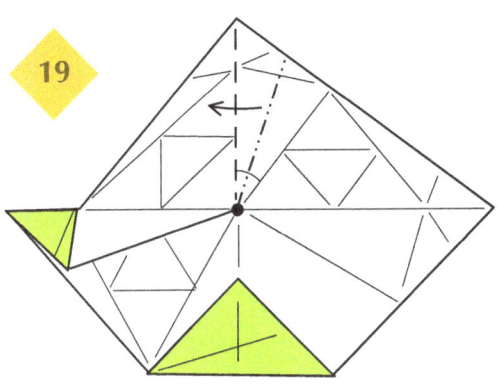

Bisect the angle and push in at the dot.

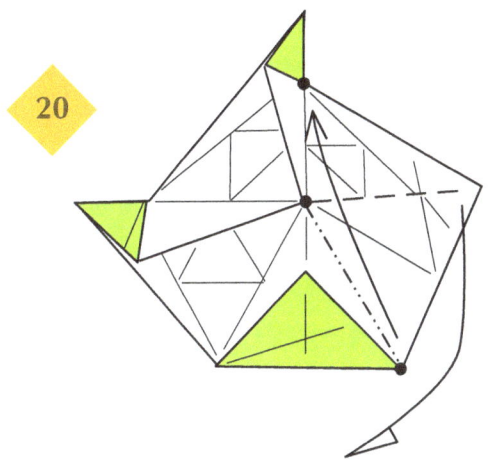

Rotate to view the outside so the center dot is at the top.

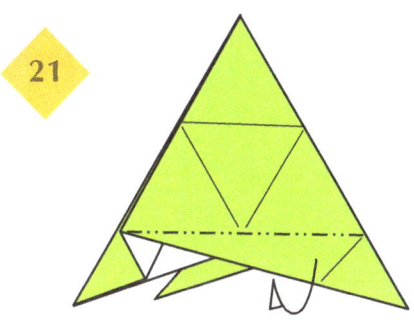

Repeat two more times.

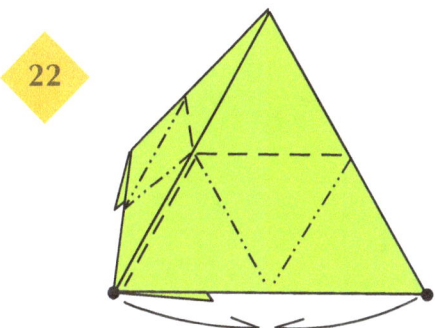

Bring the dots together. Repeat all around. Rotate to view the bottom.

Each of the three tabs creates a pocket. Interlock the tabs into the pockets.

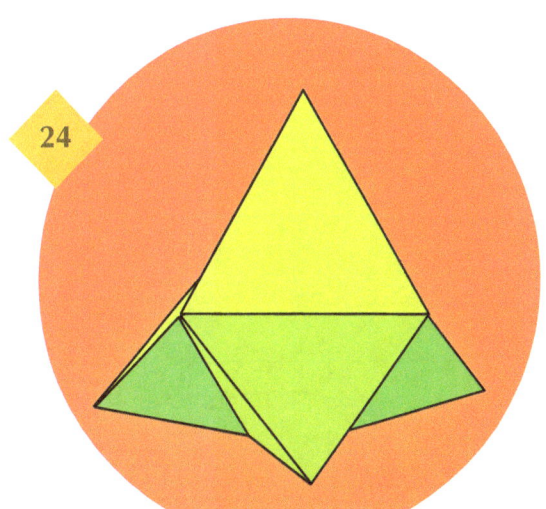

Squat Stellated Tetrahedron

Squat Stellated Tetrahedron 107

Stellated Octahedron

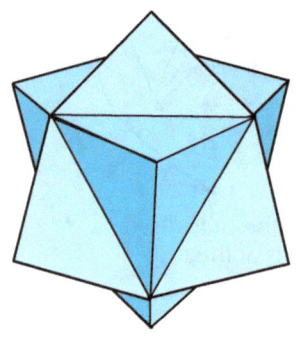

The stellated octahedron has eight points. The apex angle on each face is 90°. The paper is divided into sixths. It closes with a four-way lock.

1. Fold and unfold.
2. Fold and unfold.
3. Fold and unfold by the diagonal.
4. Fold and unfold.
5. Fold and unfold.
6. Fold and unfold.

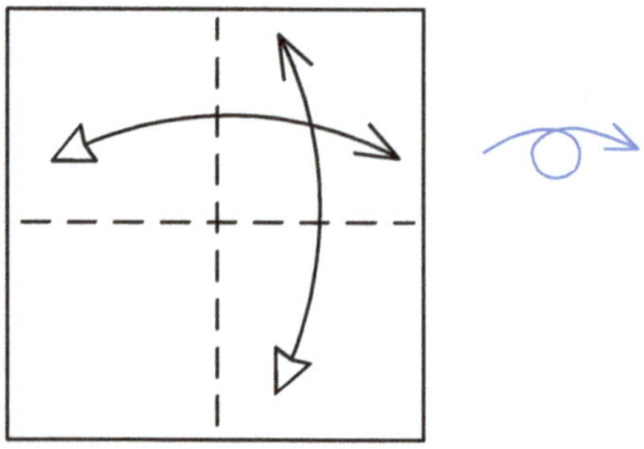

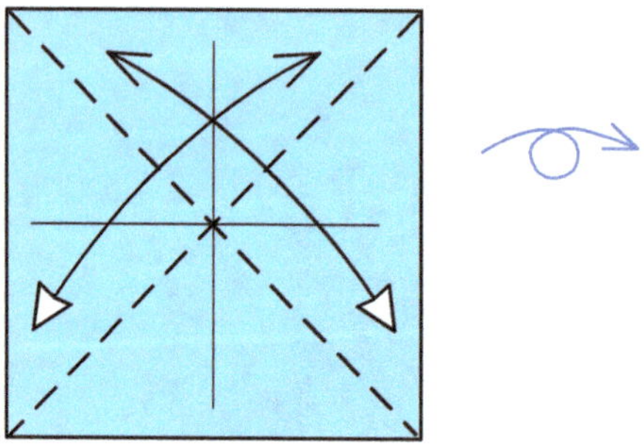

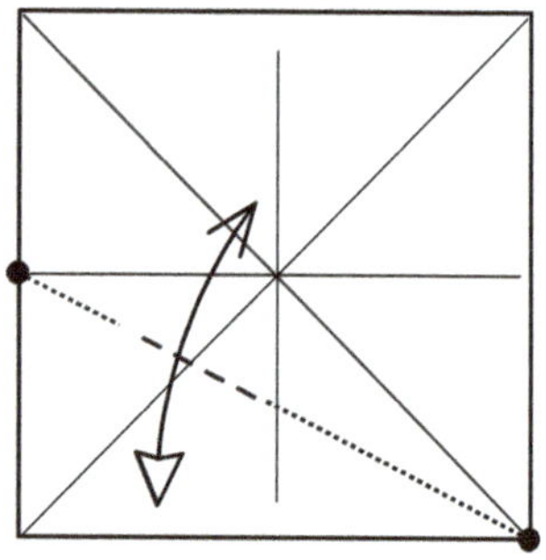

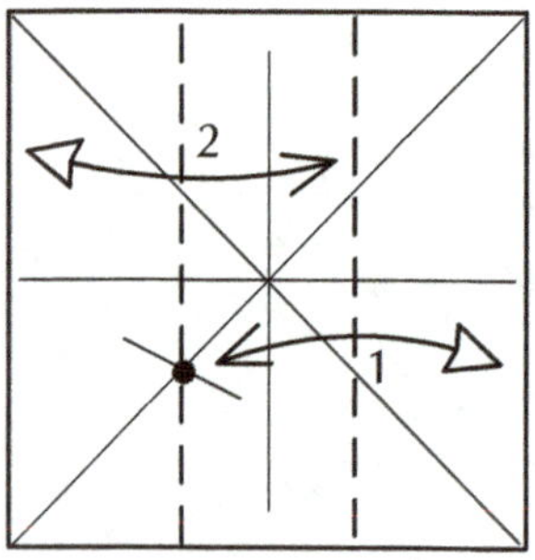

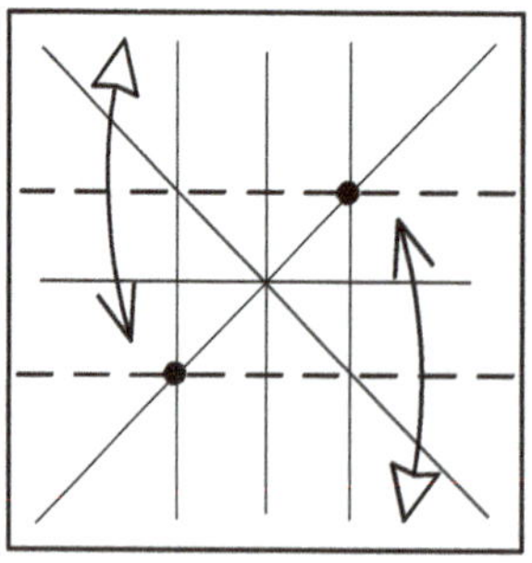

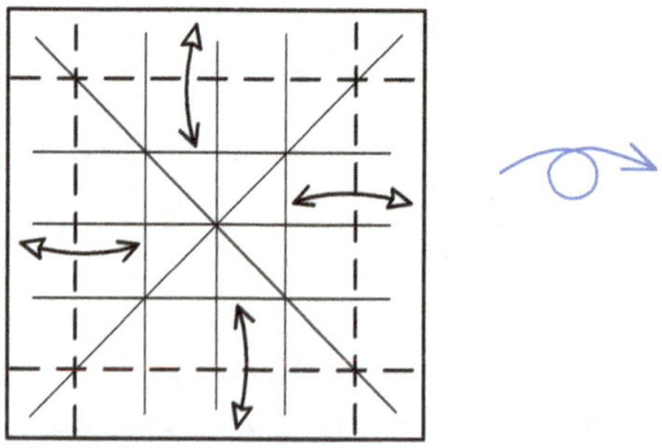

108   *Galaxy of Origami Stars*

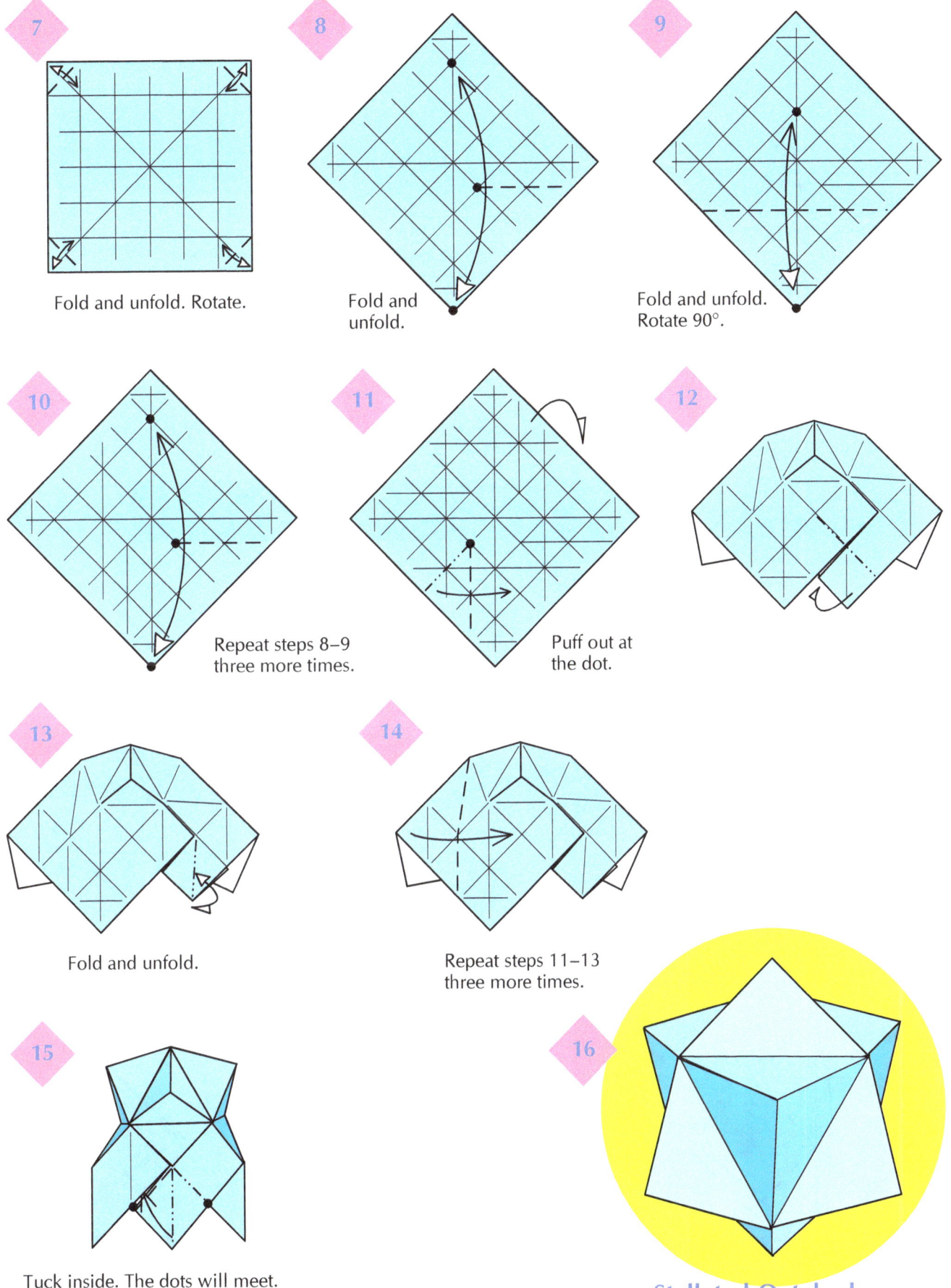

Stellated Octahedron 109

Six-Pointed Star

Stars can be formed from collapsed polyhedra. This six-pointed star comes from the six vertices of an octahedron. It was designed as a collapsed octahedron though the octahedron is hidden in the folding procedure.

1. Fold and unfold.

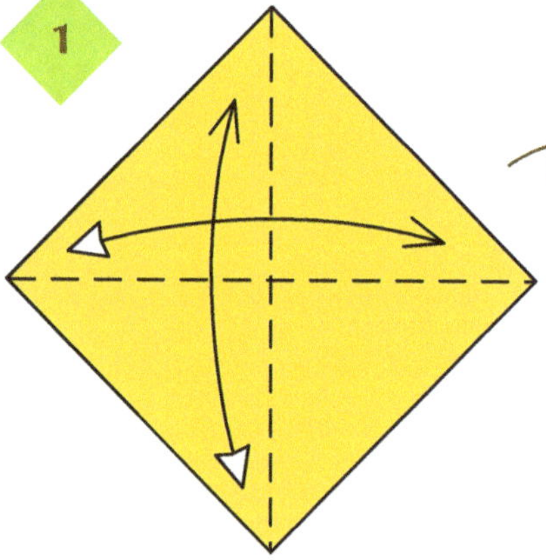

2. Fold and unfold.

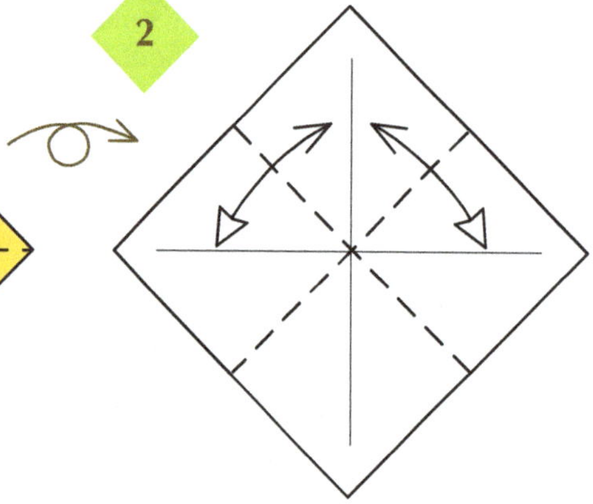

3. Fold and unfold.

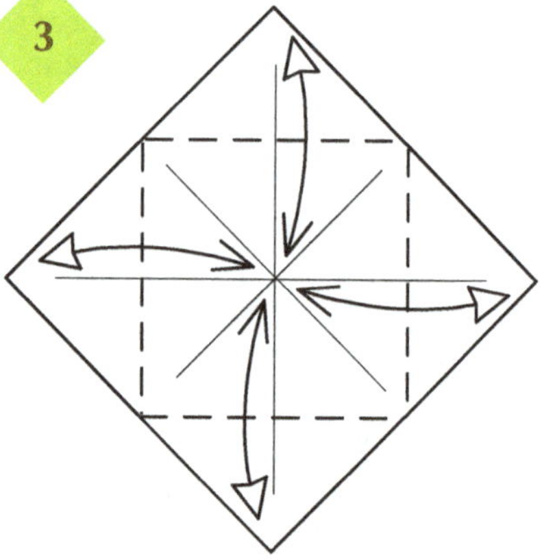

4. Collapse the square by bringing the four corners together.

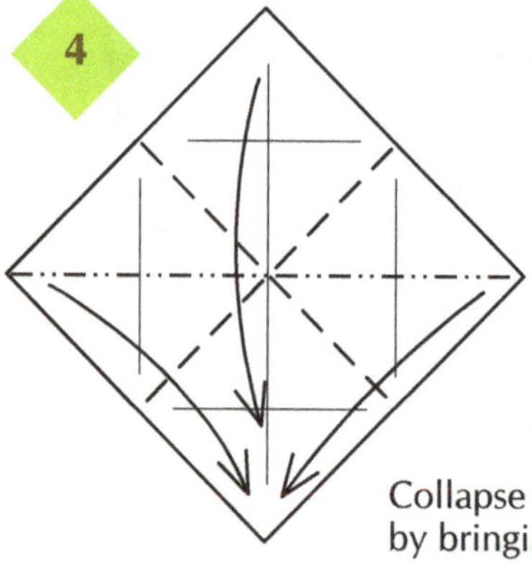

5. Only crease the top layer by the edges. Fold and unfold in half.

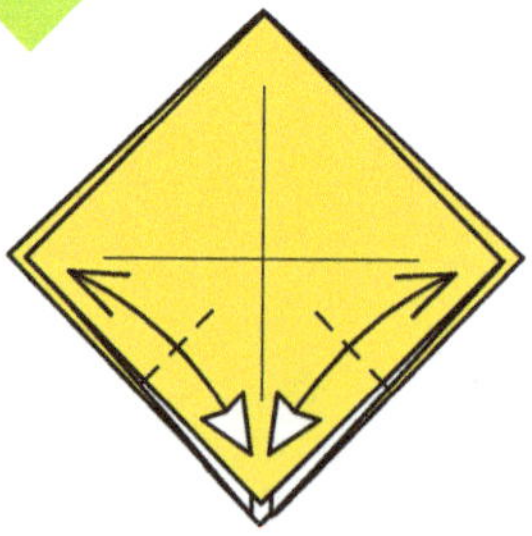

6. Repeat behind.

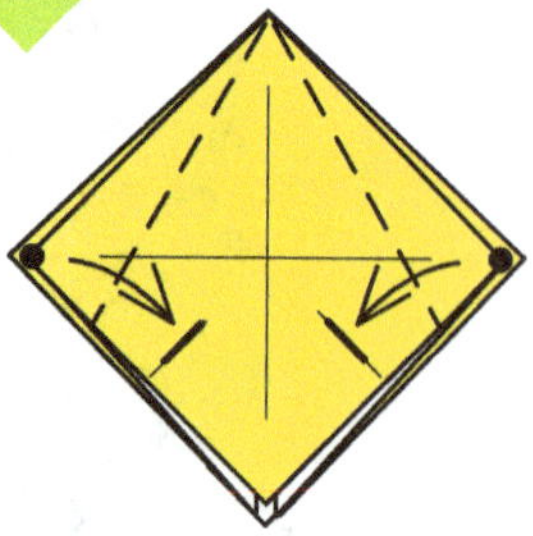

110   *Galaxy of Origami Stars*

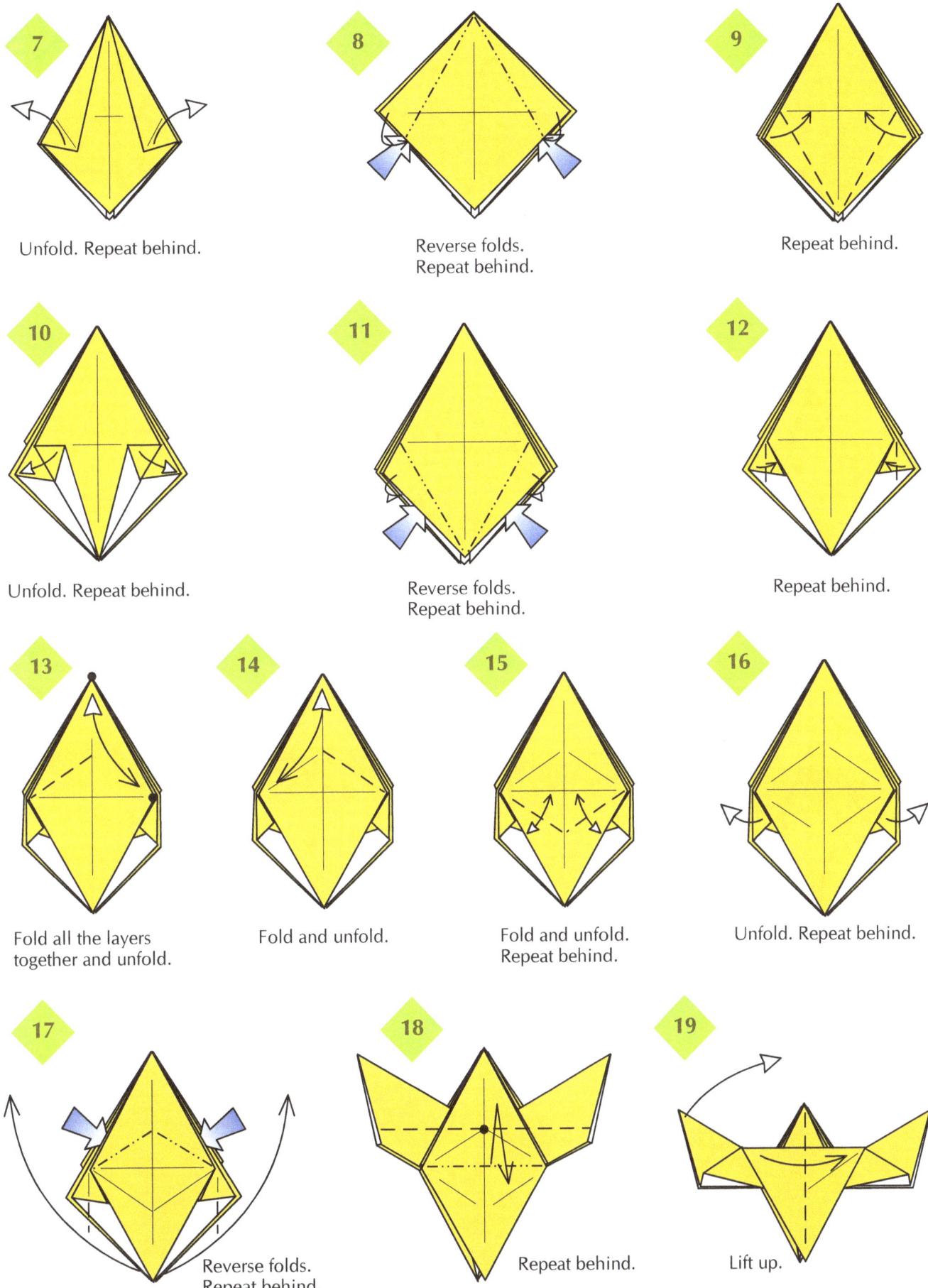

Six-Pointed Star

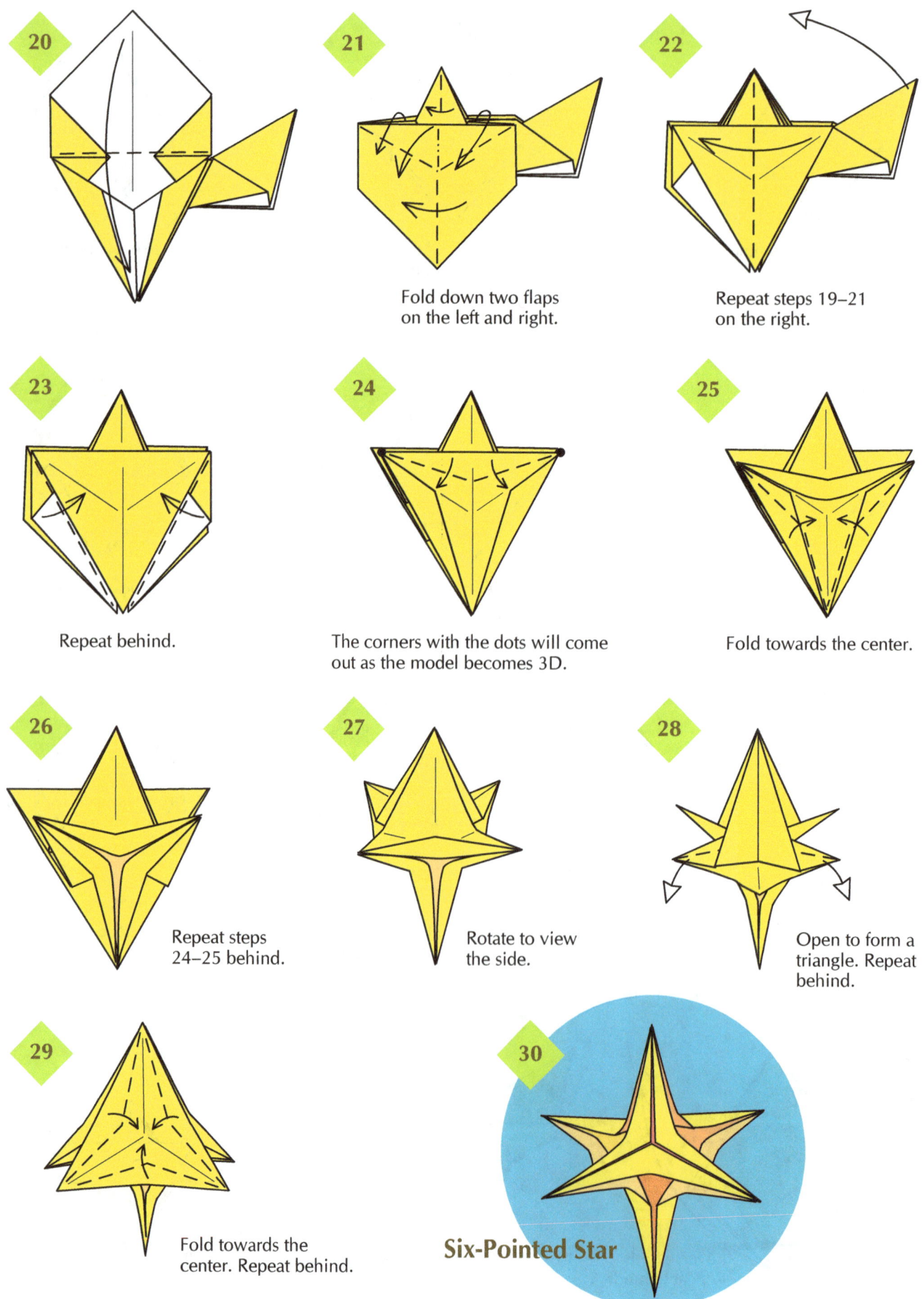

Omega Star

The omega star has twelve points. This version has four tabs which interlock. Step 26 resembles three intersecting planes in three dimensions.

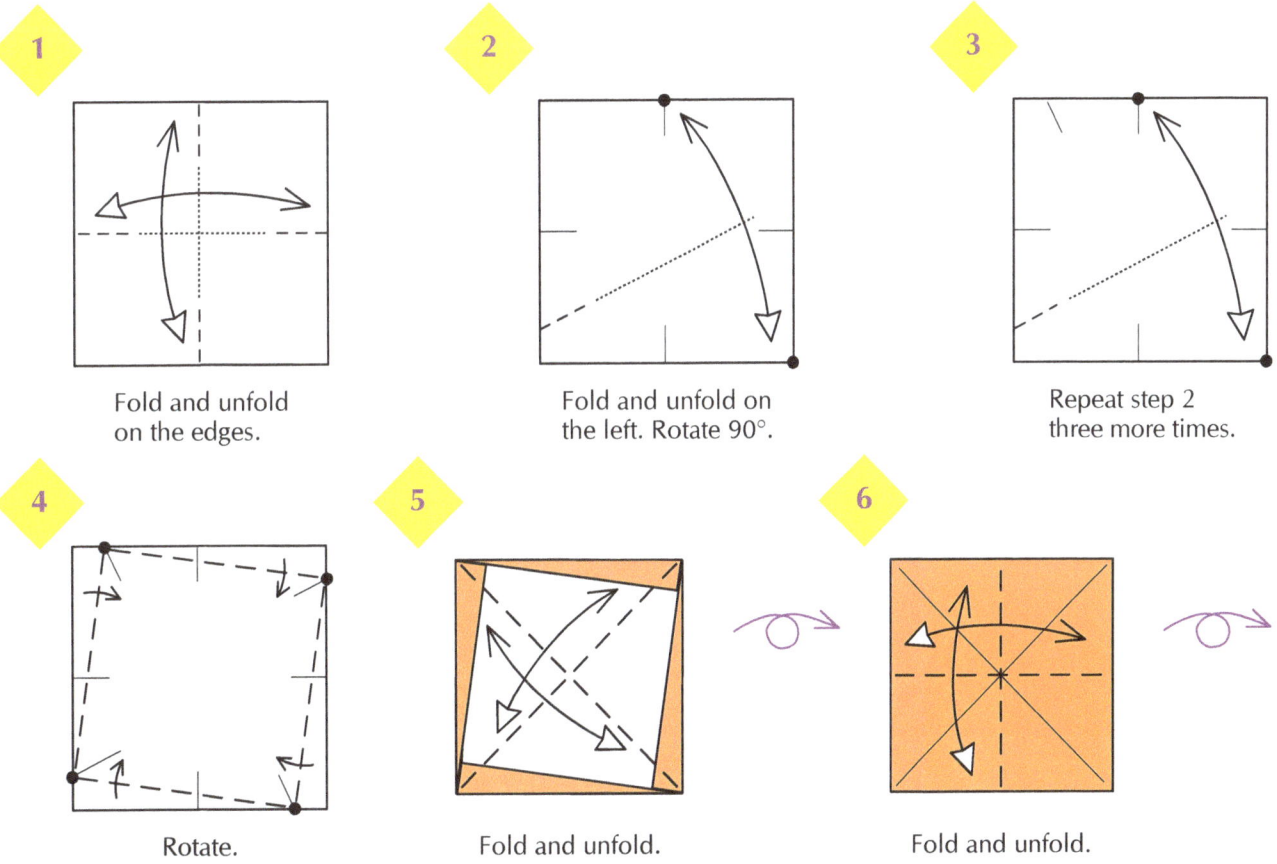

Omega Star   113

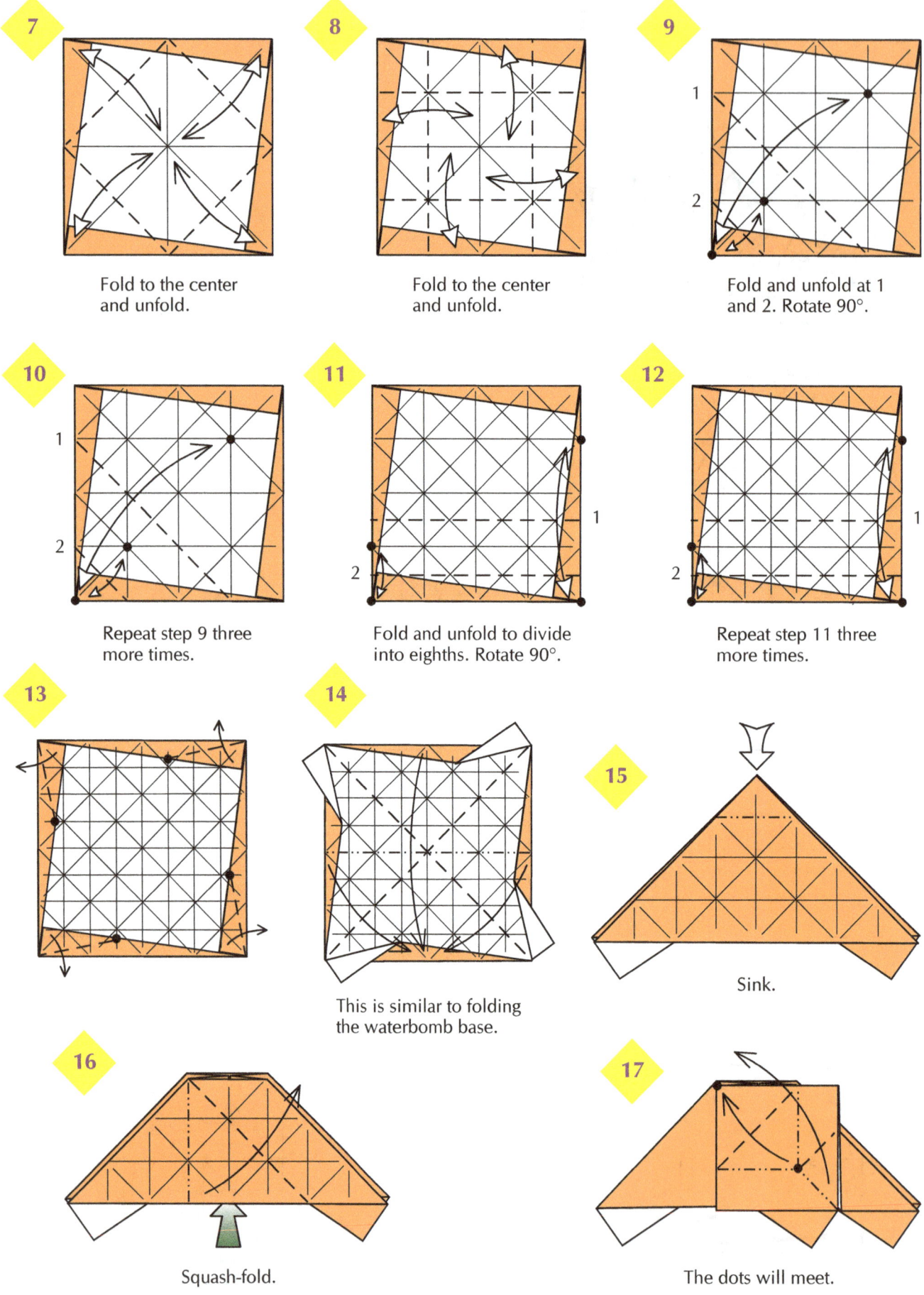

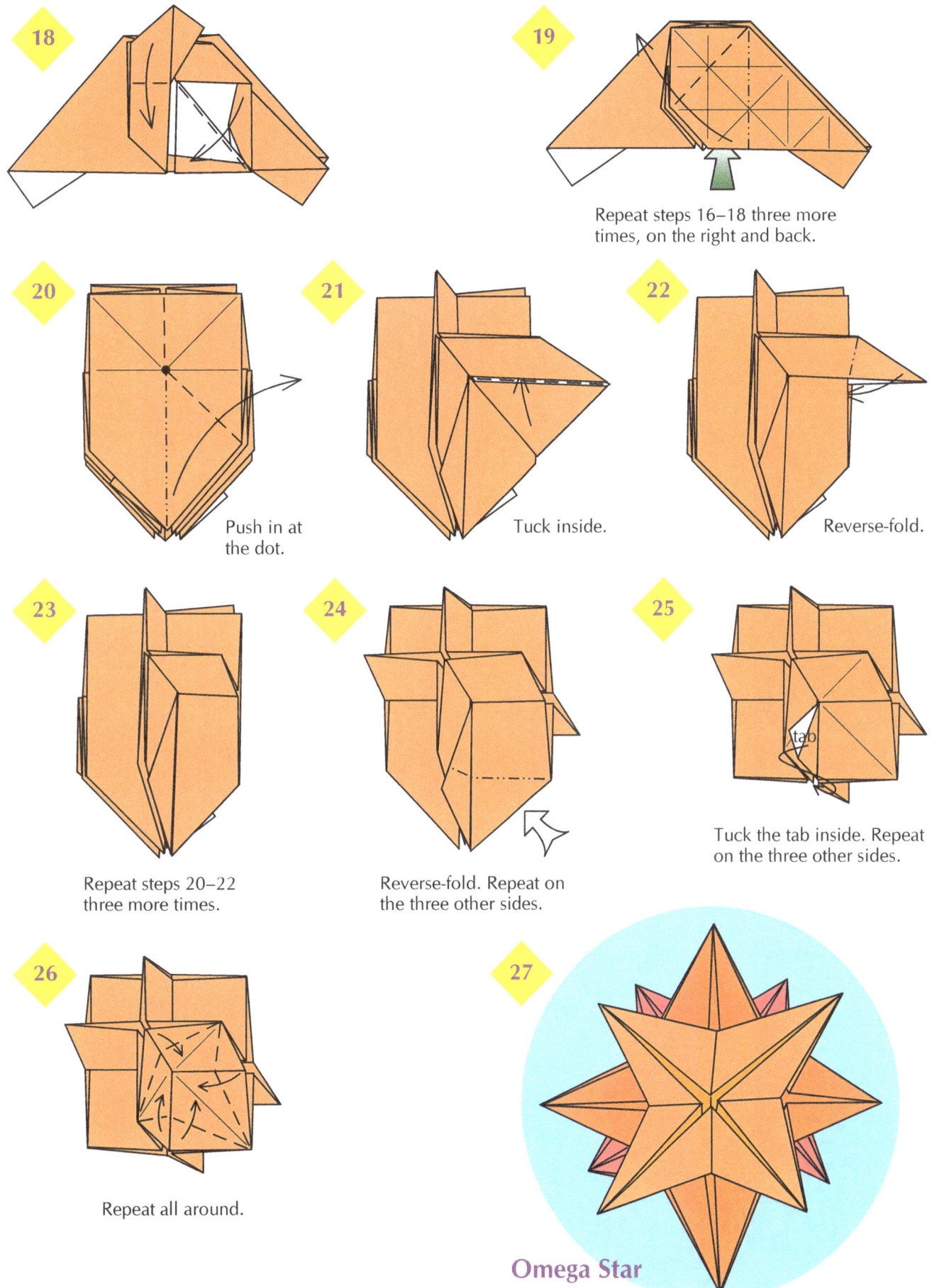

Omega Star 115

Jackstone

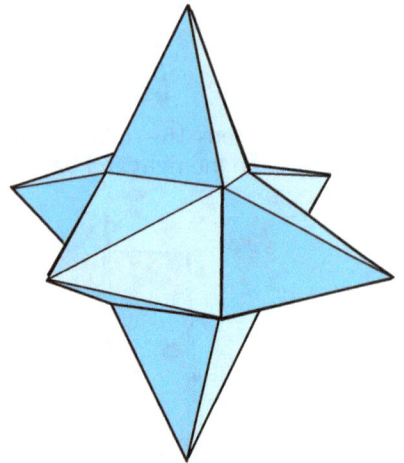

The jackstone has six points. The apex angle on each face is 45°.

1 Fold and unfold.

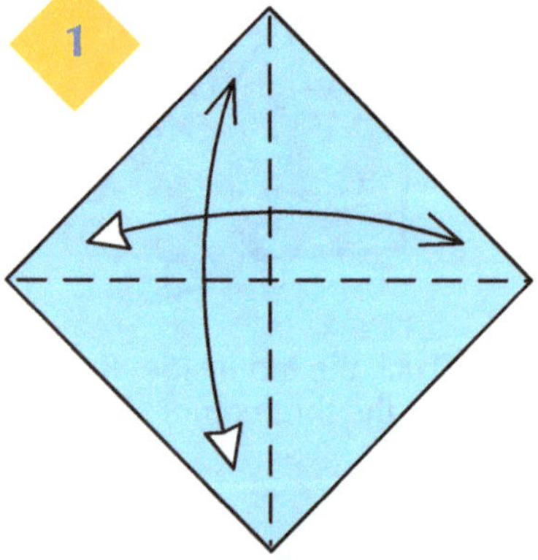

2 Crease on the left.

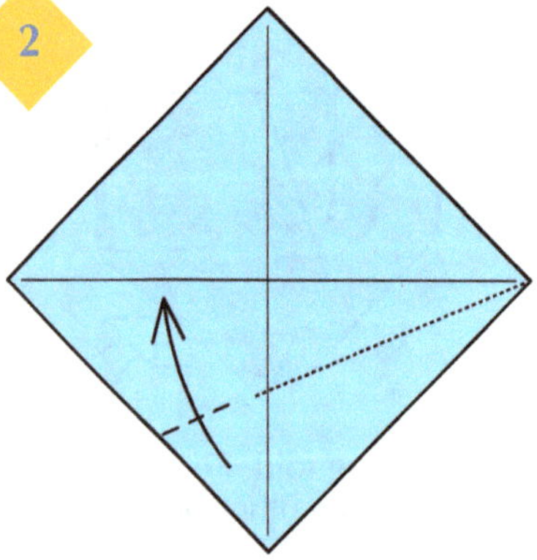

3 Unfold and rotate 180°.

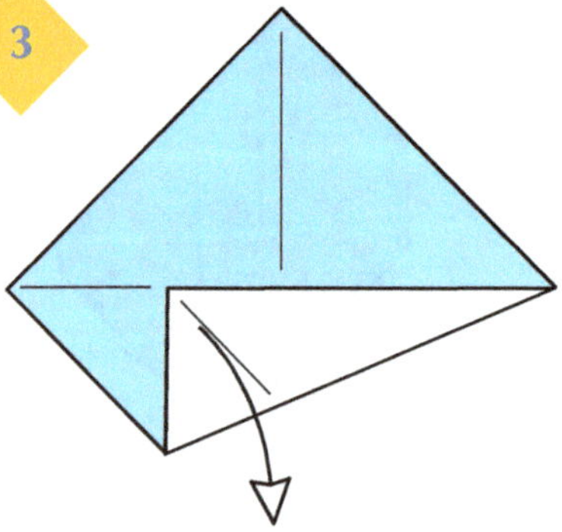

4 Repeat steps 2–3. Rotate.

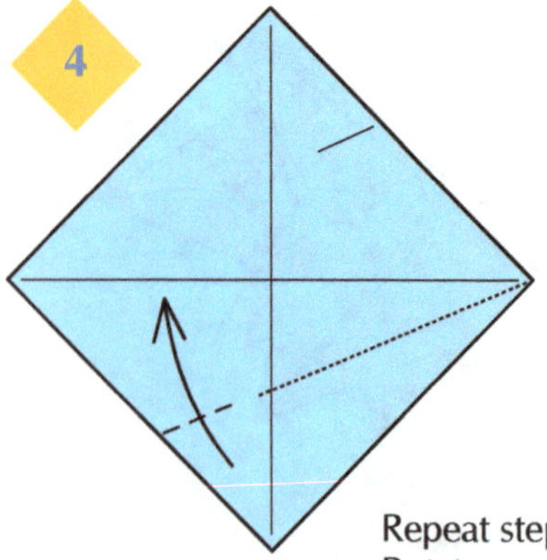

5 Fold and unfold. Rotate 180°.

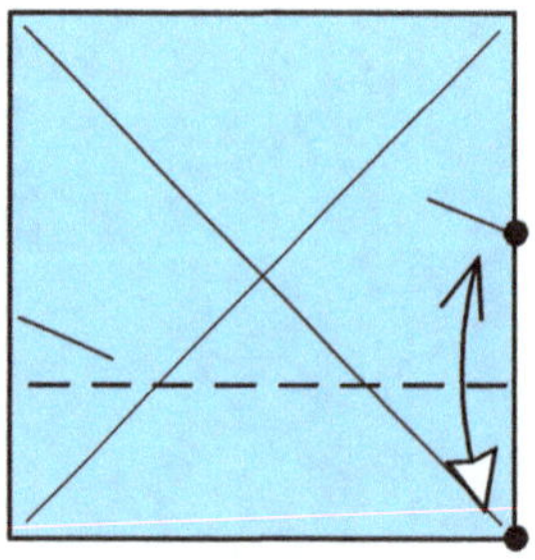

6 Fold and unfold. Rotate 90°.

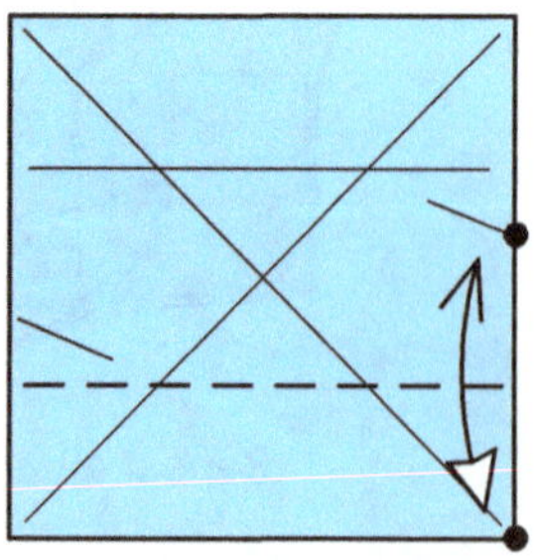

116   *Galaxy of Origami Stars*

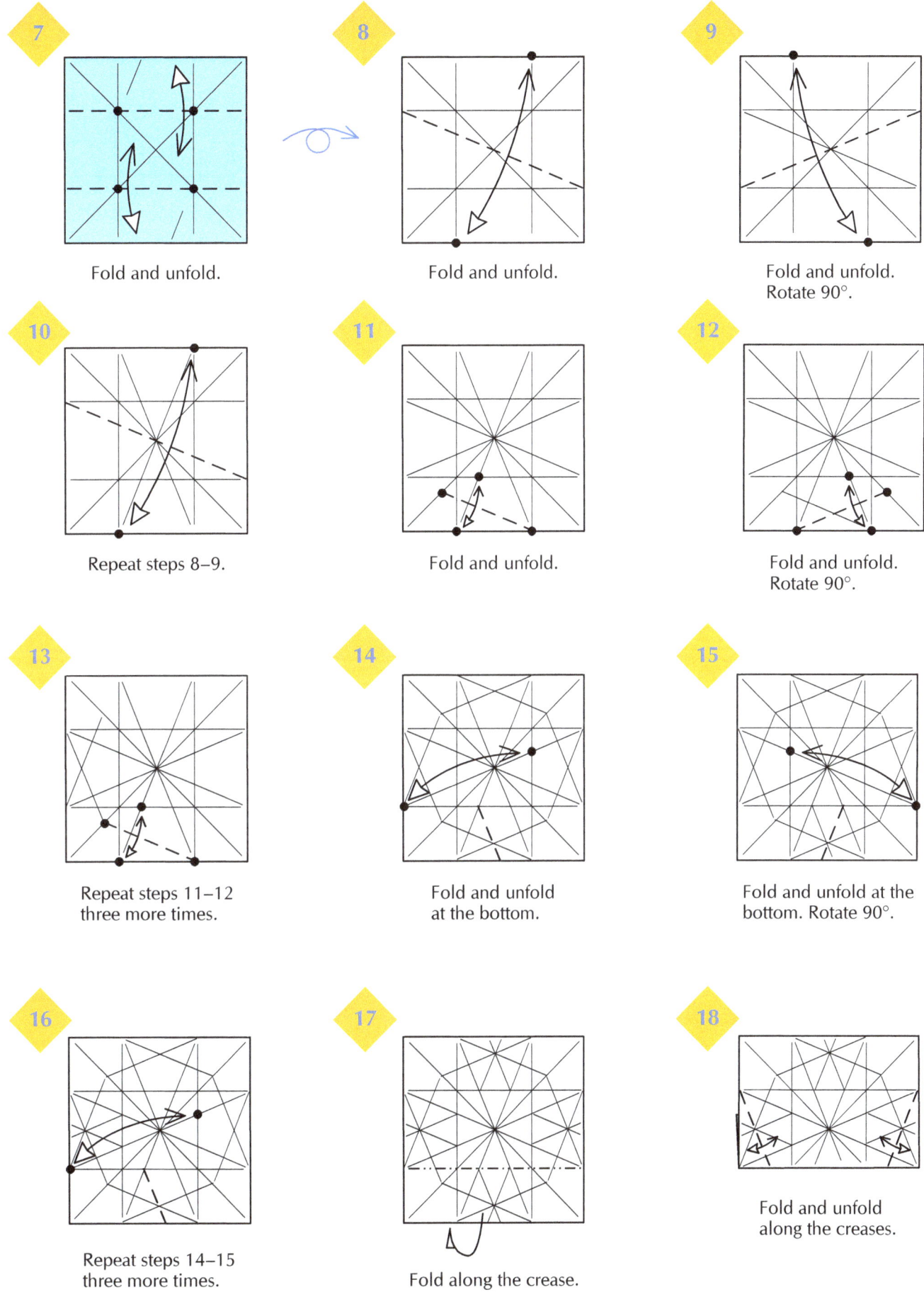

Jackstone 117

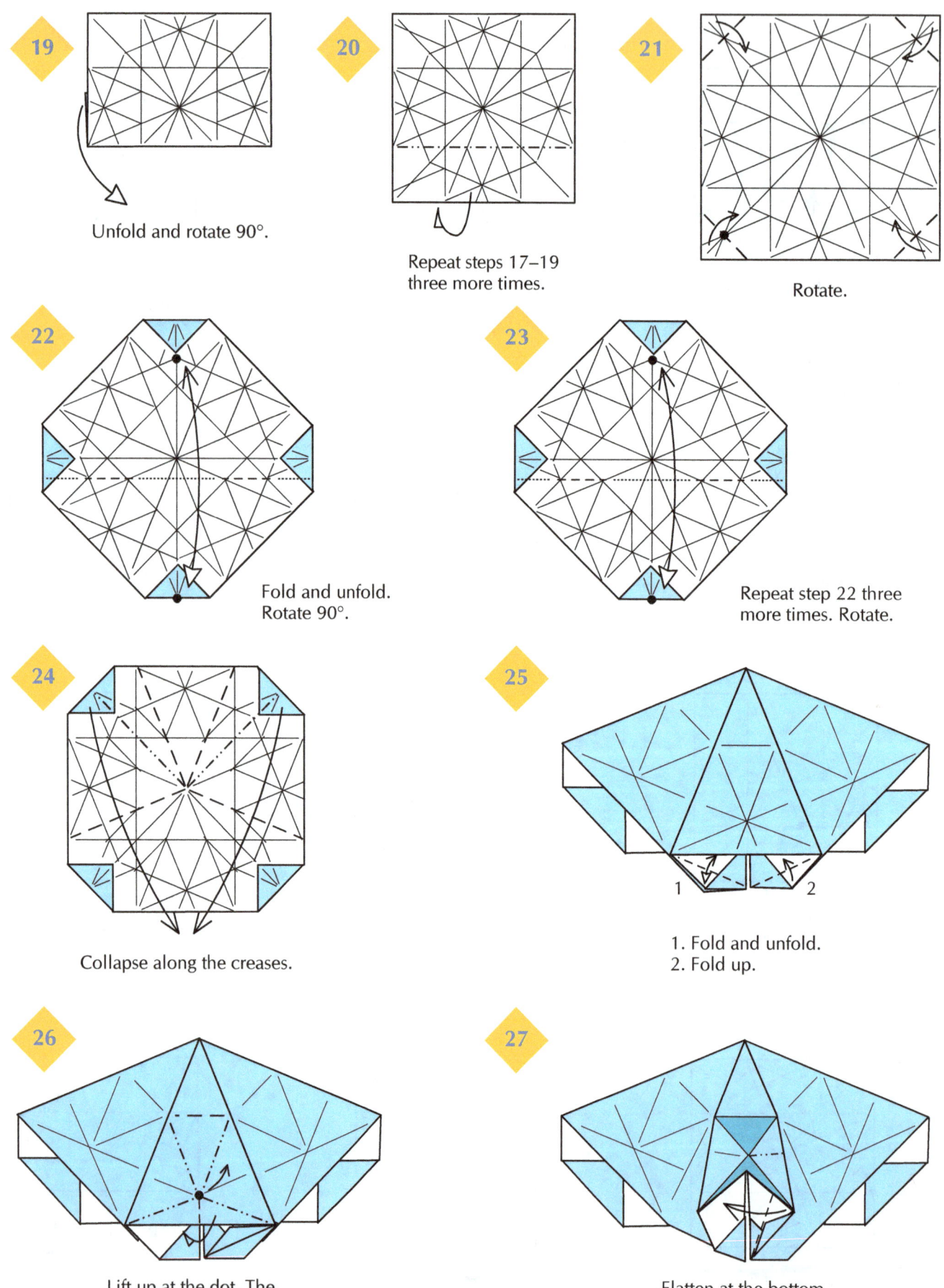

118　*Galaxy of Origami Stars*

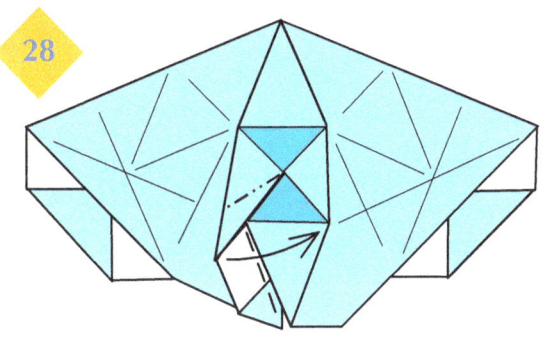

Wrap around and flatten at the bottom.

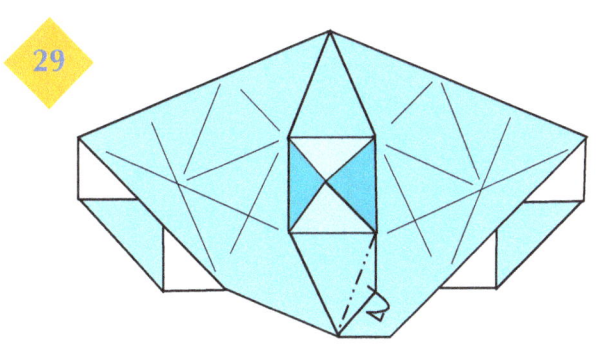

Wrap around the hidden layer.

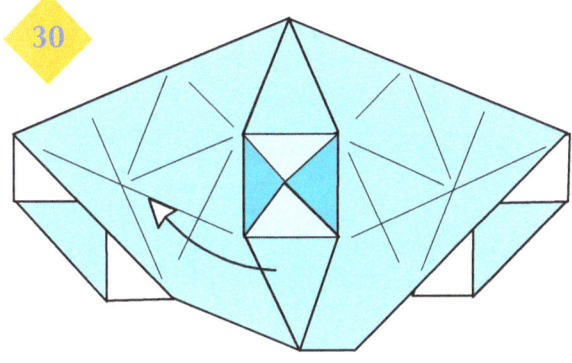

Unfold and rotate 90°.

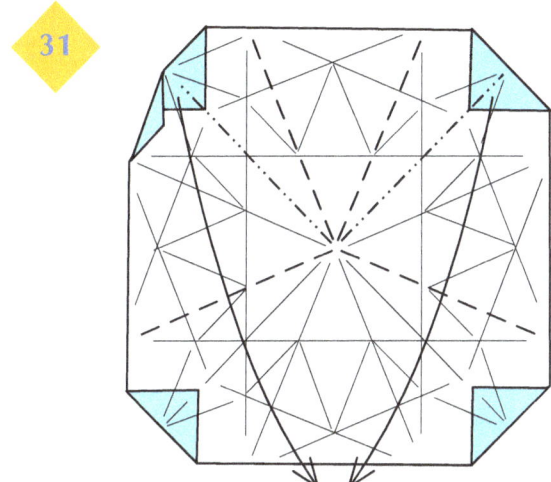

Repeat steps 24–30 on the three other sides. Do not unfold in step 30 for the last one.

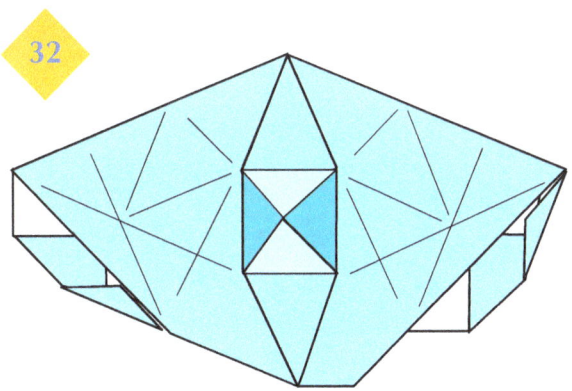

Refold on all the sides. While assembling the star, the model will continue to open.

Jackstone

www.ingramcontent.com/pod-product-compliance
Lightning Source LLC
Chambersburg PA
CBHW081116080526
44587CB00021B/3624